NIETZSCHE AND LEVINAS

Insurrections: Critical Studies in Religion, Politics, and Culture

INSURRECTIONS: CRITICAL STUDIES IN RELIGION, POLITICS, AND CULTURE
Slavoj Žižek, Clayton Crockett, Creston Davis, Jeffrey W. Robbins, Editors

The intersection of religion, politics, and culture is one of the most discussed areas in theory today. It also has the deepest and most wide-ranging impact on the world. Insurrections: Critical Studies in Religion, Politics, and Culture will bring the tools of philosophy and critical theory to the political implications of the religious turn. The series will address a range of religious traditions and political viewpoints in the United States, Europe, and other parts of the world. Without advocating any specific religious or theological stance, the series aims nonetheless to be faithful to the radical emancipatory potential of religion.

After the Death of God   John D. Caputo and Gianni Vattimo, edited by Jeffrey W. Robbins
The Politics of Postsecular Religion: Mourning Secular Futures   Ananda Abeysekara

Nietzsche and Levinas

"AFTER THE DEATH OF A CERTAIN GOD"

Edited by Jill Stauffer · Bettina Bergo

COLUMBIA UNIVERSITY PRESS   NEW YORK

COLUMBIA UNIVERSITY PRESS

Publishers Since 1893

NEW YORK   CHICHESTER, WEST SUSSEX

Copyright © 2009 Columbia University Press

Library of Congress Cataloging-in-Publication Data
Nietzsche and Lévinas : "after the death of a certain God" / edited by
Jill Stauffer and Bettina Bergo.
p.   cm. — (Insurrections)
Includes bibliographical references (p.   ) and index.
ISBN 978-0-231-14404-9 (cloth : alk. paper)
ISBN 978-0-231-14405-6 (pbk. : alk. paper)
ISBN 978-0-231-51853-6 (e-book)
1. Nietzsche, Friedrich Wilhelm, 1844–1900. 2. Lévinas, Emmanuel.
I. Stauffer, Jill, 1966– II. Bergo, Bettina. III. Title. IV. Series.
B3317.N4845 2009
193—dc22
2008020252
∞

Here I am for the others—an enormous response, whose inordinateness is attenuated with hypocrisy as soon as it enters my ears forewarned of being's essence. . . . The hypocrisy is from the first denounced. But the norms to which the denunciation refers have been understood in the enormity of meaning . . . to be true like unrefrained witness. In any case nothing less was needed for the little humanity that adorns the world. . . .

After the death of a certain god inhabiting the world behind the scenes, the substitution of the hostage discovers the trace, the unpronounceable inscription, of what . . . does not enter into any present.

—Levinas, *Otherwise Than Being*

By applying the knife vivisectionally to the chest of the very virtues of their time, [the philosophers] betrayed what was their own secret: to know of a new greatness of man, of a new untrodden way to his enhancement. Every time they exposed how much hypocrisy, comfortableness, . . . how many lies lay hidden under the best honored type of their contemporary morality. . . . Every time they said: "We must get there, that way, where you today are least at home.

—Nietzsche, *Beyond Good and Evil*

Contents

Acknowledgments

HEARTFELT THANKS to David Bertet (Université de Montréal) who prepared the bibliography and helped translate two essays, to Gabriel Malenfant (University of Iceland) and William Colish (Université de Montréal, CRÉUM) for their scrupulous editing; finally, to Tyson Gofton (University of Toronto) and Philippe Farah (Université de Montréal) for their bibliographical research. Special thanks to Babette Babich and Debra B. Bergoffen for permission to reprint a version of Claire Elise Katz's essay, "Thus Spoke Zarathustra, Thus Listened the Rabbis: Philosophy, Education, and the Cycle of Enlightenment," which first appeared in *New Nietzsche Studies,* Special Issue on *Nietzsche and the Jews,* coedited by David B. Allison, Babette Babich, and Debra B. Bergoffen, vol. 7, no. 3/4 (Fall 2007). Thanks also to Héloïse Bailly (Université de Strasbourg II, Marc Bloch and Université de Montréal) and Oona Eisenstadt (Pomona College) for their comments on several essays, and to Andréanne Sabourin-Laflamme (Université de Montréal) for her research into vitalism and mechanism. Without the criticism and insight of Gérard Bensussan (Université de Strasbourg II, Marc Bloch) and François-David Sebbah (Université de Compiègne), this collection would not have been possible. Special thanks are owed to Brian Schroeder, who helped formulate the project that led to this collection and helped in so many ways during the process of working on it. Thanks also go to the Hurford Humanities Center at Haverford College, and to all the philosophers at John Jay College, CUNY. The generous financial support of the Social Science and Humanities Research Council of Canada helped to make the material realization of this project possible, as did the CUNY Research Foundation.

Abbreviations of Works by Nietzsche and Levinas

Nietzsche

(English translation precedes the German edition cited)

AC *Twilight of the Idols/The Anti-Christ.* Trans. R. J. Hollingdale. New York: Penguin Books, 1968.

Ac *Der Antichrist.* KSA 6. Berlin/New York: DTV/de Gruyter, 1988.

BG *Beyond Good and Evil.* Trans. Walter Kaufmann. New York: Random House, 1966.

JG *Jenseits von Gut und Böse.* KSA 5. Berlin/New York: DTV/de Gruyter, 1988.

BT *The Birth of Tragedy/The Case of Wagner.* Trans. Walter Kaufmann. New York: Random House, 1967.

DG *Die Geburt der Tragödie.* KSA 1. Berlin/New York: DTV/de Gruyter, 1988.

DB *Daybreak: Thoughts on the Prejudices of Morality.* Trans. R. J. Hollingdale. Cambridge: Cambridge University Press, 1982.

MR *Morgenröte.* KSA 3. Berlin/New York: DTV/de Gruyter, 1988.

EH *On the Genealogy of Morals/Ecce Homo: How One Becomes What One Is.* Trans. Walter Kaufmann. New York: Random House, 1967.

Eh *Ecce homo.* KSA 6. Berlin/New York: DTV/de Gruyter, 1988.

GS *The Gay Science, with a Prelude of Rhymes and an Appendix of Songs.* Trans. Walter Kaufmann. New York: Random House, 1974.

Gs *Die Fröhliche Wissenschaft.* KSA 3. Berlin/New York: DTV/de Gruyter, 1988.

HA *Human, All Too Human: A Book for Free Spirits.* Trans. R. J. Hollingdale. Cambridge: Cambridge University Press, 1986.

MM *Menschliches, Allzumenschliches I und II.* KSA 2. Berlin/New York: DTV/ de Gruyter, 1988.

GM *On the Genealogy of Morals/Ecce Homo: How One Becomes What One Is.* Trans. Walter Kaufmann and R. J. Hollingdale. New York: Random House, 1967.

Gm   *Zur Genealogie der Moral.* KSA 5. Berlin/New York: DTV/de Gruyter, 1988.

TZ   *Thus Spoke Zarathustra.* Trans. Walter Kaufmann. New York: Viking Press, 1968.

AZ   *Also Sprach Zarathustra.* KSA 4. Berlin/New York: DTV/de Gruyter, 1988.

TL   *Twilight of the Idols.* Trans. Walter Kaufmann. New York: Viking Press, 1968.

GD   *Götzen-Dämmerung.* KSA 6. Berlin/New York: DTV/de Gruyter, 1988.

UM   *Untimely Meditations.* Trans. R. J. Hollingdale. Cambridge: Cambridge University Press, 1983.

UB   *Unzeitgemäße Betrachtungen I–IV.* KSA 1. Berlin/New York: DTV/de Gruyter, 1988.

WP   *The Will to Power.* Trans. Walter Kaufmann. New York: Random House, 1967.

VP I, II *La Volonté de Puissance I et II.* Trans. Geneviève Bianquis. Paris: Gallimard, 1948.

WM   *Wille zur Macht.* Stuttgart: Alfred Kröner Verlag, 1956.

DFW   *Der Fall Wagner—Ein Musikanten-Problem.* 1888. KSA 6. Berlin/New York: DTV/de Gruyter, 1988.

KSA   *Kritische Studienausgabe* (the shorter, 15-volume set). Ed. Giorgio Colli and Mazzino Montinari. Berlin/New York: DTV/de Gruyter, 1988.

KGA   *Kritische Gesamtausgabe* (the longer set, with works prior to 1870 and correspondence). Ed. Giorgio Colli and Mazzino Montinari. Berlin: DTV/de Gruyter, 1967.

Levinas

(English translation precedes the French edition cited)

TIH   *The Theory of Intuition in Husserl's Phenomenology.* Trans. Andre Orianne. Evanston, Ill.: Northwestern University Press, 1973.

TidH   *La théorie de l'intuition dans la phénoménologie de Husserl.* Paris: Vrin, 2000.

OE   *On Escape/De l'évasion.* Trans. Bettina G. Bergo. Stanford, Calif.: Stanford University Press, 2003.

DE   *De l'évasion.* Montpellier: Fata Morgana, 1996.

EE   *Existence and Existents.* Trans. Alphonso Lingis. The Hague and Boston: Martinus Nijhoff, 1978.

DEE   *De l'existence à l'existant.* Paris: Vrin, 2002.

TO   *Time and the Other.* Trans. Richard A. Cohen. Pittsburgh, Penn.: Duquesne University Press, 1987.

TA   *Le temps et l'autre.* St. Clément: Fata Morgana, 1979, and Paris: Presses Universitaires de France, 2004.

DEH   *Discovering Existence with Husserl.* Trans. Richard A. Cohen and Michael B. Smith. Evanston, Ill.: Northwestern University Press, 1998.

ED   *En découvrant l'existence avec Husserl et Heidegger.* Paris: Vrin, 1949; 1982.

TI   *Totality and Infinity: An Essay on Exteriority.* Trans. Alphonso Lingis. Pittsburgh, Penn.: Duquesne University Press, 1969.

TeI   *Totalité et Infini. Essai sur l'extériorité.* The Hague and Boston: Martinus Nijhoff, 1961 and Paris: Livre de Poche, 1990.

OB   *Otherwise Than Being; Or, Beyond Essence.* Trans. Alphonso Lingis. Dordrecht and Boston: Kluwer Academic Publishers, 1978.

AE   *Autrement qu'être ou au-delà de l'essence.* Dordrecht and Boston: Kluwer Academic Publishers, 1974, and Paris: Livre de Poche, 2004.

OG   *Of God Who Comes to Mind.* Trans. Bettina G. Bergo. Stanford, Calif.: Stanford University Press, 1998.

DV   *De Dieu qui vient à l'idée.* Paris: Vrin, 2000.

RH   "Reflections on the Philosophy of Hitlerism." 1934. Trans. Seán Hand. *Critical Inquiry* 17, no. 1 (Autumn 1990): 63–71.

QR   "Quelques réflexions sur la philosophie de l'hitlérisme." *Esprit* 2, no. 26 (1934): 199–208.

HO   *Humanism of the Other.* Trans. Nidra Poller. Chicago: Illinois University Press, 2003.

HdA   *L'humanisme de l'autre.* Montpellier: Fata Morgana, 1972.

PN   *Proper Names.* Trans. Michael B. Smith. Stanford, Calif.: Stanford University Press, 1997.

NP   *Noms propres.* Paris: Biblio essais, 1976.

EI   *Ethics and Infinity: Conversations with Philippe Nemo.* Trans. Richard A. Cohen. Pittsburgh, Penn.: Duquesne University Press, 1985.

EeI   *Éthique et infini.* Paris: Fayard, 1982.

OS   *Outside the Subject.* Trans. Michael B. Smith. Stanford, Calif.: Stanford University Press, Meridian, 1993.

HS   *Hors sujet.* Paris: Fata Morgana, 1987.

EN   *Entre Nous: On Thinking-of-the-Other.* Trans. Barbara Harshav and Michael B. Smith. New York: Columbia University Press, 2000.

ENe *Entre Nous: Essais sur le penser à l'autre.* Paris: Grasset, 1991.

GDT *God, Death, and Time.* Trans. Bettina G. Bergo, preface by Jacques Rolland. Stanford, Calif.: Stanford University Press, 2000.

GMT *Dieu, la mort, et le temps.* Paris: Grasset, 1993.

UH *Unforeseen History.* Trans. Nidra Poller, intro. Richard A. Cohen. Chicago: Illinois University Press, 2003.

IH *Les imprévus de l'histoire.* Montpellier: Fata Morgana, 1994, and Paris: LGF, 1999.

AT *Alterity and Transcendence.* Trans. Michael B. Smith. New York: Columbia University Press, 1999.

AeT *Altérité et transcendance.* Montpellier: Fata Morgana, 1995.

BPW *Emmanuel Levinas: Basic Philosophical Writings.* Ed. Simon Critchley, Adriaan Theodoor Peperzak, and Robert Bernasconi. Bloomington: Indiana University Press, 1996.

LR *The Levinas Reader: Emmanuel Levinas.* Ed. Seán Hand. Oxford: Blackwell, 1989.

CPP *Collected Philosophical Papers of Emmanuel Levinas.* Phaenomenologica 100. Trans. Alphonso Lingis. The Hague: Martinus Nijhoff, 1987.

RB *Interviews with Emmanuel Levinas: Is It Righteous to Be?* Ed. Jill Robbins. Stanford, Calif.: Stanford University Press, 2001.

DF *Difficult Freedom: Essays on Judaism.* Trans. Seán Hand. London: Athlone, 1991.

DL *Difficile liberté: essais sur le Judaïsme.* Paris: Albin Michel, 2000.

NT *Nine Talmudic Readings.* Trans. Annette Aronowicz. Bloomington: Indiana University Press, 1990. This translation regroups the lectures of 1968 and 1977.

BV *Beyond the Verse: Talmudic Readings and Lectures.* Trans. Gary D. Mole. Bloomington: Indiana University Press, 1994.

AV *L'au-delà du verset: lectures et discours talmudiques.* Paris: Minuit, 1982.

TN *In the Time of the Nations.* Trans. Michael B. Smith. Bloomington: Indiana University Press, 1994.

TdN *A l'heure des nations.* Paris: Minuit, 1988.

TR *New Talmudic Readings.* Trans. Richard A. Cohen. Pittsburgh, Penn.: Duquesne University Press, 1999.

NL *Nouvelles lectures talmudiques.* Paris: Minuit, 1995.

NIETZSCHE AND LEVINAS

Introduction

BETTINA BERGO AND JILL STAUFFER

EMMANUEL LEVINAS is no doubt the most original ethical thinker of the last century. And Friedrich Nietzsche arguably poses him the deepest ethical challenge. As such, it is often supposed that the two have little in common, not least because of the radical difference in approach and in style that separates their works. Yet while the differences between them are numerous, Nietzsche and Levinas are also thinkers with profound similarities. Both radically reevaluate the traditional ground of ethics and morality, and, further, both are united in their apprehension of the risk that nihilism poses to ethics and to life in general. In addition, both thinkers revisit the relation between embodied life and hermeneutics, and command and obedience, in an effort to overcome this danger—or at least to loosen nihilism's hold on contemporary values and culture. Both approach politics based upon a qualified return to Plato's thought, ironically the very thought that the young Nietzsche identified as the source of nihilistic *ressentiment*. Yet it is perhaps their greatest difference that draws them into closest proximity: the status of "God" in philosophy. Both thinkers lay claim to a certain atheism, and in their own ways confront the meaning of the "death of God" for contemporary humanity.

All this leads to a renewed engagement with the concepts of subjectivity and the ethical subject. Reminiscent of Nietzsche's call for the "revaluation of all values," Levinas revises the ground of traditional values and the subject, postulating ethics as first philosophy and founding his ethics on the face-to-face encounter between self and other. Nietzsche invokes the notion of a Dionysian "common faith" much the way Levinas's interpretation of ethics also lays claim to ubiquity without foundationalism. For both philosophers, the "rational" subject is heteronomous insofar as that subject is constituted by an irreducible exteriority that is paradoxically realized as such only within ourselves—as affectivity and living expression. And yet both Nietzsche and Levinas resist grounding their philosophies in any traditionally conceived authority, whether this would be particular laws, maxims, scriptural texts, or an event of revelation.

There is as much to bring the two thinkers together as there is to keep them apart, but what is most surprising about the field they share is how fertile it is for thinking. The parameters of that field include embodied subjectivity *after the dissolution of God and a sovereign Subject-substance,* a conception of writing as interpellation, the situation of goodness elsewhere than in a naïve faith in reason, and a dedication to justice without religiosity. Taking Nietzsche and Levinas together, in all the rigor and stark difficulty of their legacies of thought, leads us to the edge of what can be thought. This opens to interpretive explorations of sites, beyond divinity and subjectivity, in which ethical life arises, pointing to a different theorization of intersubjectivity and affectivity. For this reason, the present collection of essays seeks to move beyond the commonplace conception that the philosophies of Nietzsche and Levinas are fundamentally antithetical. The three sections group arguments around the following debates, which are far from being settled: What is the reevaluation of ethics (and life) that Nietzsche and Levinas respectively propose? What is the human subject— and what is substance, permanence, causality, and identity, whether social *or* ethical—in the wake of the demise of God as concept and belief? Finally, how can a "God" still inhabit philosophy, and what sort of name *is* this, in the wake of Nietzsche and Levinas?

———

Part 1, "Revaluing Ethics: Time, Teaching, and the Ambiguity of Forces," admits that it would be easy to view Levinas's ethics and Nietzsche's genealogies as presenting a choice between two opposed visions. Yet each essay shows in its own way why a simple contrast of their positions is unsatisfactory. Alphonso Lingis ("The Malice in Good Deeds") shows that it was Nietzsche who first taught us the relative crassness of our altruistic ethics—not to mention the simplicity with which we "understand" others' suffering, a simplicity that leads us to suppose we have the wherewithal to alleviate that suffering. By contrast, Levinas unfolds phenomenological presentations of the "I" in the modality of being-for-others, arguing that a subject that names itself "I" arises from individuation by the other, to whom it *experiences itself as* called upon to respond before it posits itself as the thinking self of post-idealistic philosophies. This responsibility is an affective event whose proper time works within or subliminally to the time of conscious intentionality. As affectivity, before we are fully or cognitively conscious of it, we are responsible in our interconnections, even to the point of experiencing the other as a powerful folding into oneself. The instantaneousness and subtlety of the experience means that this "I," in its affective individuation, is inhabited by and responsible to any other, regardless of the other's cognitive status: I may thus be responsible even for the irresponsibility of the other.

Leading us through the implications of that disjuncture between the ethics of Levinas and of Nietzsche, Lingis demonstrates that if we take Levinas to be urging us to *understand* the other's misfortune, ethics will unwittingly become a justification of that suffering. It is incumbent on us, then, to note the ethical ramifications of the extension of Levinas's affective responsibility into the understanding of misfortune. But even grasping the pragmatic risks implicit here does not take us far enough. Lingis takes a further, courageous step: today, as in Kant's time, we lack the rudiments of an analysis of *that imperative* through which social and economic institutions are made responsive to suffering and injustice, not to mention the imperative imposed on us by the fact of our existence in a larger ecosystem, which is not without equilibria and certain finalities. Despite the revisions and sophistication they provide for our ethical traditions, Levinas and Nietzsche miss the complex conjunction of imperatives by which responsibility could be institutional, cultural—and, as it were, naturalized.

If the announcements of the death of God are diversely made by a madman, by Nietzsche himself (the gods have laughed themselves to death), and in other guises as the legacy of the death of the Buddha, Nietzsche's "claim" is both a declaration and an observation: there is nothing more over our heads, no further hypostasis in whose image we are fashioned. This destitution of the subject, and of everything permanent that was anchored, even philosophically, in the divine principle, played itself out in the century whose advent Nietzsche regarded with apprehension. The moral destitution of the autonomous "subject" was (at least provisionally) sealed by the events grouped under the name "Auschwitz"; nevertheless, Levinas's amounts to a different conception of privation. Redefining the subject in light of heteronomy and elaborating the phenomenological *recouvrements* that show how every aspect of our existence is woven into fragilities both of body and of affectivity, Levinas reframes the very subject whose (Nietzschean) demise shook the viability and authority of liberal political conceptions of rights and freedom. Jill Stauffer, in "The Imperfect: Levinas, Nietzsche, and the Autonomous Subject," explores this challenge to liberalism, starting from its conceptions of the "state of nature" and the roots of social equality. Stauffer traces Levinas's reconceptualization back to the way he conceives desire and enjoyment, as a counterpoint to Nietzsche's emphasis on the will. We overlook that the Nietzschean "will to power" is, first, a pathos, an experience we *endure* passively. In so doing, we fail to see that Levinas's tropes—concerning embodied vulnerability to world but especially to others near to us—likewise unfold a fundamental, passive undergoing that is intersubjective in a way other than Nietzsche's intersubjectivity of forces in bodies and in nature. Levinas still aims at a certain subject; his destitution is superficially less sweeping than is Nietzsche's. However, the subject as singularity and integrity in Levinas can only arise thanks to its being acted upon by an other. Yet the challenge that Levinas and Nietzsche pose to the self-containment of conation and to the continuous, totalizing force of time's arrow also requires that they rethink the *ways* in which human existence unfolds as temporal. Stauffer underscores the work effected by the doctrine (and heuristic) of "eternal recurrence": we cannot will that the past be different, but we can will, here and now, that we willed it thus *from the outset and in every instance*. What does this mean, really? While it frees us from the bitterness of a past that cannot be refashioned, it also poses a direct challenge to the surreptitious heuristic that operates in all social-contract theory: we proceed as though the agreement given—by undetermined social actors—in the founding of a social union were also, somehow, ours to make and remake, *and as though we would have willed it thus had we been given the choice.* Yet Stauffer shows that this retroactive conception of social and political consent is neither quite "liberal" nor Nietzsche's vision; instead, it is close to a kind of revenge: I will accept that I would have affirmed the contract in this form, provided each of you also ratifies both the form and the accord it requires to exist as such. Nietzsche's innovation with eternal recurrence is close to Levinas's own discussion of the will and the other person: both oblige the will to take on a weight that only it can carry after the death of God (and all the deductive authorities attached to "God"). Levinas's later concept of "diachrony," or the *instant* of sensuous disinvestiture of the self, works similarly, provoking an affective "movement of recurrence" or recoil, such that the "self" proves to be a continuous tension, singularized because it cannot escape the emotional impact of its exposure to others and the temporal interruptions that constitute this embodied exposure. It is therefore possible—this is Stauffer's thematic innovation—to read Levinas and Nietzsche with a view to the similarities between their challenges to the liberal model of social coexistence and individual autonomy.

Jean-Michel Longneaux's "Nietzsche and Levinas: The Impossible Relation" explores the levels of Levinas's phenomenology: ipseity (oneself-ness) as enjoyment, innocent affectivity, and exploitation of resources, as well as a self-contained experience of time. Nietzsche's perspectivism lends itself to the varied layers of experience that Levinas describes under phenomenological brackets. At the root of these is revealed an active egoism that does not identify itself as an autonomous subject but that finds itself in a shiver of contentment. Nietzsche's aristocratic egoism admits comparison with the life that carries on at its level and in its particular time frame, without reference to the other person. It is crucial to the later development of Levinas's responsible subject that *this* aspect of its embodied life be phenomenologically evinced as active, unconscious innocence. And that was also Nietzsche's philological description of humans as beings with drives, prior to the inward thrust of forces that gradually produce both *ressentiment* and a "being who knows how to keep its promises" (GM I and II). The passivity and fragility of bodies, that they age first imperceptibly and always inexorably, argues that enjoyment and exploitation are nevertheless haunted by a disquiet, a concern for the morrow (Levinas). The themes of fatigue, lassitude, and a "time lost without return" allow Levinas to take a step different from—yet related to—Nietzsche's affirmation of life in the midst of suffering, Longneaux argues. The two thinkers, whose hermeneutics of innocent life unfold the layers of sensuous and affective experience *in and through time,* part company as Nietzsche grapples with a philosophy of life that would be both "pure becoming" and yet sufficiently stable to be thought. Nietzsche can only conceive a subject, Longneaux argues, provided this be qualified as a useful fiction—which returns Nietzsche to Levinas's subject that discovers its own innocent enjoyment as misplaced, somehow for naught, and even loathsome. For Nietzsche, the question thus arises: how to say "Yes" without reserve to life without affirming the unthinkable, senseless becoming? Like Stauffer, Longneaux recognizes that through the device of eternal recurrence, Nietzsche grasps will to power as pathos or as the "eternal coming of life to being" itself—and this much can, at least, be affirmed: "I am who I am" is acquiescence to the profound passivity that is not devoid of sense. *Amor fati* introduces a dimension of activity into the anonymous flux of becoming and the *bursting open* of the subject into mutually interpreting and dominating forces. Longneaux argues that the analyses of sensibility, living, and layers of selfhood or ipseity bring Levinas and Nietzsche close to each other. But ultimately, Longneaux will wonder whether Levinas has not ventured a significant divergence with Nietzsche.

Exploring a past time of the affects, which is not consciously "thematized" or represented, Levinas opens an experiential temporality different from Nietzsche's instant and his eternal recurrence. Yet, in so doing, has Levinas not constructed, differently but decisively, "an other world"? How should the Nietzschean reader understand the an-archical past in which an "I," before it congeals into the self-containment of egoity, is invested by something it cannot bring back to itself? How, again, shall the student of Nietzsche understand Levinas's arguments that hold separate the for-itself of enjoying, self-enclosed subjectivity, and the for-the-other? Nietzsche's experiments with time had not foreseen a temporality inaugurated by hetero-affection, being invested by an other. Yet Nietzsche understood clearly the distance necessary for a relationship that is neither a fiction of becoming-one, nor self-abnegation: friendship between two who are close *yet* distant enough to escape "the affect of pity." Only the problematization of the meaning and time of *relation and desire* allows us to accede to the deeper divergence between Nietzsche and Levinas.

Focusing also on the way in which the subject is persecuted, even loathed, in Levinas's work, Judith Butler looks for a place to breathe. That might not seem like the highest ethical aspiration—she admits as much—and yet breathing is a precondition for any life that could be subject to ethical reflection. Could the contemporary turn to ethics be akin to what made Nietzsche cry out about Hegel, "Bad air! Bad air!"? At any rate, we must think carefully about any threat of a heightened moralism. In her essay, "Ethical Ambivalence," Butler invites us to ponder just how much damage to the self is sustainable, and she does so by drawing our attention to the subjects given to us by Nietzsche and Levinas. Turning to Nietzsche, she shows how the noble at first appears as an individuated figure, distinct from the slave of slave morality. But these figures may not be distinct from each other. Thereupon Butler asks us to consider whether the one figure interrupts the other in much the same way that the Levinasian subject is fundamentally interrupted by its Other. If so, then we must admit that both thinkers give us a violated subjectivity. Do we not then find in the two philosophies the prerequisite for what Melanie Klein called "sustainable damage to the self"? Levinas's subject is split open by the wound of the other and persecuted by that Other. Nietzsche's animal "with the right to make promises" is given that right only when a memory is *burned* into the will. It is a "reflexive venting of the will against itself," a self-inflicted violence. Usually we understand that memory as one that creates "bad conscience" and thus is self-inflicted by the herd. But it would seem that even the noble, in keeping a promise, must remember an injury. If "something of the terror that formerly attended all promises, pledges and vows on earth is still effective" (GM 61), the noble must also subject himself to some form of self-terrorization in order to keep the promise that empowers his sovereign individuality. Now, if the noble and the herd are parts of the same subject, then there is no escape from self-inflicted violence. While these may form a fertile ground for thinking an ethics of the subject, the descriptions of subjectivity given to us by Nietzsche and Levinas are still sufficiently violent that we must ask ourselves: When we thus do violence to the self, what becomes of an ethic of nonviolence? What, really, is the ethic that we inherit from Nietzsche, and from Levinas? Might certain values, of generosity and forgiveness, be possible only through a *suspension* of their conceptions of ethicality?

Alighting on another area of our ethical ambivalence, Claire Elise Katz, in her essay "Thus Spoke Zarathustra, Thus Listened the Rabbis:

Philosophy, Education, and the Cycle of Enlightenment," turns our attention to the ethics of pedagogy. Katz finds in the standard Platonic model a constant source of failure. We inherit from this model teachers who are masters, distant from their students, and students who, in turn, aspire to become masters and continue the "cycle of enlightenment." The problem with the model is not so much its asymmetry as its lack of reciprocity: it is not open to the other and as such cannot produce subjects who respond. It reveals what Katz calls "the paradox of education": teaching, on the Platonic model, cannot teach what it is that students need in order to be able to learn—the *desire* to learn. Socrates and Nietzsche's Zarathustra both embody this model, though Zarathustra struggles against it. Katz delineates this struggle and then compares it to what she calls Levinas's Talmudic approach, where the teacher is someone who knows but also undergoes self-doubt and the student is someone who learns but also someone who teaches. The approach teaches resistance to the idea of an absolute truth, expounding a way of reading that is open to the other. Thus Katz demonstrates how Levinas gives us not only resources for ethics but a model of teaching that might actually succeed in performing ethics.

This is not just a claim about Levinas's method, however. In order to revive the Western tradition of philosophy, it might be necessary to step outside it and view pedagogy differently. In turn, the Talmudic model draws us closer to one Nietzsche envisioned, as he shares with the Talmudic rabbis a vision of how to refashion human beings—though Nietzsche, of course, was interested neither in building community nor in being open to the other in the ethical sense given to us by Levinas. Nietzsche's Zarathustra is the hermit who cannot conceive of dependence as healthy or positive, whereas the context of community, of being with others prior even to choosing, is nonnegotiable for Levinas and for the Talmudic scholars. But the rabbis (and, clearly, Levinas) were aware of something that Nietzsche also pointed out: human beings have an animal nature, are propelled by drives and instincts, and will act on these. The always-already responsible subject "competes," as it were, with the subject coiling in on itself in enjoyment, even in Levinas's prehistory of the subject. Katz argues that the Talmudic rabbis included competition, erotic desire, vulnerability, and dependence in their pedagogy precisely because these "animal" forces can foster healthy human relationships rather than contributing only destructive influences. While Nietzsche, via Zarathustra, explicitly discerned the flaws in the standard model of education, he was not able to get enough distance from it to see what the ailment was. Levinas and the Talmudic rabbis attempt to preserve philosophy from a pedagogic relation that is ultimately unphilosophical.

————

Part 2, "The Subject: Sensing, Suffering, and Responding," examines the importance of the body and its sensibilities in the work of both Levinas and Nietzsche. Bettina Bergo, in "The Flesh Made Word; Or, The Two Origins," delineates a history underlying the problems Levinas faced in his determination to deformalize Heidegger's moods without falling into the biologism of vitalist thought. The task: find some way to return to embodied states, to undercut analyses of moods like *angst*—already a form of comprehension—and to draw attention to the time lag between what we feel and how we become aware of feeling anything. In service of this, Levinas draws from Nietzsche both a reflective energy and an "aesthetic" of the other. We might say that Levinas's work on corporeal subjectivity parallels Nietzsche's attempts to deformalize the work of Kant; however, along with Nietzsche's oeuvre, Levinas inherits all of the "bad" appropriations of Nietzsche by *Lebensphilosophie*, which leaves him the unenviable task of preparing a way, along a thorny path, through what cannot be known cognitively, against a tide of biologistic understandings of the physiological self. However, if we come to "know" sensation as energy rather than as representation, understanding, or a priori synthesis, then we must question the primacy of consciousness as reason—and that is what Levinas and Nietzsche share: sensation as meaning before representation and comprehension. This is not only an innovation with regard to the lived body but has ethical ramifications. Levinas writes in *Totality and Infinity*: "*The strictly intellectualist thesis subordinates life to representation*" (TI 168). How, then, to communicate sensation without making of it an immobile "truth"?—a question for humanity living on after the death of God. For Nietzsche, sensation may already be a value judgment, but it is one made prior to cognition, spontaneously. Furthermore, for Nietzsche this is not a problem of biological mechanics but a moral problem: we humans are a synthesis of living being and intellect, with neither in ultimate control of the other. What does that make of our moralities?—another question for humanity living on after the death of God. Levinas takes the step necessary to deepen Nietzsche's reflection on the body and its forces: the upsurge of sensation, prior to its possession by consciousness, creates a surplus of meaning that consciousness on its own could not provide—it precedes consciousness and gives us a "priority" that Levinas demonstrates to be an ethical relation of the self to an other, wrought in a movement of affect. Bergo thus concludes that, for both thinkers, understanding the human body is a moral question, and this returns to what is urgent in the revisions to which the two thinkers subject the philosophical tradition.

Rosalyn Diprose, in her essay, "Nietzsche, Levinas, and the Meaning of Responsibility," brings the corporeal philosophies of Levinas and Nietzsche together to political ends. Beginning with a description of the juridico-moral concept of responsibility—understood as a determinism that requires strict continuity between past and future and as the promotion of individualism over sociality—she shows how Nietzsche simultaneously reinvents the self and the normative basis of conscience, precisely by rejecting the juridical approach. Nietzsche thus gives us a first break with determinism. Levinas later revises the same juridical concept of responsibility. He does this in part by relying on the same responsiveness we find in Nietzsche's philosophy: a corporeal, affective, futural movement of reevaluation and "self-overcoming." That movement transforms the habitual responses of a body normalized according to inherited laws and conventions. As such, conscience, for both thinkers, is a futural ability to exceed morality and custom; it is not a faculty willed in the freedom of reason by an autonomous individual. To the contrary, conscience is born in what Diprose calls "somatic reflexivity," a corporeal affective movement that precedes the faculty of reflection as the primary condition of agency and responsibility. However, insofar as Nietzsche ties the preservation of responsiveness to *sovereign* self-responsibility, Levinas would reply that Nietzsche did not delve deeply enough into the prehistory of responsibility.

Diprose combines Levinas's prehistory with Nietzsche's critique of juridico-moral responsibility, setting them in dialogue to propose an idea of responsibility between the two positions. Her aim is to diagnose how, in contemporary social relations, a failure of political responsibility precipitates a crisis of personal responsibility: when we lose the corporeal dimension of responsibility, we are left without resources for reasserting a futural conception of justice as a critique of the present, because the responsive body forms a self capable of risking an unknown future—it "goes under," according to Nietzsche, or, for Levinas, it contests the impossibility of the infinite weight of responsibility by shouldering the weight. Diprose draws our attention to how these bodies—bodies formed by somatic reflexivity, and especially the bodies of women, particular racial and ethnic groups, the socially disadvantaged, or the dispossessed—are at risk under the conditions of liberal democracy. The risk is due to the predominance of the juridico-moral concept of responsibility, which presupposes a self able to commit itself freely and definitively to a *particular* future. While this is something necessary to making promises, as Nietzsche showed, it does so at the expense of futurity itself. Rather than self-preservation, somatic reflexivity is the basis of conscience, "that felt conviction about what is right and wrong beyond convention." Thus, when we juxtapose the Levinasian intuition with Nietzsche's self-responsibility, we can pinpoint a problem with liberal democracy that neither thinker could locate on his own—in part because they both largely ignore politics. Diprose brings Levinas and Nietzsche together to show us how evasions of political responsibility affect not only those targeted but those on the "outside," by heightening their suffering (in Nietzsche's passive sense). Reading Levinas with Nietzsche reveals that when you destroy the other, you also destroy the source of that break with determinism that makes possible an ethic beyond normative conventions. Conscience born of corporeal responsiveness and capable of assuming responsibility for others helps us to reattach ethics and politics when they are wrested apart in abstract models of individualistic responsibilities and rights. The task we face, then, is to preserve somatic reflexivity against the normalizing effects of the juridico-moral concept of responsibility.

John Drabinski, in his lyrical essay "Beginning's Abyss," focuses on solitude over responsiveness—again to political ends. Solitude is another movement of subjectivity shared by Levinas and Nietzsche as, for both thinkers, beginning is marked by loss. Drabinski argues that Levinas's loss is not, or not only, "the Shoah" but the recognition that totalitarianism is not simply a form of politics but is the politics engendered by the Western tradition itself. For Levinas, the West is and has been a theory and practice of an eliminationist subjectivity. As such, our task is to begin, against the backdrop of damages that cannot be recuperated. Nietzsche's loss is the death of God—not the loss of an institution but the end of the very idea of belief. We are charged, consequently, with the responsibility of creating new values in the face of an abyssal emptiness. However, to leap over an abyss, one has to have registered the loss of what one called "home." Thus, in contrast to Heidegger, whose retrieval of ancient wisdom found loss *and then redemption,* these are losses without redemption. It makes sense, then, that for both Levinas and Nietzsche solitude is not the product of the subject's distance from the world but rather its overengagement with it. There is no escape here; the world is what we have.

To be sure, both thinkers give us melancholy discourses but, also, the possibility of hope. By reading Levinas and Nietzsche alongside Benjamin's "angel of history," Drabinski shows how they offer us the possibility of thinking a beginning even out of the most disastrous sense of loss. He writes that what Levinas and Nietzsche demonstrate is that "*life, even in its separation(s) from history, gives itself to thinking.*" The melancholic discourse produced in these philosophies evacuates an illusion that has dominated the West, leaving in its wake dead idols and, to be sure, pain. Yet it is also true that Nietzsche's work is playful and Levinas's is full of voluptuousness—both men produce work that could be read as ecstatic. Nevertheless the ecstasy is attended by pain: Zarathustra's lonely sadness, the writhings of Dionysus—self-overcoming is attached to the despondency of loss. *Totality and Infinity* promises peace against history's wars, and yet "our hands are emptied by the Other and my voice is always already violence." In *Otherwise Than Being*, obsession by the other disorients a subjectivity wrenched from its moorings in the tradition. And so we must read Nietzsche and Levinas with this melancholic thread in view, remaining sensitive to it even in the moments of transformation or release. For both thinkers, the collapse of what is foundational produces loss *and* possibility. Drabinski fittingly ends his essay with a meditation on how Levinas and Nietzsche give to us resources not only for thinking philosophical beginnings but for the real and painful task of beginning again after the catastrophe of human violence.

Picking up where Drabinski leaves off, David Boothroyd ("Beyond Suffering I Have No Alibi") asks after the meaning of the suffering of others, exploring the role of suffering and cruelty in Nietzsche's genealogy of morality and in Levinas's ethics. For both thinkers, the ancient and modern actualities of violence and cruelty—both suffered and perpetrated—constitute the context of their respective accounts of morality and moral value. Suffering may even be the ontological condition for critical thought, for both Nietzsche and Levinas. Nietzsche's noble differentiates himself from the herd by refusing the meaning attributed by the herd to suffering. Levinas's ethical relation becomes thinkable when the other's suffering is encountered as a pure passivity that places an ethical obligation on me. The "damages to self" that constituted Judith Butler's inquiry in this volume are viewed from the other side in Boothroyd's essay: What then is owed to the other who suffers? Boothroyd demonstrates that for Nietzsche and Levinas the passage of thought beyond suffering is decisive—for Nietzsche it is the "affirmation of life," for Levinas, "infinite responsibility." However, "beyond suffering" is an ambiguous movement that differs for the two thinkers. Nietzsche is concerned with the difference between how "pity" or "compassion" (*Mitleid*) is viewed by the noble (as a form of contempt for the herd's weakness) and by the herd (as self-pitying suffering). He ponders the consequences of this disparity for the fate of culture as a whole. Levinas, on the other hand, conceives "beyond suffering" in a kind of intimacy: something that cannot be "narrated as an edifying discourse"—pain resists capture in language. However, the beyond of suffering in Levinas's and Nietzsche's meditations converge in their discussions of suffering's differentiation and its ambiguity. Both thinkers "refuse" the other's suffering on some level—Nietzsche because it is a demand for pity, Levinas because one simply cannot suffer the other's suffering. In Nietzsche's work, the noble distinguishes himself from the herd and undertakes a reversal of the herd's will to ascetic idealism. But it is also true that, for Nietzsche, the other suffers "within me" because, as noble, if I do not "experience" the herd's suffering, then why should I conceive of overcoming the self I already am? Thus noble and herd are a play of opposing forces within the self. For Levinas, the differentiation of my suffering from the other's suffering is a precondition of the self's openness to others in ethical responsibility. This is so because the other also obliges me to be responsible and thus shapes what I am in a precedence of other over self—within the self. The ambiguity of suffering is tied to the self-other relation for both Levinas and Nietzsche. Boothroyd closes by asking what that implies for justice pursued through politics and whether the aim of justice implies that there can be an *alibi* for suffering.

Richard A. Cohen, in "Levinas, Spinozism, Nietzsche, and the Body," shows how Nietzsche discovered in 1881 a spiritual kinship with Spinoza, notably, around his formalist rejection of separation and transcendence. While Spinoza's philosophy of immanence proceeded on the affirmation of the "primacy and totality of context over terms," Nietzsche extended Spinoza's challenge to almost every metaphysical underpinning of morality. He proceeded by historicizing evaluations like "good" and "evil" and by insisting on a vitalist conception of embodied existence, over and against Spinoza's more intellectualist categories. Nietzsche turned from the idealism of Spinoza's *more geometrico* to a philosophical physiology of forces, health, and sickness. In so doing, Nietzsche radicalized Spinoza's *conatus essendi*—the striving of beings in their existence—introducing into that concept a perspective on life as dynamic levels of interaction. Encountered at that particular point, Levinas stands formally and emphatically opposed to both philosophies. His opposition unfolds not in indifference to life, nor in a return to a metaphysics of existence, but through a rethinking of self-sensing as the groundless origin of subjectivity. Levinas understands self-sensing as enjoyment *and* "dissatisfaction, disturbance, [even a] desire for *escape*" from one's own existence. Anguish and the repeating impulse to get out of oneself are not simply a revolt against the time or institutions that frame one's life. The repeating search for self-transcendence, informed by fleeting hopes—a theme found in Nietzsche, although developed differently by him—argues that embodied subjects tend to live as though there might be somewhere to which to escape, as though "*la vraie vie est ailleurs.*" The sources of this illusion of transcendence merit rethinking, which Levinas attempts to do in a way that distances him further from Nietzsche, Cohen argues. That intersubjective encounters, in their sensuous and affective impacts, might extract us from the immanence of physical and psychical self-containment—in which bodies are understood as "plays of vital forces"—demands a first-person phenomenology of being immediately confronted by another. That is Levinas's decisive contribution to a hermeneutics of embodiment and willing.

Thus, while both Nietzsche and Levinas work *around* the abstraction of Spinoza's concepts by means of their respective approaches to living bodies, Levinas's phenomenology leads us to question Nietzsche's conception of sensibility and his aesthetics. If, with the death of a certain God and a correlated subject, we can no longer philosophize without acknowledging the complexity of immanent drives and desires, can we sublate the gravity of shame and responsibility through a "new innocence"? Should self-overcoming be understood as giving oneself over to the play of the forces of life? Is the ultimate utility of history the intensification of the feeling of life for its own sake? Cohen entertains these questions and reminds us that Levinas's was never a mere morality of responsibility. Levinas's reinterpretation of embodied passivity and intersubjective investiture lived in the first person permits a different enlargement of the pathos that Nietzsche explored as the "subject" of will to power. If pathos and self-sensing passivity open other hermeneutic horizons, in which monadic selves are constitutively open to others, despite drives to self-affirmation, conation, and even suffering, then the Nietzschean thematics of self-transformation and overcoming can be approached otherwise—from the perspective of a being whose complex emergence requires an other-in-the-same.

———

The essays in part 3, "Heteronomy and Ubiquity: God in Philosophy," face squarely the problem that has already surfaced in the first two sections: can a God still inhabit philosophy? Focusing on the way in which both Nietzsche and Levinas take up human pain outside of teleological frameworks, John Llewelyn argues ("Suffering Redeemable and Irredeemable") that a crucial difference between the two philosophers lies in their conception of the possibility of suspending or, better, redeeming suffering. While Levinas's concern is overwhelmingly with extreme passivity as unavoidable suffering, Nietzsche's will to power enhances the beleaguered will. Levinas's exploration of the "*Moi*" as a subjectivity singularized in the accusative mode, through the face-to-face confrontation with the other, urges that the "I can" is a power and a freedom to act, "grounded" on a passivity relative neither to will nor to drives. With this claim, Levinas is close to Nietzsche, who showed that when you destroy the "true world" of metaphysics, you also abolish the apparent one. This means that unraveling the concept of an autonomous, self-causing will—whether human or divine—also undermines the mechanistic hypothesis of *unfree* wills. In fact, Nietzsche's destruction of the metaphysical ground of freedom heightened the urgency with which he sought a this-worldly redemption for suffering. An anti-Christian justice and aesthetic of life that does not foreswear all meaning must be conceived so that the nihilism intrinsic to ultimate justifications is avoided without proclaiming the inevitability of senseless misery. Llewelyn argues that if the "same" of Nietzsche's "eternal return of the same" is understood as an objective genitive, as the same for-the-sake-of ongoing returns themselves—rather than as a cosmological telos or anti-telos—then we recognize that Nietzsche's answer to the nihilism of the ideals of soul, divinity, and ultimate happiness is life's return to and for itself. Nietzsche's eternal recurrence thus takes over, for immanence, the form of an atheistic theodicy. Yet theodicy with neither God nor archè remains a doctrine of justification. Here, the justification essentially justifies its self-perpetuation, as a Yes-saying that is tragic in a particular Dionysian sense.

In Levinas's work, by contrast, no justification ransoms suffering, though we should never suppose that he is any less "this-worldly" than Nietzsche. Levinas understands suffering in its particularity, not as the (remaining) object worthy of a theodicy. He approaches suffering as a summons that we can say that we "have heard"—not the way we hear a categorical imperative but the way we discover a modification or change in us, by performing the response to it. Immediacy of this kind also points to a tragic commutativity in suffering. In enacting my responsibility to you, I recognize post facto that I fail to answer the call of other unique ones who are also "you." Thus, Nietzsche and Levinas separate in their conceptions of the tragic and how tragedy unfolds in life. The imperative of redeeming suffering—as opposed to the responsive awareness of its protean inevitability—suggests that Nietzsche was ultimately the more religious thinker of the two.

If a "*gaya scienza*" denotes a knowing both excessive and gratuitous, which comes into being with the "greatest recent event" (the death of God), then surely there is a *gaya scienza* in Levinas's philosophy as well as in Nietzsche's. While Levinas explicitly acknowledges Nietzsche's claim about the death of God, he never eschews *naming* God in his own work. Aïcha Messina ("Levinas's *Gaia Scienza*) argues that this surprising gesture of naming seeks to preserve the possibility of "giving a hearing" to a "God not contaminated by being," to a God that does not *exist* per se. Hearing "God" as limit or summons disrupts the call of existence and complicates the unfolding of existence as forces and wills. This ambiguous undertaking obliges Levinas to create a gay science of fragile expression—not wholly foreign to Nietzsche—and this constitutes his resistance to Heidegger's ontology. A chiasmus can be observed, in Nietzsche's and Levinas's works, at the point where each one breaks with being by means of a writing or an address (to us) that unravels and contests itself. It is textually and through writing's repetitive address that we are caught up in the world, but also that exceptions to the course of the "world" are stated. This is one value of history for life—as it also is of secular prophetic speech. Naming "God" has little to do with dramas of God's existence, and Levinas makes no theological appropriation of post-death-of-God thought. Writing this "name" is an oblique way of pointing toward an "outside," for Levinas. In this context, Messina explores the work done by the other in the philosophies of Nietzsche and Levinas. She shows that the attraction that the trope of the child held for both philosophers—as innocent affirmation and creativity—invites us to imagine the starting point of an ethics in Nietzsche. Yet a Nietzschean ethics could not be a morality. And for Levinas, "God" names a wager about the possibility of "goodness" that preserves a dimension of contestation at the heart of ethics of good conscience *and* metaphysical finalities. We may then wonder how the goodness of hearing and response stands with regard to Nietzsche's texts—so many of which entail an address to the friend, approached in the pathos of distance.

Working from Nietzsche's genealogy of forces, affirmative negation and negative negation—or the forces of self-affirmation versus the negation of what is unlike—Silvia Benso ("Levinas: Another Ascetic Priest?") poses an unskirtable question: Should we not consider Levinas's ethics as an expression of the values of the ascetic priest? Since Nietzsche's grand innovation, instituted with his pseudonymous declaration of the death of God, exegesis of timeless truths has been supplanted by critical genealogy and the study of signs by the analysis of symptoms. Against this displacement, Levinas insists on preserving transcendence and, with it, the distinction between interiority and exteriority. This allows him to maintain a conception of transcendence that does not foreclose the immanence, characteristic of post-Nietzschean conceptions of life. According to Benso, Levinas's essential project thus moves against Nietzsche's holism and eternity without resurrecting dead gods. Levinas can do this precisely because he shows that Nietzsche's rejection of *ressentiment*, or "negative negation," does not mean that those who negate "affirmatively"—the masters and the nobles—are free from intersubjective connectedness in their expansive affirmation of self. Self-affirmation also depends on that which it negates in order to express itself creatively. Thus, those primordial creators of value are not exempt from the interdependence that defines logics—including logics of negation. A dialectic of dependency is found on both sides of the genealogy of negative forces. Yet the side of the noble and that of the slave are neither equivalent nor symmetrical. They are both subsumed beneath a logic in which negation ensures their historical unfolding (and, later on, their corruption). Levinas eludes the accusation of asceticism and *ressentiment* by subtracting the face-to-face encounter from the logics of negation. Is this possible? Does the face of the Other not pronounce a kind of "No" to domination? Certainly, but this "passive resistance" elicits my desire—both for company and to account for myself. Again, we find the enigma of "goodness," always open to existential skepticism. Nevertheless, Levinas's interwoven descriptions of our innocent, affirmative existence ("love of life"), our enjoyments, and our experience of mutual exteriority inaugurate a sensuous "ground" of an ethics in which neither party *needs* the other, yet in whose encounter they cannot be without the other. The Levinasian innovation describes a positive "relation without relation" between two incommensurable, personal times and existences.

Proceeding from Nietzsche and Levinas's shared recognition that ethics since Nietzsche lacks all grounds that would provide it with ultimate justifications, Brian Schroeder pursues two fundamental themes in his essay, "Thinking of the Future: Apocalypse, Eschatology, and the Death of God": first, the problem of grounds as what separates and unites Nietzsche and Levinas; second, the difficulty of thinking the future, whether as hope or destiny, impossible peace or revealed reality. In theological traditions, the two approaches to the future alluded to here are sometimes called "apocalypse" and "eschatology." Schroeder explores what happens to these approaches after Hegel's philosophical synthesis of nature and spirit. Apocalypse is first concerned with a telos; it is defined by the advent of understanding and transparency. Conceptualization participates in the architecture of apocalypse, yet it may be that *naming* has a role outside of understanding and rationalization—notably, when ultimates are named. If older ethical schemas were all rooted in a metaphysics (of reason, the community, realized happiness, or destiny), then overcoming Western metaphysics and nihilism begins with the apocalyptic gesture of naming the catastrophe that is the death of God. Nietzsche would thus be a different sort of apocalyptic thinker than was Hegel. Moreover, the uncanny understanding that brings self-positing and free willing to their end is not Hegel's conjunction of spirit and nature but rather the death of the principle *and* the end once called "God." Apocalypse, in short, has run its course with Nietzsche.

Arguing that Levinas is influenced by the post-exilic prophetic tradition of messianic hope (eschatology) but *also* by Greek versions of eschatology (the "good beyond being"), Schroeder shows that Levinas has preserved eschatology in the wake of the self-undoing of apocalypse. In Levinas, eschatology appears as a way to understand subjectivity. Now, insofar as the subject emerges, affectively disturbed by something it cannot identify conceptually, and to the degree that the Other resists totalization in terms of experience, the holism of understanding implicit in apocalyptic thought is overturned by Levinas. Yet his eschatology remains as a fragile wager or a principle of hope. It is worth pondering, however, whether Nietzsche did not also open an eschatological way past the "apocalyptic death of God," notably in his "Yes," said to life, for nothing but life itself.

————

Heteronomy and ubiquity: the concepts have to be understood, here, in the ways in which they interact with each other. It is possible to deem ubiquitous a concern with the future as meaning and hope in Levinas and Nietzsche. A struggle with material suffering that slips past redemption, as it makes clear the insufficiency of responsibility to others, is also a shared thematic. For Levinas as for Nietzsche, the ubiquity of negativity is the object of a struggle, albeit engaged differently by each philosopher. Nietzsche sought to wrest nobles and the noble spirit from reactive heteronomy. Ultimately, it was the metamorphosis into the child that showed a way through the nihilisms—of a past mortgaged, of (self-)subjection, and of metaphysical projections. But it is through heteronomy that Levinas conceived a different structure of subjectivity, which, in its everyday practice, affirmed life in innocence. The surprising corporeal ubiquity of affirmation in Levinas's philosophy makes possible a heteronomy in which ethical resistance and summons neither devastate me nor elicit immediate violence. If Levinas's solution to nihilism recurs to the uncanny name of (a dead?) "God," this name remains a trope for the recurrence of the deformalized exigency that animates ethical life: I am never fully acquitted of what I owe to this one, to that one, and yet affirmation is not submerged. This ambiguous and fragile sense enlivens conceptions of justice as correction, critique, and witnessing. If the bridge beyond the human is a creative play that affirms life in Nietzsche, then Levinas sets up a kind of transition within intersubjective encounters—between innocent consumption and a memory of conscience. In neither case does the proverbial bridge *reach* the other bank of the river. It remains an opening that does not erect idols, old or new.

I

Revaluing Ethics

Time, Teaching, and the Ambiguity of Forces

I

The Malice in Good Deeds

ALPHONSO LINGIS

EMMANUEL LEVINAS locates the ethical experience neither in the rationality of the social regulation of behavior, nor in the imperative for rationality internal to the mind, but in an event, a specific form of encounter among humans: when I find another facing me. He or she who faces me is not simply exposing himself or herself to me as an object of my perception but is calling for my attention and speaking to me. Before speech is informative, it is vocative and imperative. It is the voice of a vulnerable and mortal body. In the other facing me Levinas finds the ethical imperative. It is not found in an abstract and universal form and is not an imperative for acts that are universal or universalizable. The ethical imperative is encountered in the appeal and demand the other puts on me in facing me, in the concrete exhibition of his needs.

Levinas rejects "intersubjectivity," rejects the Hegelian doctrine that it is in reciprocal recognition that each arises out of animality to free and responsible subjectivity. He posits an essential asymmetry in the face-to-face encounter. In the enjoyment of the sensuous elements, an egoism first arises as a positive event. In inhabitation and in labor, this "I" acquires a position and appropriates a range of resources. The encounter with another who perceptibly faces does not give rise to a collective being-with (*Mitsein*); instead, the other who faces intrudes upon my enjoyment and possession, contesting them, putting demands on my resources.

In *Totality and Infinity*, Levinas centered on speech, its vocative and imperative force, as the experience in which the other faces. He did emphasize that the other speaks with his needy, vulnerable, and mortal body and that I respond not with my voice only but with my body that has a position and a posture supported on a home base and that exists in appropriating the resources of my environment. But in *Otherwise Than Being*, Levinas showed that the sensitivity to the appeal and demand of another is first a being affected by, afflicted by, his needs, his suffering, and his mortality, before it is an understanding of his words. The encounter with another makes an impact on my sensibility, which, even before it is sensitive to the elements or open to things, is sensitive to the radical exteriority of the other. The sensitivity to another makes my enjoyment of the sensuous environment and my perception of things a sensitivity to the resources of the wide world.

The action that is really *my* action then is not the free action that I legislate for myself but responsible action—responsive to the needs of other humans, who are more exterior to me than the substances of the world or the fathomless elements in which things take form. In responsible action one assembles and integrates one's forces and resources and comes to exist as an integral I.

―――――

To maintain the distinctive exteriority of the other, irreducible to an alter ego, Levinas widens the gap between the phenomenal reality of the other human who faces me and that of other beings in the phenomenal environment. The elements—light, warmth, chromatic tonality and resonance, ground—are revealed in and exist for us in sensuous enjoyment. Although he refuses Heidegger's dissolution of things into relationships and asserts their existence as substances, existing in themselves, Levinas maintains that they only appear as things by being constituted in and through inhabitation, appropriation, and labor. But the other is not reducible to what I enjoy or what I inhabit and use.

To maintain the irreducible alterity of the other human, Levinas invokes infinity, or rather infinition. This dimension of unendingness seems evident in speech: every response elicits a response from the other—affirmation or contestation—and every contestation and also every affirmation require a response in turn from me. Although Levinas does affirm, in *Time and the Other*, that needs are finite and end in satisfaction, he then makes them give rise to an unending demand in the other, through his analysis of responsibility (TO 63). Against the juridical concept of responsibility that has dominated ethics since Aristotle, Levinas shows that responsibility cannot be measured by what I have foreseen and intended. To be responsible for my child is to take responsibility for what others have done to him, to take responsibility for what the debilitating or twisted conceptions that the culture that lies beyond me and existed before me have done to him. If he is born deformed or autistic, this is perhaps the result of a recessive gene from generations back, but it is I who must respond for it with all my resources.

Levinas conceptualizes this unending dimension of demand that opens in the one who faces me as infinity, and he names it "God." He invokes not "the sacred" but the monotheist God, conceived not substantively but as the "wholly Other," whose uniqueness speaks in the singularity of the one who singles me out to face me.

We can object that if the absolute alterity—absolutely other than any concrete need or want with which the other faces me—of Levinas's monotheist God is constitutive of the otherness of every other who faces me, the demand put on me loses its location in the midst of the resources of the world and its determinateness. And the otherness of the one who faces me and another who also faces me is reduced to difference—difference in time and place, difference between the empirical figure of want and need each presents.

If this vocative and imperative force is not localized and singularized, if the imperative put on me is metaphysical—issuing from the Kantian God, or the utterly nonobjective Sartrean Other which Merleau-Ponty called a "faceless haunting," or Levinas's monotheist God—it cannot give rise to a veridical response in language or a practical response in deeds. A veridical response responds to the environment open to observation and verification by the singular other who faces me. A practical response to the requirement another presents supplements the other's own resources and the resources at hand in his or her environment. The otherness of the other must be each time particular.[1]

————

Since responsiveness is constitutive of me as a subjectivity, Levinas depicts ethical acts, responsive initiatives, done by me as the acts that are genuinely *my* acts. They contrast with acts done to maintain or aggrandize myself or acts done in response to the abstract or anonymous decrees, rational or not, of institutions, or done in conformity with social mores. Levinas shows that the needs and wounds of another affect, afflict, my sensibility immediately and elicit my resources. The eyes do not view the suffering of the wounded one; they wince, feeling the pain in themselves. He affirms that before the other I am the rich one; I have always something to say, something to offer. This richness is in life that enjoys the fathomless nourishment of the elements, has a home base on the supporting ground, appropriates the resources of the environment, and labors.

Friedrich Nietzsche observes that we tend to understand the suffering and needs of another too crudely and we too quickly take ourselves to have the resources to remedy them. In our sense that we can help with our commonplace notions and resources there is a will to power, which the weak too readily seize upon. A keener eye may understand that the suffering another endures he has to endure for his own destiny. (The landlady thinks that what Beethoven needs is good soup and regular sleep.) Even the emaciated refugee needs not simply food but food that comes with acknowledgment of the justice of her wrath and with the pledge that she will see her village garden again. The suffering that we see in another's spasms and tears is not simply in his own body; it is in the coupling that body has on what it cares for. This youth is in vigorous health and has a panoply of educational and professional opportunities open to him, but he suffers, afflicted with the suffering of the oppressed in his land or in distant lands he has never seen (GS §338).

Levinas affirms that the vulnerability and suffering—the mortality—of another concerns us; the doctor, he says, is an essential dimension of our being-with-others (TI 234). Nietzsche cautions:

A physician has not now attained the highest degree of training of which he is capable when he knows the best and most recent remedies and is practiced in applying them, and can draw those quick conclusions from effects to causes that make the celebrated diagnostician—he also has to possess an eloquence adapted to every individual and calculated to touch him to the very heart, a manliness at the sight of which all timorousness (the wormrot that undermines all invalids) takes flight, a diplomat's flexibility in mediating between those who require joy if they are to become well and those who for reasons of health must (and can) make others joyful, the subtlety of an agent of police or an advocate in comprehending the secrets of a soul without betraying them.

(HA 1:§243, 2:§336)

What is more, the one we see suffering may be suffering because he inflicts great suffering on others and hears the cry of their suffering. The revolutionary finds himself unable to endure the oppression of the poor and will inflict upon them still greater oppression when he launches the struggle. Their agony intensifies his pain, which he has to suffer (GS §325).

Levinas elaborates the existence of the I as a being-for-others, responsible for others, responsible for the very irresponsibility of others. But, Nietzsche asks, if we really understand another's irresponsibility and his distress and also the misfortune that has befallen him blindly, would not our understanding convert actively into "an overall justification of his way of living and thinking"?

Consider how every individual is affected by an overall philosophical justification of his way of living and thinking: he experiences it as a sun that shines especially for him and bestows warmth, blessings, and fertility on him; it makes him independent of praise and blame, self-sufficient, rich, liberal with happiness and good will; incessantly it refashions evil into good, leads all energies to bloom and ripen, and does not permit the petty weeds of grief and chagrin to come up at all. In the end one exclaims: How I wish that many such new suns were yet to be created! Those who are evil or unhappy and the exceptional human being—all these should also have their philosophy, their good right, their sunshine! What is needful is not pity for them. (GS §289)

Nietzsche observes that we lack a name for indignation at another's unhappiness—"the more manly form of pity" (DB 1 §78). But he understands that having to receive from another what one needs is a recognition of dependence and servility; it debases the receiver. That is why the receiver often refuses any sign of the gratitude that the giver awaits as an affirmation of his power. Nietzsche also understands why Jonathan Swift said that men are grateful in the same degree as they are vengeful. In expressing his gratitude, the receiver affirms the resources and power he now has, which intrude upon the sphere of influence of the giver. The politician who publicly declares how much he has received from the great statesman is encroaching upon his place in the nation and in history. (Academics who in their "Acknowledgments" list the renowned authorities who have assisted them in their researches are hoisting themselves up to their level.) "That is why every community of the good, that is to say originally the powerful, places gratitude among its first duties" (HA 1:§44).

Levinas locates the other above oneself; his superior position lies in the force his appeal and demand have to make claims on me—and this force, in turn, lies in the unendingness of those claims, the dimension of infinity, or God, in them. Nietzsche, however, observes that "under civilized conditions everyone feels himself to be superior to everyone else in at any rate one thing" (HA 1:§509). His "under civilized conditions" would indicate that in the ever-growing complexity of skills, concretely exercised in each time's particular social and psychological conditions, each one finds that at this time and place he is best at something. We can extend that to say that in any conditions we may find ourselves best in sensitivity, sensuality, temperament, or physical strength to care for this child or this garden or to maintain ourselves composed in boredom or in suffering. "It is upon this," Nietzsche argues, "that the general mutual goodwill that exists depends, inasmuch as everyone is someone who under certain circumstances is able to be helpful and who thus feels free to accept help without a sense of shame" (HA 1:§509).

Levinas cites Pascal approvingly that "the ego is detestable"—the egoism that arises in enjoyment and materializes itself in inhabitation, appropriation, and labor. In responding to another, this egoist self gathers up all its resources and acquires the identity of an "I"; its responsible acts are its own. Nietzsche finds an egoism in apparent altruism but derives a distinctive insight from it.

> A good author whose heart is really in his subject wishes that someone would come and annihilate him by presenting the same subject with greater clarity and resolving all the questions contained in it. A girl in love wishes the faithfulness and devotion of her love could be tested by

the faithlessness of the man she loves. A soldier wishes he could fall on
the battlefield for the victorious fatherland; for his supreme desire is vic-
tor in the victory of his fatherland. A mother gives to her child that of
which she deprives herself, sleep, the best food, if need be her health,
her strength.   (HA 1:§57)

In all such instances one loves something of oneself—an idea, a desire, an
offspring—more than something else of oneself. "Man treats himself not
as *individuum* but as *dividuum*" (HA 1:§57). And just as love of another is
"understanding and rejoicing at the fact that another lives, feels and acts in
a way different from and opposite to ours" (HA 2:§75), so also self-love is
astonishment and rejoicing at a part of oneself that appears enigmatic and
acting on its own.

This explains why it is not only unmagnanimous to be always the one
who bestows; one feels shame in it.

There are occurrences of such a delicate nature that one does well to
cover them up with some rudeness to conceal them; there are actions
of love and extravagant generosity after which nothing is more advis-
able than to take a stick and give any eyewitness a sound thrashing: that
would muddle his memory. Some know how to muddle and abuse their
own memory in order to have their revenge at least against this only
witness: shame is inventive.   (BG §40)

Nietzsche finds the impulse to give not in an agent "I" that assembles
its resources, a life that in acting becomes an agent, but in the intrinsic
happiness of life. He evokes the immemorial dialogue between the wise
man and the one who comes to him, seeking happiness: "What must I
do to be happy?" The wise answer is: "Be happy, and then do what you
will" (KSA 10:195). For happiness is not something outside that is to be
sought in things; it is in life, and is the exultant upsurge of excess energies.
Happiness is not something acquired by seeking; it happens by happen-
stance, as our life, improbable result of one of billions of possible combina-
tions of the roughly 30,000 human genes, happens by chance. Happiness
is the feeling of the upsurge of superabundant energies, and this happiness
radiates and discharges itself gratuitously. The good deeds that the powerful
and joyous life realizes are done out of no inner need and ask for nothing
in return.

It is so unmagnanimous always to play the bestower and giver and to show one's face when doing so! But to give and bestow and to conceal one's name and awareness one is bestowing a favour! Or to have no name, like nature, in which the most refreshing thing of all is that here we at last no longer encounter a giver and bestower, a 'gracious countenance'!   (DB §464)

But this happiness is not innocent generosity; indeed Nietzsche affirms that "the evil of the strong harms others without giving thought to it—it *has* to discharge itself; the evil of the weak *wants* to harm others and to see the signs of the suffering it has caused" (DB §371)—but in fact the compulsion to destroy and to mock likewise issues from happiness. If magnanimous acts issue involuntarily from our nature, they do so only when this nature is a cultivated nature. Indeed, love, the pleasure over someone remote from ourselves, has to be learned. "We have to learn to love, learn to be charitable, and this from our youth up; if education and chance offer us no opportunity to practice these sensations our soul will grow dry and even incapable of understanding them in others" (HA 1:601, GS §334).

———

Emmanuel Levinas has fundamentally changed ethical philosophy in locating the ethical imperative in an experience, which he has lucidly analyzed phenomenologically. His ethical writings are largely confined to the ever more skillful analysis of this original ethical experience. There is little discussion of the social regulation of behavior and the institutions that societies elaborate. There is little attention to the conflict that arises when attending to the needs of the one I encounter results in depriving resources from those I do not encounter—the most urgent problem in today's world of increasing, institutionalized global inequality. In expending my funds on medical treatment on my son, who requires repeated and immensely complicated surgery, and in giving him all the attention and support he needs, I neglect the wants and needs of my other son and my spouse. In famine times the bread I give from my stores to the stranger is taken from my own family. What we in the rich countries think our children need is the result of turning distant lands to export-driven economies that do not supply the basic needs of their people.

Nietzsche recognizes this conflict already on the level of affective relations with individuals; we do feel hedged in when someone favors us with his affection. There arises in us a grudge against a friend or lover for his injustice in prizing us at the expense of others who are equally worthy of, and may well need, his friendship or his love (DB §488). Thus while jealous love may want the exclusive attention of the lover, this closed utopia is uneasy; there stirs the subterranean sense that we are unworthy of such exclusive valuation and that it is unjust:

> Do we not blush when we detect ourselves in the act of feeling a violent aversion? But we ought to do the same in the case of violent affections too, on account of the injustice which they too involve! More, indeed: there are people who feel as though hedged in, and whose heart grows tight, when anyone favours them with his affection only by *withdrawing* something of his affection from others. When we hear from his voice that *we* are chosen and preferred! Ah, I am not grateful for this favour, I notice in myself a grudge against him who wants to favour me in this way: he ought not to love me at the *expense* of others! I want to see how I can endure myself at my own expense! And often I find that my heart is full and I feel in high spirits—to a man who possesses such things one should give nothing that *others* stand in need, sorely in need of!
>
> (DB §488)

It is the third party, Levinas says, who judges the truth of what I respond to my interlocutor and what my interlocutor responds to my response. He or she determines a just distribution of resources for the needs of each of us. But how would he or she not simply demand of us that the zone of the environment I have shared with my interlocutor be now put in terms he or she understands and the resources I have made available to the needs of the one who faces me be offered to the third party?

Levinas inherits the phenomenology that reduces the world—the landscapes and oceans, ecosystems, and other species—taken as independently real by the natural attitude into a phenomenal world, appearing to us, existing for us. He elaborates a phenomenology that explicates the other who, in facing us, appears as not appearing to us and not existing for us. But there are imperatives in things. To see something is to see what it requires to exist in its setting. There is no inhabitation, appropriation, or labor without recognizing that to perceive what is, is to perceive what it requires to be protected, nourished, and healed. These are not simply hypothetical imperatives, derived from the imperative to answer the needs of human beings. The landscapes, ecosystems, and other species that appear to us do not appear as existing for us, for our needs and wants.

Levinas and Nietzsche have so radicalized our understanding of the experience of our encounters with others and of the good we do to them and the malice in that good that they dominate the ethical philosophy read today. But who can think of our interpersonal behaviors without thinking of the scandalously growing gap between obscenely rich countries and destitute countries, and between rich and poor in all countries? Without thinking of the global corporate powers that have been institutionalized in our societies and of the massive weapons of state terror that guarantee them, today only disrupted by terrorist acts of individuals and small commandos? Vast populations are reduced to destitution, are ravaged by plagues, and die in genocidal wars programmed and armed by neocolonial and neoimperalist policies. We urgently need an analysis of the imperative imposed on social and economic institutions and explanations of effective and institutional ways to make them responsible.

Who can think of the imperatives imposed by and in our interpersonal behaviors without thinking of ecological and climatic destruction? But neither Nietzsche nor Levinas recognizes any imperative imposed on us by nature. The earth, light, warmth, liquidity, chromatic density, sonority, and the landscapes, ecosystems, oceans, and planetary system do not appear, do not exist, as a phenomenal field constituted by human subjectivity; human subjectivity is an evolutionary part of Earth's ecosystem. The most urgent ethics of responsibility is yet to be elaborated.

NOTE

1. See Alphonso Lingis, "Theoretical Paradox and Practical Dilemma," in *International Journal of Philosophical Studies* 12, no. 1 (2004): 21–28.

2

The Imperfect

Levinas, Nietzsche, and the Autonomous Subject

JILL STAUFFER

WHAT IS clear but also surprising about the terrain inhabited jointly by Nietzsche and Levinas is its shared fixation on ethics. Levinas is the philosopher of an all-surpassing responsibility against which there has never been an opportunity to choose and that seems to be given to us by a God. Nietzsche's philosophical oeuvre stands for the will to power of free spirits who live on after the death of God. This may leave us asking: Is ethics so broad that it can house two figures who inhabit opposite ends of a spectrum that distances self from other, will from passion, constraint from freedom? Perhaps. But it seems to me more likely that while ethics may be defined by the aforementioned oppositional categories, both Levinas and Nietzsche would ask us to imagine the field differently.

At the behest of that appeal, I will focus on how each reconceives temporality, subjectivity, and ethics—and how their revisions transform certain strands of political philosophy. Both thinkers call on us to view time differently, such that synchronous temporality's "present" is interrupted by a diachronic temporality, to ethical effect. Those intersecting temporalities in turn define for us what subjectivity is or can be, leaving us with a subject we may not recognize readily. It is no accident, then, that both thinkers leave us with a philosophic legacy that is fundamentally unsettling.

Dangerous Question Mark

Levinas has written about how the modernity of modern human beings "breaks up as an impossibility to remain at home" (OB 184).That "homelessness" results from the subject's destitution, its having been desituated, "robbed" of the autonomy that, in the narrative of subjectivity that it had partly inherited, partly constructed, was guaranteed as innate, or at any rate, unquestionable. In Levinas's philosophy the sufficiency-unto-self of the "I" is radically undermined, supplanted by a new narrative wherein the subject is a hostage, always already persecuted by a responsibility to which it never had opportunity to consent. Nietzsche, on the other hand, gives us a subject inheriting a world that can no longer rely on the unifying power of a shared monotheism, and yet, Nietzsche proclaims, his world (and our world) is still ordered according to a belief in that impossible unity. Nietzsche evicts the human subject from her comfortable home and sends her wandering the frontiers of a new world so that she might learn what it means to will her way to a revaluation of all things. As such, Nietzsche accomplishes one form of the destitution of the human subject that aspires, in Nietzsche's terms, to "get there, that way, where you today are least at home" (BG 137). Nietzsche's subject then becomes, in Levinas's terms, the modernity of modern human beings that "breaks up as an impossibility to remain at home" (OB 184).

For Nietzsche, "revaluation" is the task of a "dangerous question mark." Such are philosophers who,

> by applying the knife vivisectionally to the chest of the very virtues of their time, they betrayed what was their own secret: to know of a new greatness of man, of a new untrodden way to his enhancement. Every time they exposed how much hypocrisy, comfortableness, . . . how many lies lay hidden under the best honored type of their contemporary morality, how much virtue was outlived.   (BG 137)

Nietzsche is the untimely antimoralist who dislodges established values, identifies hypocritical stances, and replaces dead forms with new creations in the service of a new world and new humanity. It is less clear, of course, how the above quotation might apply to the work of Levinas, a post-Holocaust thinker whose philosophical oeuvre introduces us to some of the most demanding ethical ideas that have ever strained at the edge of thought. It might seem that the antimoralist has encountered his opposite—a philosopher of morality. And yet Levinas draws us away from the ordered rules we associate with ethics and morality, into disorder, upsetting our ideas about what our ethical responsibilities are and how they are incurred. Levinas thereby "betray[s] what [is his] own secret: to know of a new greatness of man, a new untrodden way to his enhancement." What is innate or admirable about the human being according to what sometimes gets called "the Western tradition" is subjected by Levinas to reversal: the subject is not free and autonomous by nature but rather is shot through with vulnerabilities against which there has been neither time nor opportunity to defend itself. Vulnerabilities define us as human but also contribute to a "new greatness" that enables us to reimagine what it means to be human beings and to reconceive the basis on which we figure our ideas of selfhood and of justice. Compare that with Nietzsche's Zarathustra, preaching to his "higher men": "The most concerned ask today: 'How is man to be preserved?' But Zarathustra is the first and only one to ask: 'How is man to be overcome?' " (TZ 287).

Levinas also, like Nietzsche's philosopher, exposes the "hypocrisy" and "comfortableness" that is bound to the dominant narrative of the subject—the subject always already self-sufficient and capable of consenting to any duty she might bear. That dominant view leads to the production of theories of right that rely on universality but that grant rights only in particular circumstances, such that meaningful rights enter the world not as rights but as privileges. "How many lies lay hidden under the best honored type" of our contemporary morality, Levinas might ask along with Nietzsche. "How much virtue" is outlived? In terms more his own, Levinas asks: "It is then not without importance to know if the egalitarian and just State in which man is fulfilled . . . proceeds from a war of all against all, or from the irreducible responsibility of the one for all, and if it can do without friendships and faces" (OB 159–60). In this passage Levinas asks whether the "state of nature" narrative that helps justify the Western idea of legitimate governance could really be the basis of the just state to which that narrative claims to aspire. Could the just state emerge from the war of all against all (or even from the friendlier Lockean, Rousseauist, or Rawlsian versions of the state of nature)? In other words, can we design institutions of justice based only on a narrative of disinterested formal equality aimed at a socialized version of self-preservation? Can a just institution be created "without friendships and faces"? Nietzsche may not strike anyone as a philosopher of "the Other," but part of what I aim to establish is that his philosophy asks as much of and weighs as heavily on the human subject as does Levinas's ethics. Indeed, as Nietzsche concludes his description of the "dangerous question mark," he writes that such a philosopher "would even determine value and rank in accordance with how many things he could bear and take upon himself, how far he could extend his responsibility" (BG 137).

That responsibility will be a product of will, which for Nietzsche is largely a passivity. Of course, Nietzsche is the philosopher of will to power. That leads to two common misunderstandings. The first mistakes Nietzsche's concept of will for effective volition and thus thinks that Nietzsche merely requires of us a decisiveness or commitment that fits nicely with ideas about rational autonomy. However, it is not only Levinas who advances his arguments by describing just how impossible it is for the "I" to act as an origin: for Nietzsche, the will is a pathos. Something always precedes any ability "I" might posit to have mastered my world from the ground up. Perhaps the most important insight of all, for Nietzsche, what he often calls "the thought behind his thought," is the knowledge—or, rather, the *acknowledgement undergone*—of what the will is. In *Beyond Good and Evil* Nietzsche writes:

> Willing seems to me to be above all something complicated, something that is a unit only as a word—and it is precisely in this one word that popular prejudice lurks, which has defeated the always inadequate caution of philosophers. So let us for once be more cautious, let us be "unphilosophical": let us say that in all willing there is, first, a plurality of sensations.   (BG 25)

Sensations come first. The will is not all volition. Nietzsche counsels us that "in every act of the will there is also a ruling thought." He then adds: "the will is not only a complex of sensation and thinking, but it is above all an affect, and specifically the affect of the command. . , . A man who wills commands something within himself that renders obedience, or that he believes renders obedience" (BG 25–26). According to Nietzsche, what is "strangest about the will" is that, through a series of misunderstandings, "he who wills believes sincerely that willing suffices for action" (BG 26). But when we will we are at the same time the commanding and the obeying party[1]—"we are accustomed to disregard this duality, and to deceive ourselves about it by means of the synthetic concept 'I,'" and thus "a whole series of erroneous conclusions, and consequently of false evaluations of the will itself, has become attached to the act of willing" (BG 26). Nietzsche sought to diagnose this misunderstanding with regard to *what the will is,* but his work is as often as not subjected to misreadings because of the very same misunderstanding.

Nietzsche and Levinas both dislodge our settled ideas about subjectivity and will. However, neither the sovereign self nor the force of rational will is discarded altogether by either philosopher; rather, both concepts are unsettled in order that we might question their primordiality. Once the concepts have been displaced, they are refigured and paradoxically rendered more powerful—because we will have moved beyond the useful fiction into a franker embrace of the conditions of human life: vulnerability, sensibility, and, for Levinas, the human relationship, for Nietzsche, the will as pathos. That paradox of the vulnerable subject whose embrace of an unchosen responsibility delivers her to conditions of meaningful liberty in Levinas's philosophy is echoed in the difficult interrelation (explored in what follows) between Nietzsche's will to power and his eternal recurrence: one limits the other but in so doing gives back to what it constrained a strength it would have lacked if left to its own devices.

The Eternal Recurrence

If there is no God, and yet the world can be revalued, who will do that work? It will have to be the human subject, without its God. Nietzsche's point: if the human subject fails to take on such a responsibility, she no longer has the luxury of finding a God culpable for what is senseless in the human world—if the world, which has no inherent meaning, lacks meaning altogether, it can be no one's fault but her own. Such a responsibility weighs quite a bit. Could there be anything more terrifying than this challenge from Zarathustra when read in all the depth of its meaning? "'This is my way; where is yours?'—thus I answered those who asked me 'the way.' For *the* way—that does not exist" (TZ 195).

The human being who wants a God to blame or to praise has what Nietzsche calls "a revering heart." The aim of *Thus Spoke Zarathustra* is to break revering hearts, freeing will to power from its self-made prison by teaching the self to undergo the eternal recurrence. The eternal recurrence presses on the self the limits of what will can achieve. For instance: will that wants to change the past sinks in the impotence of revenge. "Revenge" is Nietzsche's name for a relationship to time wherein the will wants what is most impossible: to change the past. Revenge, when left unchecked, even inverts the relation between activity and passivity. Think of it in terms of revenge warfare. Someone kills my friend. No amount of will can change that fact. What I *can* do, however, is kill the person who killed my friend. That would seem to be the "active" thing to do, whereas it would be "passive" to do nothing. That is how revenge cycles proceed, with killing traded for killing, endlessly. But if all my actions are *re*actions, determined by a past event that cannot be changed, then I am acting in a determined universe where all my actions are more like fate—passivities. It would be more active, paradoxically, if I were to act otherwise or refuse to strike back, stepping out of determinism to create new values. As the Nietzsche of *Thus Spoke Zarathustra* writes:

> Willing liberates; but what is it that puts even the liberator himself in fetters? 'It was'. . . . Powerless against what has been done, [the will] is an angry spectator of all that is past. . . . that he cannot break time and time's covetousness, that is the will's loneliest melancholy. . . . What means does the will devise for himself to get rid of his melancholy and to mock his dungeon? Alas, every prisoner becomes a fool; and the imprisoned will redeems himself foolishly. That time does not run backwards, that is his wrath. . . . This, indeed this alone, is what revenge is: the will's ill will against time and its 'it was.' (TZ 139–40)

Wrath against "it was" wants to change the past. This is what might happen to a will too enamored of its autonomy and thus unreflective of the limits to what it can accomplish. But a deed once done is finished and, as finished, is no longer within the power of its creator to change. As such, will to power, thought too quickly as absolute autonomy, is defeated by time. But Zarathustra has a solution: "The will is a creator. All 'it was' is a fragment, a riddle, a dreadful accident—until the creative will says to it, 'But thus I willed it.' Until the creative will says to it, 'But thus I will it; thus shall I will it'" (TZ 141). That is Nietzsche's doctrine of eternal recurrence. It requires that the will "will backwards," which means: whatever happened in the past *is* what I willed and would will again. It is important to remark that this is not the same as deciding that what I would have willed, given what I know now, is what I did will. The distinction is weighty. I have to will that I did will what I willed. Eternal recurrence even expands the meaning of "what I did will" to include the unforeseen developments that the original will could not have predicted.

One way of understanding what matters about the distinction between "willing backwards" and "deciding that what I would have willed is what I did will" comes to us from liberal political theory. Social contract theory basically requires that we say about the consent we give to institutions that we would have willed it if we had been given a choice. So it does not matter, for social contract theory, that most of us never had opportunity to consent expressly to the rules, conventions, and institutions under which we live. What matters is that we would have consented, had we been given a choice. That allows us both to have the cake made of our arrival in the world too late to have been its creators, and to eat, too, that cake's message that we can, after the fact, represent our agency to ourselves as if we had been the world's creators. We say, "I would have willed this." But that is not Nietzsche's idea. Indeed, social contract theory's meaning is closer to the spirit of revenge. Revenge is always trying to change the past, turning a cake made out of too-late into one that we tell ourselves tastes like always-already.

Eternal recurrence makes a more difficult demand, and one as individualized as the weight on Levinas's ethical hostage—it requires of *me* that *I* break *my* revering heart. To want a world that could only have issued out of my plans is to refuse a God; to want a world wherein the past can be other than it was is to want a world redeemed . . . by a God. Such a subject wants something to revere, something to take on the weight only the subject itself can carry after the death of God. It requires a God. But it also refuses a God because it will not accept any duty to which it has not consented. In that movement we have, encapsulated, the death of God.

However, if the will frees itself from the impotence inherent in trying to change a past against which it is powerless—if it says along with Nietzsche that "what I willed" is what I now will—then the will is set free to will what it can. And though Nietzsche might not phrase it this way, the eternal recurrence makes will shoulder the responsibility it bears for being a will.

Eternal recurrence is thus a form of passivity in Nietzsche's philosophy, though it is not the passivity beyond all passivity theorized by Levinas. Nietzsche's will still has its effects. The will, for Nietzsche, must will, after all. It would rather will nothing than not will. So Nietzsche tries to save will from the nihilism of willing nothing and from the revenge spirit born in willing the impossible by teaching will to will what it can will. Passivity sets action free: once the will accepts its limitations, it is released from the endless cycle of revenge. It is a paradox: Eternal recurrence does not end up being eternal return of the *same* (as *"ewiges Wiederkehr des Gleichen"* is sometimes translated) if the will is powerful enough—and power here includes embrace of the self's subjection to passivity—to will the same's eternal recurrence.

That is how Nietzsche, in giving us the bridge to the overman, accomplishes one form of the destitution of the subject that we encounter differently in Levinas' philosophy: he evicts us from a conception of the will that is often taken to define what it means to be a human being (notably in liberal political philosophy). For Nietzsche, in order for will to be powerful, it has to admit its passivity in the face of synchronous time. It does that by embracing a different vision of time: the diachronic eternal recurrence redeems what in synchronous temporality would imprison the will in a spirit of revenge.

Synchrony and Diachrony in Levinas's *Otherwise Than Being*

In *Otherwise than Being*, Levinas describes a relation of self to other wherein the self is a hostage, persecuted by an unchosen responsibility for an Other, and owed nothing in return. That asymmetrical ethical relation transpires outside of time in a non-space Levinas terms "diachrony."[2] He makes clear that "persecution is not something added to the subjectivity of the subject and his vulnerability; it is the very movement of recurrence" (OB 111). When Levinas writes that the subject is a hostage persecuted by responsibility, he is not describing an unjust structure imposed on a subject by a corrupt agent or institution. Rather, he expresses how the human subject is formed: in "the very movement of recurrence." The self does not stay at rest in itself, is not primordially at home and comfortable, but rather is always already ill at ease in itself. Selfhood *is* persecution. As Levinas puts it, the ego, *le Moi*, "is not in itself like matter which, perfectly espoused by its form, is what it is," but rather "is in itself like one is in one's skin, that is, already tight, ill at ease in one's own skin" (OB 108). The self recurs—it does not stay at rest with itself—and it does this by contracting into itself and finding that there is no escape from itself.

It isn't that first there is a hostage-self stuck in a diachronous temporality and owed nothing in return such that at some later moment that self emerges into a synchronous temporality where it is autonomous and free. That would be too simple, as if a "state of nature" wherein the self was subject to persecution could be left behind, replaced with the greater justice of social institutions. Levinas's narrative of subject formation proceeds differently. In it the self (*soi*) is affected by an ego (*le Moi*) and also by "me" (*moi*), the part of the self we might call prepolitical. This *moi* senses the demand of an other and thus is pressed by a responsibility it never chose. Fleeing into itself (*soi*) in an attempt to evade the demands of responsibility, *moi* finds *le Moi,* and disturbs its tranquility. This movement of "me" into the self, where it encounters the ego, fractures or interrupts the sovereignty that the ego formerly thought it possessed. One might say that *le Moi* thought it was all of *soi* until *moi* came along to trouble the seamlessness of that narrative.[3] (Note, however, that none of this is meant to say that these concepts denote autonomous instances or faculties; *le Moi* and *moi* encounter each other as waves of affectivity, like the "gnawing of remorse.") The contraction into self is what Levinas calls recurrence, or substitution. The narrative cannot be construed as linear—though, of course, one difficulty is that it can only be written as linear. Rather than thinking of becoming-subject as a past event already accomplished, Levinas describes it as an affective movement that has never concluded. It's not that I was at first self-sufficient and then consented to be affected by others, but nor is it the case that at first I was riddled with unchosen responsibility only then to be offered some autonomy. The other is always already there, but it is also the case that, in order to be interrupted by the other's proximity, I have to have been an ego coiling in on itself, complacent in its enjoyment, enjoying its sufficiency to self. Levinas will not give us an origin on which to hang our theory.

Levinas has demonstrated, then, that we are hostage to a responsibility we had no opportunity to refuse. He has upset our presuppositions about how ethical responsibilities work and are incurred. Once he has accomplished this, he reminds us that the point was not to destroy the self-sufficient subject but rather to subject it to a corrective measure—to disorient it and render it less of a fact, more of a theory that participates in the give and take of the vulnerabilities, risks, and uncertainties definitive of human existence. He does this by showing us how "the third" enters the scene.

The third is another person. In diachrony there is only the self and the other, and thus no question ever arises: I am responsible; nothing is owed me in return. However, once there is a third person (and a fourth and so on), many questions arise. Am I responsible for this third person, too? If I had to choose between these two Others, how would I do so? Could there be an alliance between them against me? Or might that other Other be responsible for my Other, such that a weight is lifted from me? That is the birth of consciousness and synchrony, the possibility of cooperation and system, and all the things that make complex sociality possible. The third, then, is the transition from diachrony to synchrony. But bear in mind that between diachrony and synchrony we find interrelation rather than the linearity of cause and effect.

Temporalities of Interruption

It is easy, when reading *Otherwise Than Being*, to fail to deal adequately with the difference between diachrony and synchrony, collapsing the two at inopportune moments, and thus concluding either that Levinas's ethics is tantamount to masochism because I owe everything and nothing is owed me in return, or instead arguing that Levinas is trying to describe for us an impossible ethics we can somehow use instrumentally, right now, in building legal or political institutions. Both of those conclusions would take diachrony to transpire *in* synchrony, such that I am a hostage while everyone else is free. But Levinas does not give us an ethics that we can use instrumentally, and he is not asking us to walk out into the street and say, "Here, take my wallet, strike me on both sides of my face, and don't worry about reciprocity because I deserve no such thing." The ethical response described by Levinas occurs in diachrony, a non-space outside of time. The third and politics and people's identities enter "later," in synchrony (and that "later" is in quotation marks because these temporalities are not in linear progression—though it is also true that "later" is never figured as "sooner" because of the *priority* of ethics). When did I become responsible? Always already. When will I have discharged this responsibility? Always not yet. Responsibility does not, strictly speaking, exist. It is not coterminous with the present. But it also *is*. And that is the difficulty.

I stated that it is easy to collapse the temporalities of diachrony and synchrony and therefore to neglect to understand what separates the temporalities and the significance of their separation. However there is a way in which *Levinas* collapses the temporalities in order to demonstrate for us the movement of his ethics. The two remain distinct and incommensurable, but there is a danger in accepting that distinction as a static truth that we will go too far and think that one comes first and the other follows it, leaving the earlier time behind and replacing it with something ready for sociality. (That would be like a social contract theory, wherein a state of nature has to be left behind for the justice of institutions.)[4] Or we will get stuck asking ourselves which one is more important: justice or ethics? (That would be a false dilemma.) But justice, and especially the justice of institutions, has no sense at all if it does not issue from something beyond it. (No institution is a totality without recourse to something it cannot encompass.) And that something-beyond cannot just be beyond it at some identifiable point in the past. Diachrony is beyond the synchrony of institutions of justice *at every moment*. (At every moment. And also never. That is one sense of the risk associated with ethics.) As Levinas writes in *Otherwise Than Being*: "It is not that the entry of the third party would be an empirical fact, and that my responsibility for the other finds itself constrained to a calculus by 'the force of things.' In the proximity of the other, all the others than the other obsess me, and already this obsession cries out for justice. . . . *The other is from the first the brother of all other men*" (OB 158, emphasis mine). The third party does not enter later, after the ethical "moment." The third party is another interruption: in the midst of the interruption that calls me to an unchosen responsibility, I am also always already reminded of all the others than the other by whom I am summoned. This is when the temporalities collapse. Diachrony, though it does not "exist" (as representable experience) and has neither time nor place, in a sense does and must "coexist" with synchrony. To misunderstand that is to miss entirely the force of Levinas's ethics.

The problem with dual temporalities faces similar obstacles in Nietzsche's philosophy. It is possible to understand eternal recurrence too literally, to claim that Nietzsche thinks that all things recur in an endless cyclical time, and that we must will that to be the case as well. It is certainly possible to think that Nietzsche means that we all must will to live the same lives over and over again—he says as much, and many respected scholars of Nietzsche have argued just that. However, to my way of thinking, that misses the point: instead of collapsing the temporalities it keeps them too separate, treating them as if one had to choose between them. Eternal recurrence (or "eternal return of the same") *is* an endless cycling. But despite what Nietzsche at times says about eternal recurrence, and despite the "same" in its name, the point is that you cannot live your life over again (we have this world, this life only) and there will be no afterlife to redeem the mistakes you made within the temporal span of your life. The eternal recurrence is a cyclical temporality interacting with temporal duration to redeem the will from its tendency toward revenge.

If you undergo eternal recurrence and thereby learn how to make of your will a powerful will, you are released from cycles of revenge. But you are not thereby done with and released from the cycle of eternal recurrence. Rather, the cycle is integral to the human lifespan. Like diachrony and synchrony, eternal recurrence and life's durational span must coexist, always and never—such a feat is never accomplished once and for all. The two temporalities coexist while remaining incommensurable precisely because redeeming the will is not a one-time act but an endless path we follow—to which we are subjected—just as being responsible for the other in Levinas's philosophy could never be something a human being "accomplishes" such that she might then rest from her labors. We are always already on the way but also always not yet there.

The Imperfect

Consider this quotation from one of the English-language collections of Nietzsche's fragments published as *The Will to Power:*

> Let us think this thought in its most terrible form: existence as it is, without meaning or aim, yet recurring inevitably without any finale of nothingness: "the eternal recurrence." This is the most extreme form of nihilism: the nothing (the "meaningless") eternally!   (WP 35–36)

Nihilism wills nothingness, but when it reaches its extreme form, it hits upon something that it did not expect: there is no way out. There is no way out of "somethingness," we might say. (In a similar way we learn from

Levinas in *On Escape* that there is no escape from "*il y a*.") The extreme form of nihilism repeats its negation endlessly. But that is the point, for Nietzsche, and, I would argue, for Levinas. There is no escape: the negation, the responsibility, all this challenges the will, and renders tragic or comic our stories about the priority of our individual freedom. This is all there is, and yet it is far from being nothing. There is no one act that can be performed, and then an end reached, ethics accomplished or politics made perfect or the overman achieved. There is only the long twilight and the endless debt never contracted. Something always precedes or transcends a will and determines it or challenges it or undermines it before it begins. The key to justice or to the overman, for Levinas and Nietzsche, respectively, is a verb in the imperfect tense.[5] It has already begun and can never be accomplished once and for all. In addition, what is expressed in this imperfect verb tense, for Nietzsche and for Levinas, can never be solely the result of a will defined as something willed in the freedom of reason.

Both thinkers define for us a limit to what we could have willed, precisely so that we can redefine and then embrace the manifest responsibility for things that we do will, as well as responsibility for things we never did will and never would have willed. It reads as a simple demand, but its weight is infinite. The responsibility differs, of course, from thinker to thinker. Zarathustra tells us that eternal recurrence turns "it was" into the "thus I willed it" so that the will does not imprison itself in a past it cannot change. Levinas's subjectivity as substitution fractures any idea we might have of the priority of our freedoms or the stability of our identities. That it does this means that we can know what is valuable about freedom and identity in a sense that transcends idealism. Both thinkers want to bring ideas back to the material conditions in which they must be lived. In order to do that, both thinkers must interrupt our habits of thought. What underwrites the deepest thought of each philosophy is something imperfect: already begun, never finished, and relying on something as frail and unpredictable as a human being for its success. But that is also the point: for both of these thinkers, what matters is what we do—even though much of what we are is undergone passively. We cannot wait for a God to redeem life.[6] Nor can we step aside and hope that some other person will carry the weight. It is incumbent on *me*. What we have is the earth (for Nietzsche) and one another (for Levinas).

Though Nietzsche's redemption of the will gives little thought to the other, who is so central for Levinas, both thinkers change what it means to will, and that changes what it means to be a human being. Both imagine this transformation to be focused on the individual, though, again, they do so differently. But if we asked both thinkers just who it is who must shoulder such a burden, do we know for certain who would be the quickest to answer: "'This is my way. Where is yours?'"[7]

NOTES

Deepest thanks are owed to Bettina Bergo, Lou Reynolds, and Joshua Andresen for their comments on this essay at different points in its development.

1. Compare this with the Levinasian split subject torn between "*le Moi*'s" asserted autonomy and "*moi*'s" unchosen dependence.

2. "Outside of time" isn't exact as a phrasing. Levinas tells us that diachrony is a "*non-lieu*" outside of time, while at the same time asking us to imagine diachrony as nonspatial and nontemporal.

3. Construing Levinas's narrative of subjectivity as tripartite might, for some, resonate with the Freudian trio of superego, ego, and id. That will have to be the subject of another work. The two approaches are very different, even if there are prima facie resemblances.

4. Social contract theories do "retain" the state of nature in some way, as a reminder of its terror or as a thought experiment for arriving at an idea of justice. But Levinasian diachrony is not meant to haunt synchrony and justice with the specter of its absence the way a state of nature might; rather, it is integral to both the formation and the continuation of consciousness, justice, and all the institutions formed out of human sociality. (In this way, if any social contract theorist approaches Levinas in terms of structure and aspiration, it is John Rawls. On that, see my "Can a Theory of Justice Be Freed of Its Weight? Levinas and Rawls," in *Levinas and Liberal Democracy*, ed. Richard A. Cohen, forthcoming.)

5. If the English language permitted, it might be fruitful to consider that Levinas and Nietzsche give us a revision of voice rather than tense—that might better catch the sense of a temporality that is not about time. The famous "middle voice" of classical Greek, a voice that proceeds as neither active nor passive, strikes me as a good place to start. . . . And what better way to begin than with John Llewelyn, *The Middle Voice of Ecological Conscience: A Chiasmic Reading in the Neighborhood of Levinas, Heidegger, and Others* (New York: Palgrave Macmillan, 1991).

6. I trust that other essays in this volume will take up the theme of God and theology in much greater detail, but here is a précis of my idea on it, taken in part from an essay of mine, "Productive Ambivalence: Levinasian Subjectivity, Justice, and the Rule of Law," in *Mosaic: Essays on Levinas and Law,* ed. Desmond Manderson (New York: Palgrave Macmillan, 2008), 76–92. Nietzsche is writing after "the death of God." But what about Levinas, who makes demands that may appear to be religious? How does he solve the problem of an infinite weight weighing on a finite being? The first solution he offers is that we simply answer the demand by taking it up, and thereby undo the impossibility: "it is experienced precisely by constantly running up against it, and crossing over its own contestation" (OB 154). That is the enigma of the Infinite in Levinas's thinking. Levinas writes: "The enigma of the Infinite, whose saying in me, a responsibility where no one assists me, becomes a contestation of the Infinite. By this contestation everything is incumbent on me" (OB 154). This responsibility *is* mine despite its infinity; there can be no disputing it just as there can be no disputing the body's physiological pains (in both cases "disputation" is beside the point and almost farcical). Levinas calls this "the enigma of a God speaking in man and of man not counting on any god" (154). Nothing less is required of a post-Holocaust world wherein the certainty that no God will intervene even in the greatest human evil has been secured without ambiguity. It is not a theology.

    Everything is incumbent on me. That is his first solution. The second helps to humanize it. In diachrony, the self shoulders an infinite weight. But the self also coexists with multiple others in synchronous time, and that necessitates just institutions and stable rules that will treat all subjects equally. The subject given to us by Levinas is not a saint or a masochist and hasn't lost what liberalism names its human status, wherein it is owed rights much as it grants them.

7. There are numerous ways to read this quotation from TZ. One could read it as claiming "my place in the sun," the dreaded "usurpation of the whole world" that is one of Levinas's oft-used quotations from Pascal. Or it could be read as: "This is what I demand of myself. I cannot demand it of you. I can only hope that you will to demand it of yourself." As such, we might say that it aligns nicely with Levinas's claim that the sacrifice involved in responsibility is something one can ask only of oneself . . . because to demand it of another is to preach human sacrifice! (OB 126).

3

Nietzsche and Levinas

The Impossible Relation

JEAN-MICHEL LONGNEAUX

WE OUGHT to be able to let go of facile interpretations that make Nietzsche the herald of self-affirmation and Levinas that of the relationship to the Other. In fact, each of these thinkers attempted to reflect on the articulation between subjectivity and the opening to the other. To put these two philosophers in dialogue has nothing artificial to it, then. This is all the more true because both unfold their reflection from a common basis: a shared critique of the subject that lies in the representation of self and a common description of originary subjectivity as enjoyment [*jouissance*]. Nevertheless, as we will see, the relation between Nietzsche and Levinas rapidly proves to be impossible.

To put Nietzsche and Levinas in dialogue has nothing gratuitous to it, either. By radicalizing, each in his own way, the difference that separates them, they developed diametrically opposed reflections on the relation to the other. And the extremism that characterizes such philosophies in fact renders every concrete relation impossible or at least enigmatic. Thus the confrontation of Nietzsche and Levinas invites us to seek out a different path.

The I-Theme [Le Je-Thème]

Before underscoring the limitations of naïve subjectivity, Nietzsche and Levinas describe at length the subjectivity habitually taken to stand integrally in self-consciousness. Nietzsche's and Levinas's descriptions unfold in two stages: first, subjectivity, understood as self-consciousness thinking itself, is considered in its relationship to the world; and second, in such a relation, subjectivity gives itself to itself as object.

The Subjectivity That Institutes Its World

Levinas borrows from Husserl's phenomenology the description of subjectivity as self-consciousness, that is, as "knowledge of self by self" (OB 102; AE 130). What is a subject if not that which represents a world to itself? The subject that one establishes in consciousness inevitably gives itself as consciousness of something: it is the opening of a world and, more precisely, a power [*pouvoir*] that institutes a horizon starting from which, or on whose basis, the world is manifested.

The work of thematization is one with this power, which is the subject as *consciousness-of*. Indeed, "to thematize" the world, that is to say, to name it, is effectively to set the world before oneself, to make it "be" by assigning it an identity. The knowing subject thus never encounters any true exteriority, since all exteriority reveals itself to be merely the meaning loaned by the subject to the object. The world that is given as though it proceeded from the subject itself is a world thematized. The clarity proper to the said, to the universal logos in which everything is laid out, set forth, and assembled, is ordered and finds its place therein.

Nietzsche also describes subjectivity such as it is given in and through consciousness as *knowledge of* self and world (GS §354).[1] To be sure, Nietzsche will never speak in terms of "intentionality." He will simply show that consciousness, as knowledge of self and of world, is the work of language, thereby joining the concept of "thematization" in Levinas's philosophy. In effect, according to Nietzsche, language consists in identifying all that is foreign, all that is particular to bring it back to the known (GS §355) and the commonly held—a reduction that Nietzsche will qualify as "a herd perspective" (GS §354) or "the equation of unequal things."[2]

To identify the nonidentical or equate unequal things does not consist only in abandoning individual differences but also in fixing that which is intended or aimed at by freezing its becoming, by "main-taining" [*main-tenir*] it as immobile, that is, in *holding* it ready for the *hand* that elects to seize it or offer it. As also for the phenomenological tradition, it is through consciousness that a world is instituted and "set outside us and beyond us" (GS §354), foreign to any individuality. Shared, integrally communicable, it no longer belongs to us.

Represented Subjectivity

In unfolding his analysis within a resolutely phenomenological perspective, Levinas remarks that the subject, as master of representation, can only be defined through the Same [*par le Même*], "because in representation the I precisely loses its opposition to the object, the opposition is erased, bringing out the identity of the I despite the multiplicity of its objects" (TI 126; TeI 99, trans modified). In other words, in describing the world, it is itself that the I reaches.

The manifestation of such a subject resides, then, in the process of thematization, of its identification with the saying, or the *logos*, in which everything is disclosed for exhibition without modesty. In this way, integrally thematized or thematizable, the subject will be characterized in one of the following three ways.

First, outside its essence-as-identity, such a subject will shine through its universality, which is a universality proper to the logos with which it is identified.

Second, because it is invariably combined with what is thematized, the subject believes that it possesses itself in full; it believes that it begins and ends with the exercise of its power of thematization.

Finally, beyond the variations in its thoughts, this subject posits itself effectively as an unalterable and unaltered presence unto self. Its time is that of an eternal present that nothing could disturb, a pure synchrony in which everything is reabsorbed according to the temporal play of retentions and protentions. It is in this sense a totalitarian subject, free but alone; it is free yet prisoner of the present it gives itself.

Nietzsche, on the other hand, develops his analysis of subjectivity starting from its manifestations in science—as a relation to the world—and especially in morality, as a relation to oneself. Nietzsche sees science, in effect, as "a relatively faithful humanization of things" thanks to which "we learn to describe ourselves in an increasingly precise fashion" (GS §112; cf. GM).

The subject is given here, as in Levinas's work, as "self-consciousness" that attempts to find in this consciousness "what it has of permanence, eternity, ultimacy, of the greatest originality" (GS §11, trans. modified). Thus we find in Nietzsche—albeit in different terms—the three general characteristics highlighted in Levinas.

First, since one can only bring to consciousness what is nonindividual, the subject that apprehends itself in consciousness "ultimately [belongs] to what makes of him a communitarian nature" (GS §354). As a re-presented subject, metamorphosed into the category of the Same, and aiming at a gregarious utility that assures only the survival of the herd and the preservation of the race, Nietzsche thus defines the subject as a "neutral substratum" (GM 1:§13) that is disinterested and believes itself master of (and therefore distinct from) its acts and its destiny. It is neutral in that it can also will not to commit evil (GM 1:§13), neutral and therefore free.

Second, it follows from this that such a subject is persuaded that it is pure free will to persist in willing that which it wants willed (GM 2:§2). Having become "an animal with the right to make promises," it believes that it begins and ends with itself (GM 2:§2).

Finally, this subject lives in a time that consists in persisting imperturbably in its being, which is the time of eternity that is never finished, as it were, with anything. For such a subject, nothing should be lost, everything counts: this is the ec-static time of a seamless memory of sin [la faute] and of debt, on the one hand, and of the promise that sets the future on the path of salvation, on the other. This is an ec-static time that nevertheless does not overflow the eternal present of consciousness: everything has its place in it.

Originary Subjectivity as Enjoyment

Both Nietzsche and Levinas are sensitive to the necessity of a return to a subjectivity or an originary ipseity whose intrigue is tied up with *enjoyment*. For Nietzsche as for Levinas, such a subjectivity is given as "exploitation," a pure egoism that, because it stands back from all representation, will proclaim itself innocent, being ultimately but the play of life itself [*que le jeu de la vie elle-même*].

Enjoying Is Exploiting

To live or experience the world, to enjoy it or suffer from and through it, means for Nietzsche to despoil it, "to impose on it harshly one's own forms, to encompass it and, at best, to exploit it" (BG §259). One encompasses and exploits it to provide a new, living interpretation of it. Exploitation thus has a double implication: through it, enjoyment affirms an existence and at the same time constitutes a world.

Likewise, in Levinas's work, subjectivity as enjoyment is characterized by exploitation. More precisely, Levinas distinguishes a bidirectional intentionality: first, as determination through the world, since before belonging to the constituted, the world is the condition of life, itself constituting the subject. But thereafter, precisely through this relation, "sensibility enacts the very separation of being" (TI 138; TeI 112). It is the act by which a being tears itself out of the totality to posit itself as master *chez lui*. Dependency thus becomes independence relative to the world and, definitively, in relation to anonymous being [*à l'être anonyme*]. In effect, through enjoyment the subject does not maintain itself in being but surpasses it. Thus, what specifies the subject as a being is not, for Levinas, the act of being [*l'acte d'être*] but the fact that it could live off of this fact of being, that it could exploit it for its own benefit. The subject seems to emerge "above" ontology since it stands in the enjoyment or in the exploitation of the fact of being. A being tears itself out of being [*l'étant s'arrache de l'être*] just as Levinas described, in his first writings, the upsurge of the existent out of anonymous existence.[3] Contrary to Nietzsche, enjoyment in Levinas therefore does not constitute a world; it exploits the world only in order to assure to itself the contentment of existence (TI 135; TeI 108).

Enjoying as a Pure Egoist

What does this "contentment of existence" mean? For Levinas, one does not surpass the simple fact of being if one understands the independence of subjectivity as a hypostatic substance, the subject of the verb "to be," the support of the act of being (*that which* is), or even the support of enjoyment (*that which* enjoys). At the level of enjoying, the "I" grasps itself instead as a contraction of sentiment (TI 118; TeI 91), as an upsurge starting from enjoyment or again as an exaltation of the being or entity. This contraction is of the order of affectivity, and it is seen by Levinas as a movement of inter-nalization [*mouvement d'intériorisation*]. That is, it is seen as a movement through which the "I" identifies itself from within without recourse to des-ignations coming from outside or to that which faces the "I." In this move-ment the ipseity of the "I" is exalted, and it grasps itself as a tremor or as contentment. Thus, to posit oneself as a unique subject in enjoyment means, for Levinas, to live egoistically "without reference to the other person [*au-trui*] . . . innocently egoistic and alone" (TI 134; TeI 107, trans. modified).

Similarly, Nietzsche designates the destroying and creative affectivity, in which the ineradicable subjectivity is tied together with the expression "aristocratic egoism." This name does not single out some caste in the so-cial hierarchy. However, by way of the etymology that Nietzsche proposes for the Greek "*esthlos,*" it does designate those who *experience themselves, feel themselves* "quite simply as the happy ones," "incapable of separating activity from happiness" (GM 1:§5), that activity of affectivity that roots the latter in life. Through the aristocrat, Nietzsche is aiming at that primordial egoism that, through its exploitation of the world, necessarily undergoes the immediate experience of self.

Enjoying Outside of All Representation

Such a subjectivity "knows itself [as being] in the heights" (BG §265), that is to say, above all thematization. To the question, "Who are we, really?" we attempt to respond by accounting "for our experience, for our life, for our *being*—alas!—without finding *a just result.* . . . We remain necessarily strang-ers to ourselves, we do not understand ourselves, we cannot *do otherwise* than to take ourselves for something other than what we are" (GM, foreword: §1).

The subjectivity that is bound up in affectivity is therefore not disclosed. Its mode of revelation keeps it from being exposed since this subjectivity is without distance unto itself: "I am who I am," in the impossibility of freeing myself from me. Thus, by reason of the immediacy of its appearing, subjectivity is, in its manifestation, "that which one *feels* [ressent][4] to be contrary to the herd" (GS §213). This subjectivity, eminently personal, im-plies the "*passion of distance*" (TL §37), which refuses all publicity.

Where Nietzsche speaks of "heights," Levinas will speak of a subjec-tivity outside all consciousness. The originary subject is presented, in ef-fect, in Levinas's work, as consciousness of consciousness [*conscience de la conscience*]: a consciousness without reflection, "prior to the knowledge of this world" (TI 130; TeI 103), but that nonetheless constitutes a background starting from which things come to representation. The ipseity of the "I" stands beneath consciousness (or all unconsciousness) and thought—beneath, that is to say, elsewhere, and not related to the play of consciousness or thought.

Enjoying in All Innocence

Through the mode of manifestation specific to egoism, it follows that egoism is said to be "innocent," without the slightest trace of bad conscience or ulterior motives. Because the subject who arises out of enjoyment lives in the immediacy of its coming or return to self, there cannot be room for remorse, for Levinas. The present of enjoyment, positing itself on the basis of itself, wants only itself.[5] Likewise in Nietzsche's philosophy, this egoism cannot know doubt, remorse, or culpability, since it shows not the slightest break or fault.

Enjoying (from) Life

Because it presents this marked positivity, Nietzsche qualifies subjectivity as "self-affirmation," "glorification of self," "triumph and acceptance of the I," "egoism healthy and sacred," but also as "a Yes, said without reserve to life," "a self-celebration of life." In the final analysis, it is life itself that exalts in the drunkenness of its embrace with self, in such a way that it never ceases wanting itself ever more. This "sentiment of plenitude, of power that would overflow" in the manifestation of self (outside all representation), Nietzsche calls "will to power," which is thus first defined as pathos.[6]

Levinas's work also evinces this return to life. As in Nietzsche, the life that is in question here is not the biological life that sacrifices the individual to the species, which would be proper to an impersonal life in thrall to the anonymity of being. In Levinas's philosophy, it is a question of a personal life that is defined precisely by the independence of its happiness, that is, by its egoism. For, "to live is to take pleasure in life" (TI 115; TeI 87, trans. modified). Life is here exploitation of life, self-love, an innocent egoism that seeks only to affirm itself.

Levinas Parts Company with Nietzsche

Whereas throughout *The Gay Science* and after it, Nietzsche remains faithful to a foundation of originary subjectivity, Levinas feels the need to pursue his analysis in a more radical direction. In so doing, he adds nuance to— and some would say that he "corrects"—his early descriptions. In effect, starting from innocence subjectivity will become "hateful," loathsome. Is it a matter, here, of accounting for some sort of ambiguity in the manifestation of subjectivity to itself? However that may be, it seems certain that Levinas's analysis of the subject is guided by his elucidation of the ethical relation. This relation has, as its first requirement, in order that a face-to-face encounter be envisioned, that there be *someone* before the other, *someone* facing the other. "Egoism, enjoyment, sensibility and all the dimensions of interiority—as the articulations of separation—are necessary for the idea of Infinity—for the relation with the Other [*Autrui*], which opens forth from the separated and finite being" (TI 148; TeI 122). The analysis of subjectivity as enjoyment aimed precisely to describe the constitution of the "atheist" subject fixed in itself, on the basis of itself, who makes the ethical relation possible. However, in order that such an "atheist" subject be assigned to responsibility—of which the ethical relationship consists—a second requirement must be satisfied, that is, that this subject not be an unshakable egoism. The "enucleation" or conversion of the subject must be thinkable, in some respect already possible, starting from the separation of the subject. This turnaround will be presented under the theme of the ambiguity of the separated subject.

Whereas he earlier characterized the subject as "a being absolutely closed over upon itself" (TI 148; TeI 122), Levinas will thereafter come to rethink this affirmation: it is also necessary "that this closedness of the separated being . . . be ambiguous enough" to offer a certain opening (TI 148; TeI 122).

The Three Openings and the Loathsome I

In *Totality and Infinity*, Levinas already situates this opening in a disquiet or insecurity that arises in the very midst of enjoyment. This is a disquiet in its relation to the world—more precisely to the element—which takes the form of "concern for the morrow" (TI 150; TeI 124). Yet enjoyment can still dominate this being put into question by concern.

At a more profound level, this disquietude will be understood in *Otherwise Than Being* as the suffering tied to corporeity qua original passivity. This is not the corporeity of the body that one has or that one is,[7] but rather corporeity as an *event* in which "an identity is individuated as unique" (OB 112; AE 142).[8] This subjectivity of flesh and blood is therefore not merely enjoyment or a function of knowledge but, more fundamentally, an exposure to pain, to the other, an obsession that penetrates into the very heart of the I and comes to interrupt enjoyment in its isolation. Suffering presents itself as "the other in me" (OB 125; AE 160), as a passivity more originary than beginning, than stance, than the imperialist activity of the "I." Suffering holds integrally in its imminence: "imminence as pain arises in sensibility lived as well-being and enjoyment" only to put it into question (OB 55; AE 71).

The disquiet or insecurity that hounds enjoyment is again apprehended in the temporal passivity of the animate body. "The subject stated as properly as possible is not in time, but is diachrony itself: in the identification of the I, and the aging of him that one 'will never take up again'" (OB 56; AE 73).

This is senescence and aging as "time lost without return," as a nonintentional passivity "beyond recovery by memory" (OB 52; AE 67), giving itself simply in its refusal to be, as "an instance of the instant without the insistence of the I."[9] This "permanence of loss of self" (OB 107; AE 136) puts into question the enjoyment that is wont to assert itself in its identity. Enjoyment is thus grasped as ambiguity: that which gives itself as freedom is also humility, "a presence apprehensive before presence," "an identity" that "recoils before its affirmation or assertion" (AT 20–21; PT 42).

The depreciation of the subject, resulting from its vulnerability, requires a response. Or again the question of the salvation of subjectivity effectively imposes itself on thinking. The subject is worked, pressed, by the question of its right to be, by a justification of "its place in the sun" and so, by the problem of the meaning of its existence. Yet an answer cannot be provided by ontology, for it is precisely ontology that is here disquieted. It is thus in an "otherwise than being," understood as a beyond-ontology, that the possibility of responding for self will be given to the subject.

Why Nietzsche Cannot Follow Levinas

Nietzsche would see in such an analysis of the ambiguity of subjectivity the work of *ressentiment* or of bad conscience. How could it be otherwise, since the life that crosses through subjectivity is characterized by Levinas as all the original modes he expresses in terms of "adversity" or of "primordial lassitude" (cf. OB 51; AE 66)? It is with regard to this lassitude, to this fatigue, that "health" or the "force" of enjoyment appears arrogant, displaced, something to be repelled.

For his part, Nietzsche would assert that—in the very midst of the passivity of time, of effort, pain, labor, fatigue—there is still an affirmation of life. Or again, more precisely, to experience oneself as effort, struggle, or pain is also something proper to life, which, as will to power, never ceases experiencing the trial of self, never ceases enjoying itself and thus affirming itself. It is precisely because it is inalienable, woven into the flesh of the subject, that this affirmation reveals existence to itself as *tragedy*.

Levinas as More Nietzschean than Nietzsche?

While it condemns any thought that would try to flee the life-world, one may well wonder whether Nietzsche's philosophy does not present, in its own way, a subjectivity that is ultimately insecure, disquieted, and that would consequently be liable to experience itself as "loathsome." Already the notion of "tragedy," evoked above, appears to authorize such a reading.

Becoming and Being

In rediscovering a *living* subjectivity, Nietzsche did not remain with the subject understood merely as identity. In the last instance, what is experienced in its coming-to-self is none other than life itself—or becoming. That life is becoming is, for Nietzsche, evident in everything: our death, the course of our thoughts, or, still more simply, that which our senses reveal to us.

Yet Nietzsche's discourse oscillates continuously between the will to think the subject as life, that is, as pure becoming that implies "the refusal of the very notion of 'being'" (EH "Birth of Tragedy": §3), and as the necessity of conjoining becoming with the notion of being.

Pure becoming is evolution, "which does not want happiness but evolution and nothing else" (DB §108). The thinking of pure becoming abstracts from all that persists, including the affirmation of self, which is tied up in the drunkenness of one's coming to self. Consequently, this is a life that may only be comprehended as impermanence, annihilation, or absolute flow (GS §370). On these grounds, Nietzsche attempts to evoke the subject as that which is not but rather "is eternally directed toward the future" (GM 3:§13). In thus insisting on becoming, however, Nietzsche loses the subject. For, when he finishes, affirming that "there exists no 'being' behind doing, effecting, becoming; 'the doer' is merely a fiction added to the deed—the deed is everything" (GM 1:§13), Nietzsche leaves no room for the subject. If becoming is everything, then subjectivity is no longer anything at all.

We must then face the facts: "in order that there be a subject, there would have to exist something that persists, and even a great deal of identity and similarity. What is absolutely different in perpetual change could in no way be maintained, it would maintain itself through nothing, and would flow [s'écoulerait] like rain over stones."[10]

Nietzsche would accept reintroducing the notion of being or identity if we qualified it as an *error* or a fiction.[11] Now, insofar as such an *error* is constitutive of subjectivity, can we not ask whether Nietzsche also makes the I "loathsome" (at least in part)? Is this not a door opened to bad conscience? There is here an unavoidable difficulty that Nietzsche nonetheless seems to skirt with his "unconditional Yes," said to life. As we have seen, in rejecting every form of flight from life, Nietzsche advances the concept of acquiescing: to say Yes, "without reserve to life . . . to everything that is disconcerting and problematic in life. . . . To everything that is, there is nothing that one could do without" (EH "The Birth of Tragedy": 273). In effect, the reality to which we must consent is life, that is, not pure becoming (which is ultimately unthinkable), and certainly not being, but rather the two held together, thereby revealing the profoundly contradictory character of life. But that does not mean that an *error* to which one acquiesces becomes a truth.

The Eternal Return of The Same

Nietzsche seeks to think the contradiction that constitutes the life of the subject through the myth of the "eternal return of the same."[12] "That *everything would return* amounts to bringing together at its apogee the world of becoming and the world of being, high point of contemplation" (Granier, PV 357). "That everything returns without cease" means, for Nietzsche, "to impress the character of being upon becoming," and this labor is "*the higher form of the Will to power*" (Granier, PV 357).

As we have seen, Nietzsche understands will to power as a pathos. Thus, the eternal return of the same expresses the eternal coming [*l'éternelle adve-nue*] of life to being, and this eternal coming to being is precisely its pathos. To say that life, as eternal recurrence, is will to power is finally to set forth the idea that life is an incessant manifestation of self to self. Nietzsche will call this "an affirmation of self" (GM 1:§13) this manifestation having being as its modality (Granier, PV 357).

Subjectivity as self-affirmation is thus not the subjectivity that founds itself by itself. Besides the fact that such a self-proclamation would be the illusory work of language, the myth of eternal recurrence implies that sub-jectivity *is posited* as an affirmation of self, or, if one prefers, it *receives* itself as such. The Nietzschean notions of "eternal recurrence," "pathos" (I am who I am), "acquiescence," "*amor fati*," etc., all bear witness to this radical passivity.

If we deepen the concept of passivity that characterizes the subject fun-damentally, do we not come back to Levinas's themes of suffering and ag-ing as the direct expression of the passivity inscribed at the very heart of enjoyment? The essence of subjectivity is from the first an exposure to a fundamental disquiet or anguish.

The Love of Self

Nietzsche will stifle this ambiguity at the very heart of the life of the subject—an ambiguity that he sensed in his own way. Contrary to Levinas, he will simply hold fast to the affirmation of self as the condition of any relationship with another person, rejecting without nuance every mo-rality that decrees that "le moi est toujours haïssable" [*the "I" is always loathsome*].[13] Instead, the aristocratic morality that Nietzsche made his own has its roots "in a triumphant acceptance of the I" (DFW 52).

Such an affirmation of self could in no way be confused with "an all-too-poor, a hungry selfishness that always wants to steal, that selfishness of the sick" (TZ: "Of the Bestowing Virtue"). In effect, he who "would not love, yet wanted to live by love [that one has for him]" (TZ: "Of the Spirit of Gravity"), or he who "wants to live gratis" (TZ: "Of Old and New Law-Tables"), that man is sick. In a word, he who says, "All for me," hides an invisible degeneracy (TZ: "Of the Bestowing Virtue"). In the place of this egoism that hides a true "hatred of self and of life," Nietzsche sets forth an aristocratic egoism that should make possible a true relationship with another person (TZ: "Of the Bestowing Virtue"). It is thus that Nietzsche exhorts the self to "love oneself with a sound and healthy love, so that one may endure it with oneself and not go roaming about" (TZ: "Of the Spirit of Gravity"). For he cannot love who does not thus rest in himself.

In Nietzsche's philosophy, love of self is thus in service to the relationship with the other person. We should hardly be astonished by this since Nietzsche's philosophical project did not consist in denying the necessity of struggling against immoral actions while performing those called moral. He is simply persuaded that one should do both the one and the other, albeit "for reasons other than those held up till now" (cf. DB §103).

Nietzsche and Levinas: The Impossible Relation

The philosophies of Nietzsche and Levinas separate and grow distant at the very moment when they are about to meet. In Levinas, passivity, suffering, and the loathsome "I" become such an obsession that it appears impossible to enjoy existence: subjectivity has no horizon other than its own salvation. As for Nietzsche, he allows himself to be dazzled by that great noonday sun that is the affirmation of self. All the shadows disappear, nothing further seems liable to disturb a subjectivity everywhere at home.

There clearly follow from this two radically opposed conceptions of the relationship to the other person, both of which are mutually open to critique.

The Relation in Levinas: "The One for the Other"

Fear and Election

Levinas showed that the subject was incited to respond for its very right to be. He presents this response as accompanying the encounter with the face of the other person, who comes brutally to interrupt the complacency of the enjoying subject. This interruption converts the loathsome character of subjectivity into "fear *for* the other." In facing the other person [*Autrui*], bad conscience is born, as is the fear of occupying the place of an other [d'un *Autre*], a fear "of all that my existence—despite its intentional and conscious innocence—could enact that is violent and murderous" (PT 42). This is a fear prior to any sin or fault, and prior to freedom; such an apprehension accuses me and requires a response from me. The other [*l'Autre*] intrudes, enters irrevocably, returning the subject to a responsibility caused by no engagement on its part. To be chosen before I could choose—an election undergone before any beginning—is the responsibility Levinas aims to reach; this power [*emprise*] constitutes one otherwise than "as a substance contemporary with itself, like a transcendental I [*un Moi transcendental*]" (OB 56; AE 73).

The Dis-inter-ested Self

Because it cannot flee the encounter, the identitary "I" of enjoyment becomes a self, an elected subjectivity, unique, irreplaceable, and responsible for the neighbor before having so much as recognized this. For-the-other without possible flight, responsible from the outset, and this despite myself, not against my will but prior to freedom and nonfreedom of any kind: in effect, this subjectivity as the one-for-the-other does not identify itself in its responsibility. Its uniqueness as elected is caught up in a past without memory; it holds it in the incapacity of "separating from self to contemplate and express itself and, consequently, to show itself" (OB 107; AE 136). In this sense, the self "in proximity is absolute exteriority," without common measure with the present, "unassemblable in it . . . always 'already in the past'"—in this the present is postponed or held in check (OB 100; AE 127): thus the self dis-inter-ested, otherwise than being.

From Persecution to Expiation for the Other

Despite that, the expression "the other for whom I am responsible" does not signify *rapprochement* or confusion of terms, as in reciprocal relations. For, "between the one who I am, and the other for whom I am responsible, opens a difference without common ground [*sans fond de communauté*]" (OB 166; AE 211). Responsibility for the other is constituted as a "face-to-face" (TO 93–94; TA 88–89) that nothing could totalize.

Such a face-to-face, which nothing could reabsorb, supposes first that the subject could maintain itself in its being, even in its encounter with the

other person [*Autrui*]. If this were not the case, the subject would be absorbed by that other [*Autre*]. Moreover, in *Otherwise Than Being*, this face-
to-face, because it is a trope whose terms have no common time but are "a
diachrony and refusal of conjunction" (OB 11; AE 14), cannot be lived or
experienced as reciprocity but only as an investiture by the other that arises
from persecution. We have to recur to this limit situation, because "without
persecution, the I [*le Moi*] raises its head and covers over the Self" (OB 112;
AE 143). That is, the *for-oneself* would again become sovereign in regard to
the *for-the-other*, and the ethical would be absorbed into the ontological.
Rather than assigning the self, to give it the present time of a commencement or beginning, the suffering of persecution undergone turns into expiation for the Other, for the fault or wrong of one's persecutor. Substitution
for the other is precisely what it is "to be in-self [*en-soi*]," lying deep "in
oneself 'beyond essence'" (OB 116; AE 148).

The I, Rid of Itself

Nevertheless, even in substitution the subject does not lose the uniqueness
acquired during the separation it realized in enjoyment. As long as the subject is a "man who is hungry and who eats, entrails in a skin," he is "capable
of giving the bread out of his mouth, or giving his skin" (OB 77; AE 97).
Since the very possibility of giving has no "meaning except as an extracting
from self, *despite* oneself, and not only *without* ego [*sans moi*]" (OB 74; AE
93, trans modified), substitution concerns an ontological identity only to
displace it, in suffering, or at least to convert it. Subjectivity is not broken,
then; its meaning is simply inverted. It is not the uniqueness of the being
that insists and persists heavily in its identity, but rather the uniqueness of
the one elected: a subject who receives itself from without and does not
come back to itself, who does not begin with itself but departs for the other
[*s'en va pour l'Autre*].

Yet at the same time, the conversion of this subject is radical. Between
the "I" that plays the game of essence or Being, and the self that, filled
with alterity, is swept up in responsibility, there is no common time: the
first cannot understand the second and the second can only interrupt the
first. Between the for-itself and the for-the-other opens "the distance of diachrony without *a common present*" (OB 89; AE 113, trans. modified). This is
"the marvel of the ego [*moi*] rid of itself and fearing for the other" (PT 43).

Nietzsche as Critic of Levinas

The subjectivity Levinas aims at, the for-the-other, is opposed to the subject understood as a neutral substratum or master of its destiny, even as it presents itself as without-return-to-self. Although it is already foreshadowed through the passivity or vulnerability of corporeity, this subjectivity is caught up in an intrigue that Levinas situates outside of life, that is to say, outside of every present time, in that "time" of the encounter with the face of the other person who commands to responsibility: an irrecoverable, immemorially past time.

It is true that Levinas emphasizes the ambiguity of this "before." Irreducible to any present time, by its very irreducibility it disturbs the present. Thus, "an-archy does not reign but holds itself in this way in ambiguity, in enigma, and leaves a trace" in speech (OB 194n. 4; AE 128n. 4). However, if the notion of a trace suggests the idea of a passage that perturbs the present, it is nevertheless without letting itself be invested by it. In other words, despite the ambiguity of the "an-archical past," Levinas poses an "other world"[14] *in the form of another time,* offering no synthesis, refusing any present. Does he not write that this beyond "is absolute exteriority, without common measure with the present, non-assemblable into the present, always 'already in the past'—behind which the present delays—over and beyond the 'now' which this exteriority disturbs or obsesses" (OB 100; AE 127)?

Despite Levinas's protest to the contrary, Nietzsche would find in his thought the need for being and stability that this recourse to an elsewhere intimates. In effect, in Levinas, the intrigue of subjectivity is ultimately understood as a disturbance, on the basis of a ground that we sense has an absoluteness and, in Nietzsche's sense of the term, a reassuring stability— whether it be the face of the other person, defined precisely by its absoluteness because it stands in the preeminence of a past irreducible to consciousness, or whether it be the stability likewise found in that unflagging responsibility, that unconditional "Thou shalt," which is imposed without any possible flight.

The Relation in Nietzsche: Virtue That Gives

That the lonely height may not always be solitary and sufficient to itself; that the mountain may descend to the valley and the wind of the heights to the lowlands—Oh who shall find the rightful baptismal and virtuous name for such a longing! "Bestowing virtue."[15]

Nietzsche envisions the fulfillment of this virtue in a perspective that could not fail to make us think of Aristotle's "friendship among equals."[16] Two cases are considered by the author: love and friendship.

Love

Love enshrines two egoisms: one that experiences the need to give and another, to take. "The one is empty and wants to be filled, the other overflows and wants to pour forth, each of these will go in search of an individual who allows them to do this. It is this phenomenon, taken in its highest sense, that we designate in both cases with a single word: love. How is that? Love ought to be something unegoistical?" (DB §145; trans. modified).

Love is doubtless the site where egoism triumphs without bad conscience. And it is precisely because egoism is safeguarded here, as the condition of such a relationship, that the latter could not dissolve in fusion or in an asymmetrical rapport. The one who pours forth does not crush him who seeks to be filled. And the latter does not absorb the one through whom his thirst sought to be quenched. For the act of taking that is lived by both of them is perceived by each one as a gift.

Because it leads to no affirmation of self but instead presupposes such an affirmation, a love relationship is not motivated by quests for glory or sanctification: there is no one here to save, only one to love.

Friendship

Friendship is for Nietzsche the archetype of a relationship fulfilled, for it is not encumbered by any form of need that would risk bringing about the dependency we might nonetheless fear occurs in love.

"Are you a slave? If so, you cannot be a friend. Are you a tyrant? If so, you cannot have friends" (TZ: "Of the Friend"). The slave, subjected, depends on a master. He *is not* self-affirming and therefore could not enter into a relation of friendship. The tyrant, who no doubt affirms himself, cannot *have* a friend because he subjects everyone around him. Two conditions must be fulfilled, therefore, for us to speak of friendship. The first condition: friends must be two "hale and hearty egoisms." The friend could thus not be the "neighbor," him upon whom we lay hands out of pity: he is on the contrary him "in whom the world stands complete, a vessel of the good—the creative friend, who always has a complete world to bestow" (TZ: "Of the Friend"). Friendship does not know the affect of pity (dear to Schopenhauer).[17]

The second condition: friendship must respect the "distance" (as Nietzsche will say [see TL §37]) that separates the partners in the relationship. To be sure, friendship brings friends closer together and sometimes to such a degree that "one might have said that they had reached their goal and [never had but] one goal" (GS §279). And yet, despite appearances, a certain distance is maintained and confirmed. Firstly, it is necessary to remain solidly fixed in oneself, otherwise the friendship is lost. One slides back into the situation of slave or tyrant. Furthermore, because such a relationship does not attach the other to the self but respects the distance, one must be able to accept that friendship, eventually, be but a provisional relationship. It is thus that Nietzsche can write: "But thereafter, the irresistible call of our mission drove us far from one another anew . . . that we had to become estranged, is the law above us: by the same token we should also become more venerable for each other—and the memory of our former friendship more sacred" (GS §279, trans. modified).

Levinas as Critic of Nietzsche

As we have seen, Levinas sets down as condition for the relation to the other that the subject be "a being who lacks nothing" (HA 29). No doubt on this point he is following Nietzsche's own thought. Likewise, Levinas might agree that to understand the friend as a complete world is, in a certain way, to underscore his irreducible alterity. The friend is pure exteriority.

But precisely because he posits an "I" [un moi] and an other as pure affirmation of self, as the pure exteriority of the one relative to the other, Nietzsche is, in reality, incapable of thinking a relationship of some kind. There is lacking to him a thinking of passivity as insecurity or disquiet, which would lie at the very heart of the subject, that is to say, ultimately, a thinking that concerns the "desire for the other person" (HH 29, trans. modified).

Opposing any philosophy of the *one-for-the-other*, Nietzsche cannot think relationships in a mode other than "the-one-with-the-other," that is, as "the-one-beside-the-other." Does he not make the friendship that he praises so highly precisely into a *"star-friendship"* (GS §279)? Yet stars are incapable of friendship—or any other relation—because their frozen light is blind. They shine, but they cannot illuminate one another: only the night reveals them, to themselves.

Rethinking Relation

Nietzsche and Levinas, each in his way, have rendered problematic the relation to the other. To put it simply, either the relationship does not exist or it is a one-way relation.

We should retain from Nietzsche the pure affirmation of self without confusing it with the life of some monad. From Levinas, we would like to preserve the "Desire for the other person," but without presupposing from the outset a loathsome "I." Rather than envisioning a subjectivity as enjoyment that ought to be dismissed in order that the opening to the other emerge, could we not envision the desire for the other as precisely one of the sites of enjoyment itself? For, if desire is not to be an unconscious mechanism that would be activated without me, without the *moi*, it must come to be [*il doit venir à l'être*]. In order to do this, in order that it be mine, we must allow that it always already have experienced the trial of the Self, that it thus be a pathos, which is also to say an enjoyment of self. Could not the affirmation of self stand in this manifestation of desire to that self?

If the opening to the other is given to itself [to the opening] in the enjoyment of self; that is, if therein lies the fundamental condition to be preserved, then, first, the mode that will determine the relation will be that of contemporaneousness (and not that of the antecedence or preeminence of the one vis-à-vis the other): a relationship not to another person (with all that Levinas and Nietzsche imply in this word) but, as it were, a relation between brothers. But thereby, all angelic dimensions must be excluded; that is my second point: it is the wealth—or the disquieting ambiguity—of every relation (between brothers) that will have to be assumed before any consideration of an ethical kind. Third, as to responsibility, election, etc., these would no longer be understood as interrupting affirmations of self but as coming to venerate or sanctify it. In this way, one would, no doubt, still be indebted to the other not because one would be loathsome but rather because a grace or a gift is received, one that consists in being confirmed in one's ownmost being.[18]

NOTES

This essay first appeared in French in 1998. Translated by Bettina Bergo; edited by Gabriel Malenfant, Université de Montréal.

1. Longneaux uses the French translation of the Colli-Montinari edition of Nietzsche's collected works. See *Œuvres philosophiques complètes: Textes et variantes établis par Giorgio Colli et Mazzino Montinari* (Paris: Gallimard, 1967). This edition was updated in 1984, with significant changes in its pagination. Thus, I have eliminated the outdated 1967 pagination in favor of section numbers, while keeping the translation close to the French text used.—Trans.

2. Friedrich Nietzsche, "On Truth and Lies in a Non-Moral Sense," trans. Daniel Breazeale, in *Philosophy and Truth: Selections from Nietzsche's Notebooks of the Early 1870s* (Atlantic Highlands, N.J.: Humanities Press, 1979), 83. Longneaux uses the French translation, *Le Livre du philosophe* (Paris: Garnier Flammarion, 1993).

3. See EE 67–70.

4. Author's italics.

5. It does this without referring to anything else. The egoistic "I" cannot conceive itself in reference to an alterity of some, really, of any kind. We understand this easily when that alterity is another person [*Autrui*].

  Contrariwise, one might believe in the alterity of the world, in its exteriority relative to the subject. For, in the first place, holding itself entirely in enjoyment, the subject in no way identifies itself with that from which it draws enjoyment; and, in the second place, because the world which gives itself to enjoyment—a world that Levinas calls "*the element*"—consists only in the instant of enjoyment. The alterity of the world consists not in the heterogeneity of that world, but in its perpetual vanishing. This is to such a degree the case that enjoyment would ultimately be distracted from itself. Disturbed by the fundamental insecurity that the inconsistency of the element inspires, enjoyment would even be concerned with, and worry about, its tomorrow.

  Nevertheless, this alterity and the distraction it occasions will be resorbed into the order of the Same. For, on the one hand, the insecurity that appears here does not really undo enjoyment, nor does it really follow it. Insecurity arises, rather, in its midst precisely to disquiet it. In other words, enjoyment is not interrupted; it persists despite the disquiet that works on it from within [*la taraude de l'intérieur*]. On the other hand, the "I" that ties itself together in enjoyment may well have recourse to work and open itself to representation to convert the elemental into a *world,* that is, into an object able to be possessed (see TI 141; TeI 114–115). Its alterity is surmountable, not to say always already surmounted. The "I" of enjoyment thus lives in the innocence of its egoism, foreign to all alterity, knowing only itself qua "enjoyment-of."

6. Cf. Nietzsche, KSA, vol. 13 (1888), 259: "der Wille zur Macht nicht ein Sein, nicht ein Werden, sondern ein *Pathos* ist die elementärste Thatsache." Cited by Michel Henry, *Généalogie de la psychanalyse, le commencement perdu* (Paris: Presses Universitaires de France, 1993), 279; in English, *Genealogy of Psychoanalysis: The Lost Beginning,* trans. Douglas Brick (Stanford, Calif.: Stanford University Press, 1998).

7. "Will it be said that . . . in the internal sensibility there is inwardness [*une intimité*] that can go as far as identification . . . that I do not only have a body, but am a body! But even then the body is still being taken to be a being, a substantive, eventually a means of localization, but not the way a man engages in existence, the way he posits himself" (EE 69–70; DEE 122–23).

8. Translations have been modified for fluency with the French that Longneaux cites.—Trans.

9. Emmanuel Levinas, "Philosophie et transcendance," in *Encyclopédie philosophique universelle. L'univers philosophique* (Paris: Presses Universitaires de France, 1989), 38–45. Hereafter abbreviated as PT. Translated as "Philosophy and Transcendence," in AT.

10. Nietzsche, KSA, vol. 9 (1880–1882), 11 [268], p. 543.

11. See Friedrich Nietzsche, *Twilight of the Idols and The Anti-Christ,* trans. R. J. Hollingdale (New York: Penguin Books, 1990), 139.

12. As Jean Granier shows, Nietzsche uses the myth of eternal recurrence to approach several different problems, none of them entirely foreign to the others, whether this be at the "level of the critique of metaphysical finalism" or to express an "ecstatic nihilism" and in regard to the status of becoming, or in relation to "the absolute affirmation." For the sake of clarity, in my text I will refer to the last two problematics. See Jean Granier, *Le problème de la vérité dans la philosophie de Nietzsche* (Paris: Le Seuil, 1966). Hereafter cited as PV.

13. Nietzsche cites Pascal in French; see epilogue in DFW 52.

14. It is obvious that we must not speak of an "other world" in a naïve sense (which Levinas also repudiates) but rather in a form much more subtle and

pernicious, which is remarkable in that it again reveals the unsatisfying character of the present world. See ED "*A priori* et subjectivité": 194.

15. TZ "Of the Three Evil Things": 208. Nietzsche calls this "*Schenkende Tugend.*"
    This is the unnamable virtue ["*das Unnennbare*"], virtue that gives.—Trans.

16. Aristotle, *Nicomachean Ethics,* trans. Terence Irwin (Indianapolis, Ind.: Hack-
    ett, 1999), book 8, chaps. 6–8, 125–29.

17. See Arthur Schopenhauer, *The World as Will and Representation,* trans. E. F. J.
    Payne (New York: Dover Publications, 1969), 271 ff.

18. Every relationship based on opposition, by contrast, will be lived as some
    nonconfirmation of our being.

4

Ethical Ambivalence

JUDITH BUTLER

I DO not have much to say about why there is a return to ethics, if there is one, in recent years, except to say that I have for the most part resisted this return, and that what I have to offer is something like a map of this resistance and its partial overcoming that I hope will be useful for more than biographical purposes. I've worried that the return to ethics has constituted an escape from politics, and I've also worried that it has meant a certain heightening of moralism and this has made me cry out, as Nietzsche cried out about Hegel, "Bad air! Bad air!" I suppose that looking for a space in which to breathe is not the highest ethical aspiration, but it is there, etymologically embedded in aspiration itself, and does seem to constitute something of a precondition for any viable, that is, livable, ethical reflection.

I began my philosophical career within the context of a Jewish education, one that took the ethical dilemmas posed by the mass extermination of the Jews during World War II, including members of my own family, to set the scene for thinking of ethicality as such. The question endlessly posed, implicitly and explicitly, is what you would have done in those circumstances, whether you would have kept the alliance, whether you would have broken the alliance, whether you would have stayed brave and fierce and agreed to die, whether you would have become cowardly, sold out, tried to live, and betrayed others in the process. The questions posed were rather stark, and it seemed as if they were posed not merely about hypothetical past action but of present and future actions as well: Will you live in the mode of that alliance? Will you live in the mode of that betrayal, and will you be desecrating the dead by your actions, will you be killing them again? No, worse, you are, by your present action, effectively killing them again. It was unclear whether any sort of significant action could be dislodged from this framework, and whether any action could be dissociated from the ethical itself: the effect on action was generally paralysis or guilt with occasional moments of hallucinatory heroism.

We know this particular form of ethical thinking from Woody Allen films, the humor of Richard Lewis, and others. And, despite its gravity, or rather because of it, I can barely restrain myself from driving the logic into the sometimes hilarious extremes it achieves in the U.S. context (Did you brush your teeth? Are you betraying the Jews?), but I will try not to—and not only from fear of enacting that desecration again. It was with reluctance that I agreed to read Nietzsche, and I generally disdained him through most of my undergraduate years at Yale until a friend of mine brought me to Paul de Man's class on *Beyond Good and Evil* and I found myself at once compelled and repelled. As I read further I saw in Nietzsche a profound critique of the psychic violence performed by impossible and relentless ethical demands, the kind that takes whatever force of life affirmation that might be available and turns it back upon itself, spawning from that negative reflexivity the panoply of psychic phenomena called "bad conscience," "guilt," and even "the soul." I read Nietzsche's *On the Genealogy of Morals* with difficulty, since what I wanted most from it was his critique of slave morality, and what I hated most in it was his persistent association of slave morality with the Jews and Judaism. It was as if the moment of the text that offered me some release from the hyperethical framework that I derived from a postwar Jewish education was the very one that threatened to implicate me in an alliance with an anti-Semitic text. The bind seemed almost airtight: to go against the hyperethicality of Judaism, I could go with Nietzsche, but to go with Nietzsche meant to go against Judaism, and this was unacceptable. If only he had left the anti-Semitic remarks aside, if only we could read him in such a way that those remarks really didn't matter!

I read since the age of fourteen a series of Jewish thinkers and writers, and if I am to be honest, I probably know more about them than I know about anything written in queer theory today. They included Maimonides, Spinoza, Buber, Benjamin, Arendt, and Scholem, and especially the work and letters of Kafka, whose ethical dilemmas impressed me as no less than sublime. But I clearly turned away from pursuing Jewish studies formally for fear, no doubt, that somewhere in those texts the crushing force of the unappeasable law would be upon me again. And I was drawn toward those kinds of readings that suspended the law, exposed its illegibility, its internal limits and contradictions, and even found Jewish authorization for those kinds of readings. I was also compelled to show that this kind of reading did not paralyze ethical or political action, to show that the law might be critically interrogated and mobilized at once.

When I first read some Levinas, I found a hyperbolic instance of this su-peregoic law. I read, for instance, about the demand that is imposed upon me by the face of the Other, a demand that is "before all language and mimicry," a face that is *not* a representation, a demand that is *not* open to interpretation. "I am as it were ordered from the outside, traumatically commanded, without interiorizing by representation and concepts the authority that commands me, without asking myself: what then is he to me? where does he get his right to command?" (OB 87). What would it mean to obey such a demand, to acquiesce to such a demand when no critical evaluation of the demand could be made? Would such an acquiescence be any more or less critical and unthinking than an acquiescence to an ungrounded authoritarian law? How would one distinguish between a fascist demand and one that somehow affirms the ethical bonds between humans that Levinas understands as constitutive of the ethical subject?[1]

For the Levinas of *Otherwise Than Being*, the reverse question seems to be paramount: Given that we reflect ethically on the principles and norms that guide our relations to others, are we not, prior to any such reflection, already in relation to others such that that reflection becomes possible—an ethical relation that is, as it were, prior to all reflection? For Levinas, the Other is not always or exclusively elsewhere; it makes its demand on me, but it is also of me: it is the constitutive relation of this subject to the ethical, one that both constitutes and divides the subject from the start. For Levinas, this splitting of the subject, foundationally, by the Other establishes this nonunitary subject as the basis for ethical responsibility.

The subject is, moreover, from the start split by the wound of the Other (not simply the wounds that the Other performs, but a wound that the Other somehow is, prior to action). The task of this fundamentally wounded subject is to take responsibility for the very other who, in Levinas's terms, "persecutes" that self. That Other delivers the command to take responsibility for the persecution that the Other inflicts. In effect, I do not take responsibility for the Other who wounds me after the wound has appeared. My openness to the Other is what allows for the wound and what also at the same time commands that I take responsibility for that Other.

When I first encountered this position, I ran in the opposite direction, understanding it as a valorization of self-sacrifice that would make excellent material for a Nietzschean psychological critique. This was clearly the will turned back upon itself, the reflexive rerouting of the *conatus* against its own strength, possibly for affirmation, and desire, a position that quite literally called into question self-preservation as the basis for ethical reflection. As an exercise, I would ask my students to take the above lines from Levinas and compare them with Nietzsche's from *On the Genealogy of Morals:*

> Hostility, cruelty, joy in persecuting, in attacking, in change, in destruction—all turned against the possessors of such instincts: *that* is the origin of the "bad conscience." The man who, from lack of external enemies and resistances and forcibly confined to the oppressive narrowness and punctiliousness of custom, impatiently lacerated, persecuted, gnawed at, assaulted, and maltreated himself: . . . this deprived creature, racked with homesickness for the wild, who had to turn himself into an adventure, a torture chamber, an uncertain and dangerous wilderness— this fool, this yearning and desperate prisoner became the inventor of the "bad conscience."　　　　　　　　　　　　　　　　　　　(GM 85)

Thus, it was with some wryness that I became aware of the sudden and enthusiastic turn to Levinas among the deconstructively minded after the Paul de Man affair broke into the public press. If the popular conclusion drawn from de Man's wartime writing was that something in the mode of deconstruction leads to Nazi sympathizing, then perhaps there is a way to show that deconstruction is on the side of the Jews, that it can be made to serve an ethical demand that would put deconstruction on the side of responsibility, resistance, and antifascist ethics. My sense was that it made no sense to rush to a slave morality to avert the charge of fascism and that there had to be some other way to navigate these alternatives besides heaping reaction formation upon reaction formation.

I don't know whether I have arrived at an alternative, or whether that is what I propose to offer you in the final pages of this paper. But I have come to think that the opposition that I saw between Levinas and Nietzsche was, perhaps, not quite as stark as I thought. I was going to write about the consonant meanings of "yielding" in Levinas, and "undergoing" in Nietzsche, but I am only able to clear the ground for a future reflection on the topic. I would like to point to two moments, instead, in which the subordinated becomes identified with the subordinator and where this identification is not simply an identification with the oppressor but appears to be a paradoxical basis for a different order of commonality that puts the distinction between subordinator and subordinated into a useful crisis.

In the first essay of *On the Genealogy of Morals,* Nietzsche introduces the noble to us as someone with the capacity to forget; the noble has "no memory for insults" and his forgetfulness is clearly the condition of his capacity to exercise his will. (As he elaborates in the second essay, forgetfulness makes room for new experience, nourishes the "nobler" faculties, and keeps us from being preoccupied with what has happened to us [GM 58–59]). The slave and the man of *ressentiment,* we are told, remember every insult perfectly and develop a clear memory in the service of vengefulness.

Nietzsche then starts the second essay by introducing the animal who is bred with the right to make promises, and this animal turns out to be the noble in a new form. What is paradoxical, and Nietzsche marks this, is that to make a promise means to have a memory, indeed, to have a continuous memory that lasts through time. If I say that I promise at one time, then my promise fails to remain a promise if, at another time, I forget what it is I have said. A promise is the sustained memory of an utterance, a memory that becomes instilled in the will, so that I not only say what it is I promise to do, but I also do precisely what I said I would do. The temporality of the utterance must, in the case of the promise, exceed the time and occasion of its enunciation. The linguistic deed of promising is "discharged" into the nonlinguistic deed precisely by virtue of this memory that becomes the resolution of the will.

Thus, the animal who requires forgetting also breeds in itself a capacity *to make and sustain a memory.* Forgetfulness is thus "abrogated"— Nietzsche's term—in those cases in which the need to sustain a memory of a promise emerges. He will tell us that within slave morality, a mnemonics of the will is prepared, that a memory is *burned* into the will, and that this burning is not only violent but bloody (thus, Nietzsche's famous quip that Kant's categorical imperative is steeped in blood). The way in which this memory is burned into the will, however, is precisely through a reflexive venting of the will against itself. In other words, morality for the one within slave morality requires a self-inflicted violence. But is this actually different from the kind of memory of the will that the noble crafts for himself?

At the moment in which the noble seeks to have a memory, a continuous memory through time, is the noble acting like those who belong to the sphere of *ressentiment?* Can the noble keep his promise without *remembering an injury*, even if the injury that he remembers is one that he inflicts on himself?

The result of this self-infliction is a continuous and trustworthy will: "between the original 'I will,' 'I shall do this' and the actual discharge of the will, its act, a world of strange new things, circumstances, even acts of will may be interposed without breaking this long chain of will" (GM 58).[2]

The will of the promising animal is one that is extended through time, figured as "a long chain of will," suggesting that there are different interlocking links of the will that remain unbroken by new things and circumstances or other acts of will. Whatever it is I promise, I do. And I renew that promise in different circumstances, and keep that promise *despite all circumstances.*

Of course, the figure of a chain with discontinuous links is an odd one to stand for this putatively "continuous" will. Indeed, pages later, Nietzsche reinvokes the figure of the chain to support a contradictory conclusion. Writing of the law, he argues that it makes no sense to determine the function of the law in terms of the origins of the law, the original reasons why the law was made, the original purposes it sought to serve (GM 77). As a social convention, the meanings and purposes of law change through time, they come to take on purposes that were never intended for them, and they no longer serve the original purposes for which they were devised. Nietzsche writes:

> The cause of the origin of a thing and its eventual utility, its actual employment and place in a system of purposes, lie worlds apart; whatever exists, having somehow come into being, is again and again reinterpreted to new ends, taken over, transformed, and redirected by some

power superior to it; all events in the organic world are a subduing, a *becoming master*, and all subduing and becoming master involves a fresh interpretation, an adaptation through which any previous "meaning" and "purpose" are necessarily obscured.[3]   (GM 77)

What happens if we return to the question of the status of the promise, if we understand promise as one of the conventions that Nietzsche mentions above? Can it be said that the cause and origin of a promise lie worlds apart, if promising is understood as a custom and its eventual utility, its actual employment and place in a system of purposes are in no necessary way linked to the act of promising itself? What does promising become if it is understood as one way to exercise a superior power, in Nietzsche's view, to reinterpret the promise to new ends, take it over, transform and redirect it? Or are we to conclude that promising as a customary act cannot exercise or manifest this superior power?

According to the above quotation, it seems that the "masterful" and "noble" thing to do is precisely to *revise* the meaning and purpose of a thing, an organ, or a custom according to new circumstances. And this power to reinterpret a convention to new ends not only requires becoming forgetful about the past, but characterizes the noble exercise of will.

The quotation continues:

The entire history of a "thing," an organ, a custom can in this way be a continuous *sign-chain* [*Zeichenkette*] of ever new interpretations and adaptations [suggesting an adaptation to new circumstances] whose causes do not even have to be related to one another but, on the contrary, in some cases succeed and alternate with one another in a purely chance fashion.   (GM 77)

The second use of the "chain" (*Kette*) seems to reverse the first, figuring the will as a chain of signs, a long sign-chain of the will, that indicates its uneven history. When the text makes this shift, the will, still called noble, not only adapts to new circumstances but endows its customary utterances, including promises, with new meaning, divorcing it from its original and animating intention. Indeed, therefore, to be noble is precisely *not* to keep one's promise regardless of circumstance.

But here Nietzsche wants the noble to elude the self-terrorizing practice of the slave at the same time that he elevates the promise as the right and entitlement of the noble. What remains unclear, however, is whether the promise can be kept without some measure of self-terrorization. Nietzsche proposes that "something of the terror that formerly attended all promises, pledges, and vows on earth is still effective" (GM 61). If the noble's promise does not elude that terror, is it a result of a certain self-terrorization, a terrorization of the will? And if so, is the conscience that is said to belong to the noble any different from the conscience that is said to belong to the slave? Can the noble, in other words, forget his terror and still sustain his promise?

The promise in Nietzsche's work seems to arise, then, from a necessary self-affliction, a terrorizing that was originally directed against the other and that now preserves the other, one might say in a Kleinian vein, precisely through a certain kind of sustainable damage to the self. Levinas's explanation clearly differs insofar as the wound is not understood as the reflexive form that aggression toward the Other takes, but constitutes something of the primary violence that marks our vulnerable, passive and necessary relation to that Other. Indeed, for Levinas, the "I" is split from the start precisely by this yielding to the Other that is its primary mode of being and its irreducible relationality. Nietzsche's noble at first appears as an individuated figure, distinct from the slave, but are these figures actually distinct from one another? Indeed, does the one figure interrupt the other in much the same way that the Levinasian subject is fundamentally interrupted by its Other? Is Nietzsche's wounded relation to the promise that is, after all, invariably a promise to the other any different from Levinas's wounded relation to alterity?

Just as, for Nietzsche, the injury to and by the other is "burned in the will," so Levinas writes, "The Other is in me and in the midst of my very identification" (OB 125). The Levinasian subject, we might say, also bears no grudges, assumes responsibility without *ressentiment:* "In suffering *by* the fault of the Other dawns suffering *for* the fault of Others." Indeed, this self is "accused by the Other to the point of persecution," and this very persecution implies a responsibility for the persecutor (OB 126). Thus, to be persecuted and to be accused for this subject are that for which one takes responsibility: "the position of the subject . . . is . . . a substitution by a hostage expiating for the violence of the persecution itself" (OB 127). Importantly, there is no self prior to its persecution by the Other. It is that persecution that establishes the Other at the heart of the self, and establishes that "heart" as an ethical relation of responsibility. To claim the self-identity of the subject is thus an act of irresponsibility, an effort to close off one's fundamental vulnerability to the Other, the primary accusation that the Other bears. Levinas writes:

> The accusation is in this sense persecuting; the persecuted one can no longer answer for it. More exactly, it is an accusation which I cannot answer, but for which I cannot decline responsibility.[4]   (OB 127)

This primary responsibility for the persecutor establishes the basis for ethical responsibility.

Levinas dedicated *Otherwise Than Being* "to the memory of those who were closest among the six million assassinated by the National Socialists, and of the millions and millions of all confessions and all nations, victims of the same hatred of the other [*la même haine de l'autre homme*], the same anti-Semitism." And just when it appears that Levinas has installed the Jew as the paradigm of all victimization, he warns on the next page against Zionist persecution, citing the precautionary words of Pascal: "'That is my place in the sun.' That is how the usurpation of the whole world began [*Voilà le commencement et l'image du l'usurpation de toute la terre*]." And if it were not enough that the Jew figured here is *both* victim and persecutor, Levinas cites from Ezekiel the direct address of a God who bears the same double status, requiring violence and repentance at once: "if a righteous man turn from his righteousness . . . his blood will I require at your hands," and then, "pass through the city—through Jerusalem—and set a mark upon the foreheads of the men who sigh and cry for all the abominations that are done in the midst of it." But then of course God commits an abomination himself, instructing another man to follow the man he just instructed: "pass through the city after him and slay without mercy or pity. Old men, young men and maidens, little children and women—strike them all dead! But touch no one on whom is the mark. And begin at my sanctuary!" Thus, God endeavors to save from destruction those who bemoan the abominations, but he commits an abomination precisely in the act of providing salvation. Thus, God cannot condemn abomination without the condemnation being an abomination itself. Even with God, good and evil are less than distinct.

The subject who might seek to become righteous according to the ways of such a God will be one who is not only accused and persecuted from the start, but one who is also accusing and persecuting. In this view, there is no innocence, only the navigations of ambivalence, since it seems to be impossible to be persecuted without at once being or becoming the persecutor as well. What remains to be considered is how this scene of ethical inversion nevertheless leads to a responsibility that is, by definition it seems, constantly confounded by self-preservation and its attendant aggressions. If there is no becoming ethical save through a certain violence, then how are we to gauge the value of such an ethics? Is it the only mode for ethics, and what becomes of an ethics of nonviolence? And how often does the violence of ethics, seen most clearly when in the act of righteous denunciation, pose the question of the value of the ethical relation itself? Certain kinds of values, such as generosity and forgiveness, may only be possible through a suspension of this mode of ethicality and, indeed, by calling into question the value of ethics itself.

Levinas recognizes that it is not always possible to live or love well under such conditions. He refers to this primary ethical relation to alterity as "breathless," as if the Other is what is breathed in and preserved within the hollow of the self, as if this very preservation puts the life of the ethical subject at risk. I don't know whether air that is not exhaled comes close to becoming "bad air," but certainly the ethical bearing in this instance degrades the biological conditions of life. Given that the Levinasian subject also rehearses an "insomniac vigilance" in relation to the other, it may still be necessary to continue to call for "good air" and to find a place for the value of self-preservation, if one wants, for instance, to breathe and to sleep.

NOTES

This essay originally appeared in the volume *The Turn to Ethics,* ed. Marjorie Garber, Beatrice Hanssen, and Rebecca L. Walkowitz (New York: Routledge, 2000), 15–28.

1. The ethical relation is that of a passivity beyond passivity, one that escapes from the binary opposition of passive and active; it is an "effacement," a "bad conscience," a primordial exposure to the Other, to the face of the Other, to the demand that is made by the face of the Other: "To have to respond to [the Other's] right to be—not by reference to the abstraction of some anonymous law, some juridical entity, but in fear of the Other. My 'in the world' [alluding to Heidegger], my 'place in the sun,' my at-homeness, have they not been the usurpation of the places belonging to the other man already oppressed and

starved by me?" (quoted from "Bad Conscience and the Inexorable," in *Face to Face with Levinas,* ed. Richard A. Cohen [Albany: State University of New York Press, 1986], 38).

2. In German: "so dass zwischen das ursprüngliche 'ich will,' 'ich werde tun' und die eigentliche Entladung des Willens, seinen Akt, unbedenklich eine Welt von neuen fremden Dingen, Umständen, selbst Willensakten dazwischengelegt werden darf, ohne dass diese lange Kette des Willens springt" (Gm [293]).

3. In German: "Dass nämlich die Ursache der Entstehung eines Dings und dessen schliessliche Nützlichkeit, dessen tatsächliche Verwendung und Einordnung in ein System von Zwecken *toto coelo* auseinander liegen; dass etwas Vorhandenes, irgendwie Zu-Stande-Gekommenes immer wieder von einer ihm überlegenen Macht auf neue Ansichten ausgelegt, neu in Beschlag genommen, zu einem neuen Nutzen umgebildet und umgerichtet wird; dass alles Geschehen in der organischen Welt ein Überwältigen, Herrwerden und dass wiederum alles Überwältigen und Herrwerden ein Neu-Interpretieren, ein Zurechtmachen ist, bei dem der bisherige 'Sinn' und 'Zweck' notwendig verdunkelt oder ganz ausgelöscht werden muss" (Gm [314]).

4. "Accusation, en ce sens persécutrice, à laquelle le persécuté ne peut pas répondre—ou plus exactement—accusation à laquelle je ne peux répondre—mais dont je ne peux décliner la responsabilité" (AE 202).

5

Thus Spoke Zarathustra, Thus Listened the Rabbis

Philosophy, Education, and the Cycle of Enlightenment

CLAIRE ELISE KATZ

ONE NARRATIVE in the history of philosophy is a story about the search for truth. This narrative reveals an underlying story about a particular model of philosophical education and how that truth can be attained. Yet, in spite of its own attempts at self-critique, and in spite of the variations on how truth and knowledge are defined, philosophy continually appropriates the same model of education. Although it appears to take different forms, the model of education, which doubles as the model of philosophy, expresses the same features: a master teacher who not only does not learn but who also has trouble teaching, and a student who, in spite of being taught by a master teacher who has attained wisdom, needs to be self-motivated in order to learn what the teacher knows—and this is something that cannot be taught by the master teacher. The student is unable to hear what the teacher wishes to convey, and the teacher is unable to identify what the student needs in order to learn. The model reveals the paradox of education: teaching cannot teach precisely what is needed to learn—the student's internal desire to learn. Additionally, insofar as the roles are discretely circumscribed, the real teaching that takes place goes unacknowledged. Teachers continue to remain ignorant of why their students misunderstand them and the message they wish to communicate, and students remain frustrated in their attempts to attain the knowledge that their teachers wish to convey.[1]

Briefly, we can describe the dominant, Platonic model as follows—we are presented with a master teacher, although we have no idea from where he originates,[2] and someone designated as the student, or there are many students or disciples. The problem with the imbalanced relationship between teacher and student is less that it is asymmetrical than that it is nonreciprocal. The boundaries and the tasks of each in his respective role are tightly circumscribed. A "learner" leaves the community, although the mechanism and the means for doing so vary in each education narrative. He then attains enlightenment or knowledge, which is often thought to be a form of self-knowledge. The educated one then returns to the masses in order to convey this knowledge or simply rule over them. The model often follows this equation: community equals mass thinking equals corruption of creative, individual thinking. Thus, the teacher has something to offer, or simply rules over, the students. Here again the motivation and means for the return also vary. However, in almost all of the narratives, the process is a failure, at least with regard to its stated goal. My concern lies in this cycle of enlightenment, or this description of the process of education.[3]

This essay explores this model of education, which is still viewed as the standard today. My interest lies in why it remains so seductive and why it is ultimately ineffectual. I return to two teachers: Socrates as portrayed by Plato and Nietzsche's Zarathustra, in *Thus Spoke Zarathustra,* both of whom exemplify this model. Both are of interest precisely because of how each teacher presents himself to others: Socrates presents himself as open to learning, as not knowing anything, and as someone who is aware of both of these facts about himself. Although scholars disagree about Plato's presentation of Socrates and whether it is intentional, anyone who has taught the dialogues to unsympathetic audiences knows that Socrates' method of teaching, for all its novelty and insight, is frequently received as patronizing.[4] Finally, I turn to Levinas's philosophical work, which I argue embodies a Talmudic model of education, in order to provide an alternative to the standard philosophical model of teaching and learning.

———

Plato's dialogues are carefully, and artfully, crafted, and we are led to believe that Socrates is the hero. He is more frequently than not referenced as the ideal teacher, and many of us secretly wish we could choreograph our classroom discussions so that we too could gently lead our students to see the error of their own arguments and unsupported beliefs. For me, that wish is often tempered by an accompanying discomfort with the model. What if we were to consider that Socrates simply upholds a model of teaching that is not only ineffective but also dishonest? Is Socrates who he presents himself to be? Similar to the problems encountered by Zarathustra, what does this mistaken identity mean for Socrates? What does it mean for the teacher in general? Additionally, and not unrelated to these other questions, we can ask what role listening plays in teaching. In what ways do students have something to teach teachers, not simply about the material at hand but about who the teachers are as individuals? How might students' responses reveal that identity? What if the image we think we convey about ourselves is not the one that our students see, and what if our students can give us a more accurate accounting? How might we understand the relationship between teacher and student differently? How might we understand the model of education differently? My point in raising these questions is to acknowledge, on the one hand, that both Socrates and Zarathustra are pivotal figures in philosophical education. Socrates is offered as the model teacher, the exemplar of teaching; Zarathustra is presented as a radical critic of philosophy and education. Yet, on the other hand, both reveal that they subscribe to a model of education that is conventional and ineffective.

What is common to both Socrates, as represented by the Platonic model of teaching, and Nietzsche's Zarathustra is an emphasis on the privileged position of the teacher of virtue who, as a result of this position, stands above his students.[5] As Daniel Conway notes, the teacher of virtue "views the construction of his position as neither contingent nor arbitrary. He consequently exempts himself from his own teaching on the grounds that [in Zarathustra's case] he has already renounced his belief in God."[6] But as Conway also notes, Zarathustra has "invented" the conditions of his success as a teacher.

I do not dispute that Zarathustra is searching; his frustration with his students, which leads him to rethink his teaching methods, is a sign of this searching. However, his search lacks inward reflection; he does not search himself. His focus on his students as the location of the flaw in the teaching leads to the second level of the pedagogical problem. In order to correct

the teaching, Zarathustra journeys alone in the search. The reciprocity necessarily inherent in an effective and sophisticated model of education is
disregarded. These models assume that education is static for the teacher.
The teacher is oblivious to the other, the student, and therefore remains
untouched and unchanged by the other—or, at least, is unable to acknowledge these changes as a result of contact with the other.

We see this model throughout the history of philosophy. In light of the
little attention philosophy of education is given by philosophers today, one
might be led to believe that education is not important to philosophers. Yet,
the history of philosophy is in fact a history of the philosophy of education:
someone has gained an insight, or attained wisdom, and the all-consuming
question is how to convey this insight to others. The paradox of this model
lies in the manner in which one attained the wisdom and the pedagogical
stance one now assumes. Thus, the educational model begins in, to put it
mildly, a flawed state.[7]

Who is Nietzsche's Zarathustra? Heidegger raises this question in an essay in which he investigates the relationship between two of Zarathustra's
teachings: the overman and the doctrine of the eternal return.[8] The question is not so easily answered. Heidegger presents a compelling case that
while Nietzsche thought he was bringing an end to metaphysics, *Zarathustra* reveals a fundamental reliance on metaphysics. I am convinced by Heidegger's reading of these two teachings and their link to each other. However,
my interest lies not in the unity of the teachings but in the project as a
whole: the link between these teachings and Zarathustra's pedagogy. In the
end it does not matter what the teachings prove if Zarathustra is not equal
to the task of trying to teach them. Put more simply, I am interested in the
unity of Zarathustra himself. And we see this problem revealed in the representation of Zarathustra's identity to others. For example, in part 2 of *Thus
Spoke Zarathustra,* Zarathustra says, "My friends I do not want to be mixed
up and confused with others" (TZ 100). Although Zarathustra implores his
disciples not to confuse him with others, his demand is too late. Throughout part 2 we continually see that Zarathustra is trying to distinguish himself, even if unsuccessfully. What then is the source of this confusion?

Zarathustra's question at the end of part 2, "Who am I?" indicates that
Zarathustra himself is confused about his own identity. The confusion then
can be seen from two perspectives: who he is as seen from the point of
view of his disciples, and who he is as someone whose identity remains obscure even to himself. It is not clear that these two perspectives are mutually

exclusive, and they might even be necessarily intertwined. The disciples' "confusion" might not be a confusion at all but rather an identification of the Zarathustra that is presented to others even if unwittingly so by Zarathustra himself.

We see evidence of this problem early in part 2 when a child holds a mirror to Zarathustra, and in the reflection he sees himself as a demon.[9] The mirror could be said to represent his disciples, and the image reflected back to Zarathustra represents how his disciples see him. But we cannot ignore the level of self-reflection—Zarathustra sees this image of himself also, or put even more simply, this image is the one that he in fact unintentionally projects.

There are several sources in part 2 that aid in this confusion: Zarathustra's teaching of the doctrine of justice; the characteristic of revenge that he may have in common with those from whom he is trying to distinguish himself; and his understanding of himself, attributed in part to his inattentiveness to what his disciples say to him. We find Zarathustra's doctrine of justice in the seventh speech, "On the Tarantulas." Here Zarathustra asks, "What would my love of the overman be if I spoke otherwise?" (TZ 101). But the teachings of Zarathustra with regard to such a doctrine have led his disciples to misunderstand him and reveal how tightly they cling to the old ideal of justice, i.e., justice as equality. Those who preach equality are also preachers of Zarathustra's doctrine of life—but what distinguishes them from Zarathustra is that they also preach tarantulas (TZ 99). Those who preach equality—though they claim to love life—in actuality, harbor a hatred of it. Thus, the justice of equality reveals the jealousy that ultimately breeds revenge.

In order to distinguish himself from others, Zarathustra must be clear about his doctrine. He must be clear that justice is a justice of inequality. Yet, his disciples still misunderstand him, since they hear within his teaching the justice of equality. At the end of "On Tarantulas," Zarathustra is bitten by a tarantula, symbolizing that he has been infected with the spirit of revenge. If he now embodies the spirit of revenge, we can ask whether Zarathustra is actually similar to those he has called the teachers of revenge (TZ 99).[10]

This experience of revenge plays a role in Zarathustra's confusion.[11] At the end of part 2, Zarathustra's *ressentiment* evolves into bad conscience—"I am ashamed." According to Gilles Deleuze, each of these reactive types are made bearable, as well as possible, by an ascetic ideal.[12] These "moments" of revenge parallel Zarathustra's movement toward self-realization. During the time when Zarathustra is caught in the spirit of revenge—*ressentiment* or bad conscience—he is confused about who he is.

The necessity of first moving through revenge is revealed in Deleuze's comment that "our knowledge of the will to power will remain limited if we do not grasp its manifestation in *ressentiment,* bad conscience, the ascetic ideal and the nihilism which forces us to know it."[13] The spirit of revenge gives us insight into spirit itself and thus gives us insight into the will to power. As part 2 progresses, Zarathustra begins to move out of revenge toward self-discovery.

The final source of his disciples' confusion can be found in the later speeches of this second part. We see emerging from this confusion Zarathustra's initial awareness regarding his own confusion. Zarathustra shakes his head at his disciples in three particular speeches, "On Poets," "On Great Events," and "On the Soothsayer," indicating his own disappointment with his disciples' inability to understand him. In "On Redemption," we are given the means to understand the soothsayer's prophecy; Zarathustra's confusion over his own identity becomes apparent.

"On Redemption" hints at the eternal return, although it is not mentioned explicitly. We learn that what will redeem has been transformed. The will to power was first expressed as self-overcoming; the self is connected to the body and the body to life. Life must continually overcome itself (TZ 115). This moment of linking the will to power to the eternal return is the key to Zarathustra's own identity, to his own discovery about who he is. His confusion regarding his own identity is more apparent in light of his moments of self-discovery. As the hunchback notices in "On Redemption," Zarathustra speaks differently to others, to his disciples, and to himself. Yet, this could be an indication that Zarathustra is not only misunderstood by his disciples, if indeed he is misunderstood, but that Zarathustra misunderstood them.

At the end of part 2, Zarathustra believes that he must make a complete split from his disciples; he must make the journey to the overman alone. He misunderstood his disciples when he believed that the way of the overman was for them. It was not; it was for him alone. Yet, in spite of his new awareness, in spite of knowing what needs to be done, Zarathustra "reflected for a long time and trembled. . . . But at last [he] said what [he] said at first: I do not want to" (TZ 145). His identity unfolds at the end of part 2. Nonetheless, we are left with a less than satisfying answer to the question regarding Zarathustra's success at distinguishing himself from the other "false prophets." How different is he from his disciples and from how his disciples view him?

The confusion about Zarathustra's identity is significant since it is upon Zarathustra's discovery about who he is that he also recognizes his mistaken assumption about whose task it is to go on the journey to the overman. Upon realizing who he is, Zarathustra also sees his disciples for who they are, and, more important, who they cannot be. At the end of part 2, Zarathustra realizes that it is he alone who must assume this task. I use the term "realizes" with hesitation, since it is not clear his realization is accurate or even authentic. This belief, however, grounds what we see as a standard model of education, and, more specifically, teaching. The teacher must go the distance alone, without the students. And the intended message sent by the teacher is not always the message received by the students. In spite of Zarathustra's insistence that he will not return from his journey to the overman, he does return.

We find a similar return in Plato's cave allegory in book 7 of his *Republic*. The allegory poses the possibility of the "return" as hypothetical—what *would* happen if the escapee who now has seen the light were to return to the cave? However, Socrates can certainly be viewed as the most famous escapee, who not only returns to the masses repeatedly but whose return eventually motivates others to kill him. Like Zarathustra, Socrates cannot help himself. We see his return in Plato's *Republic, Euthyphro, Meno,* and *Apology,* to name only a few. The *Republic* begins with Socrates' announcement that he went down to Piraeus. The *Euthyphro* shows him engaged with a young man who, returning from the courthouse, tells Socrates that he has just charged his father with impiety; *Meno* elucidates the problem with teaching virtue; and the *Apology* recounts Socrates' final act of the return—that of trying to convince a jury of his peers that he is innocent of the charges against him.

————

Levinas is acutely aware of the paradox—of how to convey philosophical insight to others—and in this sense embodies the Talmudic approach to education.[14] The Talmudic approach rejects the equation set out above. Instead, it views a community of learners as precisely how one cultivates a creative, thinking mind.[15] In their essay "The Babylonian Talmud in Cognitive Perspective," Jeffrey Kraus and Marjorie Lehman demonstrate this point.[16]

Kraus and Lehman begin with a discussion of the Talmud's structure, which they see as argumentative as opposed to dialogical. In addition to this argumentative structure, the polyphony of opinion in the text is also emphasized or noted as fundamental to the structure of the text. Talmudic scholars do not see this polyphony as undermining the significance of the text. Rather, they believe that it indicates that the Talmud is teaching the more important point—that truth is often indefinable. Ironically, this point brings Nietzsche into a closer relationship with the rabbis than he, or we, might have thought. The *method* of learning takes precedence over the content, without undermining or erasing it. In answering the question, Why have a sacred text that does not even pretend to give the answers? the authors cite Talmudic scholars who speculate that the text must be about something more than providing dogmatic responses. The text actually models the way we are to think about the questions of daily life—ethical questions that require us to think about how to treat other people.

Additionally, within the process of this kind of learning, the questioning between the two study partners requires each participant to admit that there is always something more to be known and that truth is indefinable. This process intends to develop humility and a certain integrity regarding truth. The interaction between the study partners aids in developing the respect one has for the other, in addition to building a close bond of friendship. If nothing else, this process teaches both partners that dependency and vulnerability and the willingness to be open to learning from the other are not only a good thing but are necessary for any real learning to occur. The Talmudic model explicitly rejects the model we found in Plato. Not only is the polyphony of views not a form of mediocre thinking; it is viewed as precisely the way that creative, independent, and critical thinking is produced.

If we look at Levinas's work, we see that not only does he, too, repeatedly reference teaching and the teaching relationship but his project also assumes a model of education that is necessary for cultivating the very ethical subject he describes.[17] Additionally, his philosophical writings perform a similar task to that of the Babylonian Talmud (*Bavli*). Levinas's references to the Hebrew Scriptures ask us to think about the context in which we find these references and what they might mean. His repeated references to the Other ask us to think not only about the human other but the text as other. To use Levinas's term, the text becomes a third in the relationship with the other. Teaching and learning are transformed. The teacher is someone who knows but also someone who engages in self-doubt. The student is someone who learns but also someone who teaches. It is not that the roles are so confused that the student does not learn and the teacher has nothing to teach. Rather, the journey undertaken by both is part of a dynamic and transformative experience; the journey is something that must be taken together even if the second level of learning, the individual level identified by the Russian psychologist Lev Vygotsky, is a dimension of learning that happens "intrapsychologically," that is, within the child—or the adult.[18]

Levinas's view of the ethical relation not only points to a pedagogy that includes reading biblical narratives Jewishly; it also relies on this model of education to cultivate an ethical subject. Levinas's insight reveals the role that alterity plays in midrash, since the role of midrash is to open up the text and allow voices that are otherwise muted to be heard. Thus, for Levinas, to read Jewishly is precisely to read such that one is open to the other. Additionally, the process of questioning that we find in the Talmudic tradition is intended not only to teach students to question in order to be attuned to the material at hand. The Jewish tradition of learning recognizes something unique about the journey one takes in the educational process—it reveals an approach to education that is less concerned with the notion of absolute truth. Instead, its role is to engage the mind and to join the learners in a community of education. It might be that this role is what philosophy always intended—that philosophy was less concerned about a single truth than it was about identifying wisdom by inflaming the creative mind—and that this kind of learning was to be done communally. Unfortunately, this is not the standard view of philosophy or of education.[19]

The Talmudic model of learning outlined above radically challenges the model we find throughout the history of philosophy. It not only resists an absolute truth; it also explicitly teaches this resistance. This point draws the rabbinic pedagogical model closer to one that Nietzsche might have envisioned. In both cases, the context for pedagogy would be an opposition to many of the values we find in modernity. These values emerge out of an extreme liberalism that cannot offer a positive vision in the cultivation of humanity but only a view of individuals as free to make choices on their own, and out of a society that is engineered to guarantee the widest range of these freedoms. Both Nietzsche and the Talmudic rabbis would agree that, left to their own devices, people, though free, frequently do not make good choices, or even choices that would best serve them. Freedom, while an important part of humanity, cannot be the overriding value that determines how individuals are cultivated. Both Nietzsche and the Talmudic rabbis have a vision of how to refashion human beings. However, this is the point at which Nietzsche and the Talmudic rabbis would part company.

For Nietzsche, "community" is negotiable. Although Zarathustra rejects the life of the hermit, it seems clear that most of his teachings reflect a view of humanity that is at least suspicious of dependence if it is anything other than propadeutic or temporary. He cannot envision dependence on others as healthy or positive. By contrast, for the Talmudic rabbis, the context of the Jewish community and the larger community in which they live is nonnegotiable. The community is what drives the entire Talmudic project in its positive vision of cultivating humanity. What the Talmudic rabbis discovered and exploited is the way that individuals contribute not only destructively to relationships but also positively. Healthy competition, vulnerability and dependence, and erotic desire in learning fundamentally drive healthy human relationships. For the rabbis, these are not simply "facts of life," though they are that. They are also what it means to be human. Like Nietzsche, the Jews do not deny their animal nature, nor do they deny the unhealthy tendencies that can accompany that nature. Instead, the Talmudic tradition is geared precisely toward constructing a community that takes all of these elements of human life into account.[20]

In his essay "Hegel and the Jews," Levinas analyzes a few of Hegel's writings, presented by Bernard Bourgeois, that were intended to be incorporated into the Hegelian system (in DF). As is familiar to most of us, neither Christianity nor Judaism is at the end of the Hegelian system. They are steps along the way, but both are superseded by something else. Levinas observes that while it is true that both are superseded, each is represented quite differently from the other. Christianity, though not necessarily recognizable to some Christians, is not offensive either. The critical discourse surrounding Judaism, Levinas notes, has nurtured anti-Semitism.[21]

Levinas's primary concern is that Hegel's characterization of Judaism as the negation of spirit leads to an anti-Semitism that "is based within the System" (DF 236). The most common charge against Judaism is that it is "particular" as opposed to "universal." It is tribal and exclusive. But the more damning comments from these Hegelian meditations are the ones that refer to Judaism, and in particular Abraham, as material and bestial, focused only on self-preservation and animal needs. And, of course, this is put in opposition to freedom. This essay was first published in 1971, but in

1935 Levinas had already countered these simplistic critiques of both Judaism and materiality.

In *De l'evasion,* Levinas teaches us that the seductive call of freedom presented to us by modern philosophy is a mythology.[22] First and foremost, our bodies require food, nurturance, and warmth. Our bodies betray us. Levinas's ethics, the response to the other, which recognizes the possibility of sacrificing one's life for the other, is prior to any sense of freedom or choice. And here Levinas sees the mythology of freedom in the same way that he sees the mythology of autonomy.

Levinas nonetheless recognizes that even before the call of the other, before any ethical response, we are not free. Thus, it is on this model that we can see how a Jewish pedagogy, how a Jewish model of education would be founded. And we can see that unless one is willing to step out of the tradition set forth by modern philosophy, and step out of it radically, this kind of pedagogy might not reveal itself. Levinas's implicit identification of the Talmudic approach to learning not only radicalizes his philosophical project; it also transforms how we think about education, our understanding of both teaching and learning.[23] The individualism that dominates theories of education and the philosophical journey itself, in spite of their attempt to portray themselves in terms of the social, can now be understood in its social dimension. The radical individualism that is valorized throughout most of the history of philosophy, even if also unwittingly undermined by those same philosophers who champion it, is critiqued and transformed through the influence of Jewish philosophy and theology in Levinas's philosophical work. Levinas's use of Jewish wisdom in his philosophical discourse transforms how we might think about education.

The Jewish religion described by the Torah, the Talmud, and the Jewish philosophers who followed them does not describe a religion of asceticism. It is a religion that enjoys and celebrates life, from the birth of the child to the sexual encounter that made that child possible. It encourages us to enjoy food, dance, music, wine, song, and relationships with others. I do not dispute that contemporary Judaism and many contemporary Jews have fallen prey to the values of modernity that contribute to *ressentiment* and asceticism. Nor do I dispute that strains of asceticism can be found within traditional Judaism—either as theological opinions fundamental to the religion or in the practices of Jews who have adopted the cultural practices and attitudes of the milieu in which they live. However, this is a very different matter from what Judaism might have to offer, in spite of and even because of its association with modern culture. Judaism's commitment to include the minority position as part of its theological canon not only allows Judaism to resist being characterized as monolithic; it also provides the very substance and model for the educational process.

Nietzsche represents someone who almost gets it right. Like Rousseau before him, he can identify the problem, but he cannot solve it on his own. Nietzsche's *Zarathustra* clarifies, more than any other book in the history of philosophy, the flaws in the standard model of teaching and philosophical education; it seems that this is precisely Nietzsche's intention. Nietzsche's description of and admiration for the agon might have led him to admire the Talmudic approach to education, which is often criticized for its competitiveness.[24] The primary problem with Nietzsche's analysis is his apparent conflation of Christianity and Judaism. No doubt, Christians have their own complaints about how Nietzsche has characterized Christianity. My concern here is how he has characterized Judaism. Much of this characterization results from Nietzsche's own ambivalence towards Judaism, some of which is probably the result of his lack of knowledge of it. Most readers of Nietzsche recognize that his admiration for Judaism is the Judaism of the Torah—the Kingly Jews, the Jews who were warriors, and Yahweh, a God whose wrath was feared. It is the post-Diaspora Jews, the Jews represented by the Prophetic and Priestly periods, whom Nietzsche does not completely respect (AC §25). For Nietzsche, the rabbinic period is simply more of the same.[25] To his unschooled eyes, these later stages of Judaism simply look like Christianity. Yet it is precisely in these periods that we find the radical distinction between Judaism and Christianity, for it is in the rabbinic period that gave rise to the Midrash and then later to the Talmud that we find Jewish wisdom, a love of life, and a unique educational model. Nietzsche's disdain for this Jewish period and his naïve view that it resembled Christianity precluded him from seeing precisely how Judaism was different in one of the most significant ways. Judaism does not begin with an ascetic ideal.[26] As a result, problems like *ressentiment* are pseudo problems.

However, if I am right that the radical critique of this model of education could only come from wholly outside of it, then the solution is one that Nietzsche could have only have glimpsed. He might never have been able to find it on his own. In fact, one might even say that this is precisely the moment where Nietzsche's ambivalence with regard to Judaism betrays him. Nietzsche's diagnosis of the problems in philosophy and philosophical education is correct, but he needed the help of the Jewish "doctors,"[27] whom he dismissed as part of the problem, to help him cure the disease.

NOTES

Another version of this paper is published in *New Nietzsche Studies,* Special Issue on "Nietzsche and the Jews," coedited by David B. Allison, Babette Babich, and Debra B. Bergoffen, vol. 7, no. 3/4 (Fall 2007). I would like to thank Bettina Bergo, Debra Bergoffen, Daniel Conway, and Jill Stauffer for their comments on previous drafts.

1. See Claire Katz, "Witnessing Education," *Studies in Practical Philosophy* 3, no. 2 (2003): 107–31.

2. More often than not the person designated as the teacher is male. However, one of the recurring themes throughout these treatises on philosophy of education is that it is the women who are ultimately the most effective teachers — and who in fact know more about themselves and others — even if these points are not acknowledged explicitly.

3. Philosophy is itself the story of the return to the masses and the cycle of education. The problem of the return and the issue of what can and cannot be taught, first seen in Plato's Cave Allegory, reappears in Eugen Fink's analysis of phenomenology and the phenomenological turn. How do those who have made the "turn" convey to those who have not, the dogmatists, the significance of making the turn? The problem, as Fink indicates, is that the motivation for making the turn is the turn itself. The problem of motivation reveals the problem with teaching.

4. A typical exchange in an introductory philosophy class includes the students condemning Socrates for his arrogance — in the *Apology* — and his insensitivity in the *Crito* and *Phaedo.* The typical response to this view, even if muttered to oneself, is for the teacher to declare that the students simply do not get it. While admittedly this is true, part of the problem lies in delivery of the message. It often does not occur to us that the models for instruction are, quite simply, ineffective at best and misleading at worst.

5. See Daniel Conway, "Nietzsche *Contra* Nietzsche: The Deconstruction of Nietzsche," in *Nietzsche as Post-Modernist,* ed. Clayton Koelb (Albany: State University of New York Press, 1990), 91–110, 304–11.

6. Conway, "Nietzsche *Contra* Nietzsche," 95.

7. We do not need to return to the ancient Greeks to find the flaw. We can see it in the modern period exemplified by Rousseau's educational treatise, *Emile*. For a longer analysis of *Emile*, see Claire Katz, "Teaching the Other: Levinas, Rousseau, and the Question of Education" *Philosophy Today* 49, no. 2 (Summer 2005): 200–207; Claire Katz, "Educating the Solitary Man: Dependence and Vulnerability in Levinas and Rousseau," in *Levinas Studies: An Annual Review*, vol. 2 (Pittsburgh, Penn.: Duquesne University Press, 2007), 133–52.

8. Martin Heidegger, "Who Is Nietzsche's Zarathustra?" in *The New Nietzsche*, ed. David Allison (Cambridge, Mass.: MIT Press, 1995), 64–79.

9. It should not be lost on us that references to the devil are often anti-Semitic references—references to Jews. Is Zarathustra worried that there is a Jew in their midst?

10. Heidegger wonders if Zarathustra's doctrine delivers him from revenge ("Who Is," 76). For Heidegger Zarathustra himself is not free from the spirit of revenge until he recognizes the Being of beings as represented in the eternal return. It appears that the deliverance from the spirit of revenge is the crossing over to the overman (74). In Heidegger's view, Zarathustra's doctrine does not actually bring deliverance from revenge.

11. This view is supported by Gilles Deleuze's reading of Zarathustra in *Nietzsche and Philosophy*, trans. Hugh Tomlinson (New York: Columbia University Press, 1962); *Nietzsche et la philosophie* (Paris: PUF, 1962). Hereafter cited by the English and the French page numbers unless otherwise specified.

12. Deleuze, *Nietzsche*, 146 (not in the French version).

13. Deleuze, *Nietzsche*, 172/198.

14. See Claire Elise Katz, "Levinas—Between Philosophy and Rhetoric: The 'Teaching' of Levinas's Scriptural References," *Philosophy and Rhetoric* 38, no. 2 (2005): 159–72.

15. This community of learners is typically in the yeshiva, which is first and foremost filled with male members of the community. Moreover, there is a distinction made between those who study in the yeshiva and those who do not. My point is that the rabbis nonetheless see the value of a communal approach to education.

16. See Jeffrey Kress and Marjorie Lehman, "The Babylonian Talmud in Cognitive Perspective," *Journal of Jewish Education* 69, no. 2 (2003): 58–78.

17. Levinas was associated with the Alliance Israélite Universelle for more than fifty years, and he directed the Ecole Normal Israelite Orientale for about forty years.

18. See Kress and Lehman, "The Babylonian Talmud."

19. Also see Claire Elise Katz, "'The Presence of the Other Is a Presence That Teaches': Levinas, Pragmatism, and Pedagogy," *Journal of Jewish Thought and Philosophy* 14, nos. 1–2 (2006): 91–108.

20. We see this demonstrated by the very substance of the Talmud, which raises questions about all aspects of daily life from the food we eat to our obligations in marriage.

21. DF 236. Unfortunately, Hegel's characterization of the Jews has influenced not only non-Jews but Jews themselves. For more on anti-Semitism in both Hegel and Nietzsche, see Yirmiyahu Yovel, *Dark Riddle: Hegel, Nietzsche, and the Jews* (University Park: Penn State Press, 1998).

22. See RH. This essay was originally published in 1934 in *Esprit,* and *De l'evasion* was published just one year later in 1935.

23. He makes this reference explicit in his writings on Jewish education, some of which are collected in *Difficult Freedom.*

24. See for example, Friedrich Nietzsche, "Homer's Contest," *The Portable Nietzsche,* ed. and trans. Walter Kaufmann (Middlesex, U.K.: Penguin, 1976).

25. For more on this "ambivalence," see Yovel, *Dark Riddle.* In particular, see 145 ff. In this discussion, Yovel asserts that Nietzsche is clear—all ambivalence is gone and Nietzsche "decries" the priestly period just as he decried anti-Semitism and Christianity (145). However, even here we see a more complex ambivalence. For Nietzsche, the Jews of the Diaspora are the "promise" of the cure for Christianity. While Nietzsche blames the Jews—precisely for bringing Christianity into being—it is the Jews of the modern period whom he believes can cure modernity of its ills. Thus, the children are to cure what the ancestors wrought. My intent here is not to solve the problem of Nietzsche's ambivalence nor of his attitude toward the Jews. Rather, I call attention to it and ask us to think about the ways in which Nietzsche remained trapped within the very system he hoped to escape.

26. Although there are dietary restrictions and rules governing sexual activity, the enjoyment of both food and sexuality for its own sake is neither prohibited nor frowned upon. Admittedly, there are conflicting rabbinic views on sexual activity—to be sure, Judaism is not monolithic. Nonetheless, the canon explicitly maintains the minority views precisely to indicate the nuances of Jewish tradition.

27. Levinas refers to the Talmudic and midrashic rabbis as "doctors."

II

The Subject

Sensing, Suffering, and Responding

6

The Flesh Made Word; Or, The Two Origins

BETTINA BERGO

WE ARE now a half century away from the last writings of Martin Buber and the first magnum opus of Levinas, *Totality and Infinity* (1961). While both thinkers deformalized consciousness, Buber explicitly took up Nietzsche's heritage to this end. He did this as late as *I and Thou* (1923).[1] Writing in the 1940s, Levinas will face the prospect of deformalizing Heidegger's Dasein through a return to embodied states (nausea, lassitude, shame), even to significant dimensions of life itself (fatigue, labor, pleasure, sexuality). His multiple experiments with embodiment in *On Escape* (1936) and *Existence and Existents* (1947) are clear evidence that Levinas was seeking to undercut Heidegger's cerebral *Stimmungen* of angst and boredom. Even if later on Heidegger speaks of "moods" like serenity following the trial of Being, anxiety and boredom remain close to resoluteness as the revelatory modes through which the question of Being comes into view—while requiring that we confront courageously our (and Being's) mortality. To deformalize Heidegger's moods, which *are already a kind of comprehension*, Levinas has to show that at the depths of living embodiment lies a gap, between *what* we feel and the way we *become aware* of actively feeling anything. This also meant contesting the primacy Husserl attributed to transcendental consciousness as passive temporal synthesis. In this deformalization, the deeper question is: *how* can we approach living embodiment without recourse to *Lebensphilosophie,* with its sometimes perverse appropriations of Nietzsche?[2] I am thinking here of the German reception of Nietzsche in the 1910s and 1920s, notably under the pen of Johann Bachofen (1815–1887), Ludwig Klages (1872–1956), and Alfred Baeumler (1887–1968).[3]

Levinas was not only aware of this reception but understood the potency of calls to return to life and to creativity. Nevertheless, he was skeptical about *Lebensphilosophie* in any of its forms. The challenge he faced was, thus, *how* to unfold a conception of embodiment in which sensation carried meaning before it became re-presentation and understanding. The living body had to be approached in a way that resembled Nietzsche's own deformalization of Kant but repelled its *lebensphilosophische* extensions. In this, Levinas had to go Buber one step better. He had to avoid the passion for energy, mythology, and Nietzsche's creative individual while working with forces and sensations and their sublimation in ethical practice (EE 93–96). For Levinas, the way to proceed was to reinterpret Nietzsche's pathos out of the "*pathos* of distance" and that of power (*Macht*) as sublimated force (*Kraft*), privileging responsibility over affirmation or resistance, on the inner side of those unconscious movements. Like Buber, Levinas will draw from Nietzsche's return to bodies both a reflective energy and a kind of aesthetic of the other (first, through the other sex, later, through the figures of the widow and the stranger). But Levinas will avoid the biological and psychological reductions of Nietzsche. This leaves him with the question of conceiving sense, where "life" is typically adumbrated as forces in conflict (Nietzsche and Darwin's German reception). How to rehabilitate corporeity, if not to make the flesh *word,* signification, rather than the word, *flesh?*[4] In what follows, I will show the way in which Levinas worked this out, and some of the difficulties he faced.

The Two Origins: Sensation and Energy Versus A Priori Synthesis

Understanding sensations poses us no difficulties until we ask how they became conscious in the first place. In his *Nietzsche et l'ombre de Dieu* (1998), the French phenomenologist Didier Franck observed that Nietzsche anticipated phenomenology with his perspectivalism, which implied the ever-present possibility of expanding one's approach to an entity.[5] "The correlative analysis of the body and of the will to power [in Nietzsche] is thus accompanied necessarily by a critique of the privilege of consciousness whose essential form is reason; it is accompanied . . . by an anticipated subordination of transcendental phenomenology" (NOD 200). Perspectivalism in Nietzsche assumed a host of forms, notably, an examination of the "intelligences" of the body: "guided by the thread of the body . . . we learn that our life is possible only thanks to the combined play of numerous intelligences of highly unequal value."[6] Nietzsche understood that mechanistic physiology had gotten this much right: consciousness and the body were the product of systems working with energies or forces that remained mysterious to us. If physiologists of his time adopted a model of "*neural irritations*" in the place of the old "humours" (e.g., F. Broussais, 1772–1838),[7] while some neo-Kantian philosophers like Johann Friedrich Herbart (1776–1841) spoke of force as the *noumenon*, Nietzsche objected: there is no "noumenon" and no "will"; nevertheless materialism obscures the fact that mechanism requires a first mover (VP I frag. 42, 231; WP frag. 688, 366–67; KSA, vol. 13, 300–301). That we are bodies constituted of energies—even active and reactive forces—was not in doubt.[8] The consequence of Nietzsche's "philosophical" approach to nineteenth-century biology (i.e., forces, in light of will to power) was a portrayal of the correlations of forces whose epiphenomena, from consciousness to social groups, naïvely took themselves to be sovereign. Despite its difficulties, from holism to anthropomorphism, Nietzsche's "structuralist" approach to life answered a question that Levinas also posed to Husserl. If basic consciousness, as the continuous flow of internal "time," is the fundamental, a priori synthesis, in which all "data" find a place, then how can we understand the spontaneous upsurge of sensation? Where does it come from; how does it connect with previous, flowing "moments" of consciousness?[9] Is this upsurge not *extra*-temporal? Can we really approach the continuum that goes from embodied operations to emergent conscious sensation as if this were just another *intentional* object? That approach accounts for a mentalist quality in Husserl. To avoid this, we have to entertain the possibility that "sensible contents (or primary contents, according to the *Logical Investigations*) are not phenomena—except in being interpreted as *objects post facto*—since, though I certainly see the tree in the garden, I do not see my sensations."[10] But how does sensation present itself to itself without becoming a phenomenon? It occupies a metaphoric middle, between lived immediacy and its thematization. It cannot simply be a phenomenon, lest we spiritualize our living being, which is sensible and affective before it is fully conscious of these. "How could sensation present itself to itself without *intending* itself . . . without a certain dislocation of the felt in relation to the feeling . . . without a tiny setting-out-of-phase [*déphasage*] that is both another sensation *and* the gap in which the *origin* of time and intentionality resides?" (DDP 115; emphasis added).

Levinas thematizes this *déphasage* in the 1940s, distinguishing what he calls the *soi* (of feeling) and the *moi* of the feeling-intended (*moi se visant*). Such attempts go back to Kant's conundrums of representation. But it was Nietzsche who subjected them to the most radical hermeneutic. For Nietzsche, sensation is already a value judgment, except that it is such spontaneously and without cognition. There is no essential difference between the interpreting activity of consciousness and the collaboration and ordering of forces in the body. The great difficulty concerns the way in which we approach these "unknowables" with metaphors.

How Levinas Rethinks Nietzsche's Legacy of the Body

Unlike Buber, who was fascinated by Nietzsche's self-creating individual, Levinas faced the Nietzschean heritage, in its emphasis on "elementary sentiments,"[11] with two objectives: first, to deepen one side of Nietzsche's explorations of bodily forces; second, to despiritualize Heidegger's hermeneutic transformation of Nietzsche's thought.

When he focuses on the passive side of the body and its sensations, Levinas makes a paradoxical but legitimate move. The paradox lies in the fact that speaking of passivity requires reconstruction, which implies an abstracting characterization of active and passive forces woven together by intentionality. Something we call "I"—which has accompanied modern philosophy since the *cogito*—feels the pressing of our drives. Yet, our drives *are* we. Passivity is never "present" in us devoid of some activity. Levinas knows this. But his move is legitimate insofar as it is not meant to be an epistemology of sensibility, much less of passive synthesis. It is a description of being-affected by something that disturbs: an other-in-the-same. Yet the problem of a continuous movement between the affectable self and the thematizing "I" (*moi*) remains because, for Levinas, the emergence and possibility of a divided subject depends upon the co-origination of primordial sensation and temporal synthesis. In other words, two ongoing psychic processes are inseparable: the becoming-conscious of sensation and the flowing, extra-conative dimension Husserl called time-consciousness. Without the upsurge of sensation, the interruption that is the source of Levinas's ethics would simply be turned into an event that the "river" of formal time engulfs and situates in its flow. There would not be transcendence in the sense of an event of pure alterity, which Levinas framed against Heidegger's transcendence. In the absence of the possibility of *this* transcendence, there would not be "a surplus of meaning of which consciousness all by itself would be incapable" (OB 152).

Therein lies the wager of Levinas's philosophy: in-finite alterity is no longer the Absolute but an enigma (OB 152). Transcendence is yoked to the skin as feeling, with or without accompanying emotion. For Levinas, this passivity—contracted into the instant of sensation's upsurge—has for its cognate an emotion called "sincerity" (OB 150). Through this affect, sense appears to arise even before it is integrated into the temporal synthesis, open to phenomenological inspection. The flesh made word: "It is the bottomless passivity of responsibility, and thus sincerity. It is the meaning of language, before language scatters into words . . . dissimulating in the Said the openness of the Saying exposed [sincerity] like a bleeding wound" (OB 151). There is an inductive chain (whose origin is the enigma), moving from the structure of the flesh in its passive depths all the way to the possibility of bearing a witness that does not so much believe in a god as it "enacts god" by speaking to the other person. The speaking-to may be concessive, it may be a response to a command, or a demand for justice. Levinas's is the phenomenology of the meaning and possibility of prophetism. This is one of two sides, interiority and exteriority, approached in his philosophy. The latter side was addressed in *Totality and Infinity*. There, alterity was not so quickly situated in the flesh but, rather, in a radical exteriority, which did not exclude its effectivity in immanence. The decisive claim is this: before I can thematize it, I am affected by something I do not recognize as my own, as "me." If this exteriority phenomenalizes as expression (the face is not mere phenomenon, but expression), then the disturbance affects me with a violence that is nonphysical—*yet, for me, sensible, preconscious:*

The Other—the absolutely Other—paralyzes possession which he contests by his epiphany in the face. He can contest my possession only

because he approaches me not from the outside [really], but from
above. . . . But the . . . negation of murder is announced by this dimension of height, where the Other comes to me concretely in the ethical
impossibility of committing this murder.   (TI 171)

The ethical impossibility is *not* an ontological impossibility. Ontology in
Levinas is as beset by forces and wills as it is in Nietzsche. Caught between
ontology and ethical resistance, I desire the company of the face. I suffer
more from the event of its death than I do from the fear of my own. But
despite that, I can seek to murder that being who faces me. It is the only
"being" who effects a violence such that it elicits the desire to murder. The
other who faces is like a contradictory force from without. Unanticipated,
nonphenomenal, it impacts the "I" or *moi,* thrusting it inward, as if the skin
could be made concave without being transpierced. We must think in these
metaphoric terms: "the body is in fact the *mode* in which a being, neither
spatial nor foreign to . . . physical extension, exists separately . . . it is not
that to an intention called theoretical . . . would be added volitions, desires,
and sentiments, so as to transform thought into life. *The strictly intellectualist thesis subordinates life to representation*" (TI 168). Without the body, there
is no signification prior to thematizing consciousness.[12] Levinas must thus
preserve both bodily immanence and that tenuous first consciousness that
glimmers, in the time lag of sensations, between *soi* and *moi.* It is here that
a different structure of time, based exclusively on the interruption and the
instant's ability to alter events, allows Levinas to speak of "an extreme vigilance" and even a "messianic consciousness" (TI 285). This innovation with
regard to time rethinks Husserl's holistic passive synthesis and introduces
the heteronomy of time-as-flow to time-as-recommencement (TI 284);
here, something not identifiable—not thematizable, not objectifiable—
brings novelty. If the body were not aligned with, characterized by, living
forces, the idea of an ethical interruption, much less Being as chaotic preda-
tion, would be obviated.

Lebensphilosophie

There is not space, here, to examine the history of Nietzsche's complex influence on Jewish thinkers from Benjamin to Buber to Levinas. The young
Buber embraced Nietzsche for his emphasis on self-overcoming and the

mythic wellsprings of cultural existence, though Levinas clearly never envisioned using Nietzsche that way (NAZ 172–73). Two closely related themes make Nietzsche's thought fundamentally unembraceable for Levinas: the genealogy of moral life and the question of forces. In Nietzsche, the precursor of moral autonomy is the creditor-debtor relationship, so widespread that it is virtually pre-cultural. Levinas' entire argument about the heteronomous origin of responsibility implies the sociality of the Third and a sensibility that undercuts the sadistic jubilation of creditors and punishments. Buber argued as much in 1938 (NAZ 179); a transhistoric, sadistic *jouissance* fuels the punishment that evolves into the autonomous modern subject or morality.

While it is physiologically enlightening to follow Nietzsche (a throng of French philosophers from Deleuze to Michel Henry have done so) in speaking of active and reactive forces in the body, Levinas cannot accord Nietzsche the totalizing decomposition of bodies and societies into interpreting and conflicting forces. While Nietzsche argued that "consciousness is the last born of the organs, and therefore, still a child—let us pardon it its childishness [*Kindereien*]! Among many others, we include morality" (KSA, vol. 10, 1883, 284–85; AC §14), it was the domination and *hierarchy* of forces that characterized becoming and perhaps self-overcoming. Yet hierarchy is also necessary to assure a stability sufficient for the development of an entity. Thus Levinas cannot so much reject this perspective as displace it. He will focus neither on Nietzsche's hierarchy structuring the development of organisms (borrowed from German Darwinists "of struggle," such as Roux),[13] nor accept the hierarchy that privileges the individual over the herd. However, insofar as hierarchy is an affair of "instances," Levinas will speak of the height and the command of the other. Moreover, the Nietzschean body, with its interpreting forces that supplanted more spiritual conceptions, as "the *Zeichensprache*" of the body (cf. KSA, vol. 10, 1883, 285; NOD 385), will help Levinas to immanentize alterity, notably by 1974. It was this conception of forces that made it possible for Nietzsche to rethink, on a new ground, every ethics unfolding from Christianity and related metaphysics: the cultivation of life over Christian hope, charity, and equality of believers. The Nietzschean body, traces of which we find in Levinas, opens the possibility of a different gospel, which explains why a messianic tone is present in Nietzsche, especially in *Zarathustra*. We might even say that Nietzsche's naturalistic messianism is more obvious than is Levinas's rationalist messianism.

Nietzsche's messianism—even if it remains formalist[14]—consisted of seeking a new justice that should overcome the Christian equality of members within the "church," returning us to consistency with the natural unfolding of natural processes. Whatever we make of this justice, Nietzsche was troubled by the question early on (cf. NOD 33–38). He sought to show how the revaluation of values alone—passing through the body as through the history of morality—could allow us to conceive a justice that takes up where Paul's messianic Christianity had come to an end. Didier Franck argues:

> Saint Paul is not Nietzsche's only adversary, but he is . . . the greatest, and when the Antichrist declares that "Nihilist and Christian [*Nihilist und Christ*]: these rhyme and not only rhyme . . ." Nietzsche says . . . absolutely nothing other [than that Christianity itself must now be overcome]. It is therefore on the resurrection of the body that Nietzsche's transvaluation must be effectuated, whose principle is the Eternal Return.   (NOD 468)

Eternal recurrence, combined with life as will to power, where *Macht* is already a sublimation of *Kraft*, enables us to shake free of that weight from which even the death of God did not liberate us: guilt tied to "original sin." The entire weight of scripture situates humanity under a fait accompli whose ransom, faith in the crucified God, is almost worsened by the catastrophe of the death of God. Even the end of idealism unfolded under this anguish. If, for Paul, the human soul endures the tribulation of the possibility of evil, Kant and Schelling will translate original sin philosophically into a fundamental human tendency called egotism. In this way, they perpetuate the anguish. Yet, as Nietzsche argued, *this* God has perished, so we face a new necessity: daring to attribute to ourselves the qualities hitherto projected onto our god.

> There is no superior instance over us: insofar as God could be such an instance, we are now ourselves God . . . we must attribute to ourselves those attributes that we once attributed to God.[15]
>   (KSA, vol. 13, 1888, 143; quoted in NOD 91)

Facing such a task, there are two possibilities. First, that of saying "Yes" in a single instant and to all of existence.

For nothing exists for itself alone, neither in us nor in things; and if our soul has even once resonated like a note of joy, then all eternity has collaborated in determining this single fact—and in this unique instant of affirmation, all of eternity finds itself confirmed, ransomed, justified, affirmed.

(WP frag. 1032, 532; trans. modified; KSA, vol. 12, 1885–1887, 307)

The other possibility, which also extends the first, is either to create new gods or to perish, with nobility.

I have sought a new *center*. . . . Advancing still farther on the path of decomposition, *I have discovered there for individuals new sources of forces. We must be destroyers!*—I have recognized that the state of *decomposition*, in the midst of which individual beings may arrive *better than ever at their own perfection*, is an image and a *particular case of existence*. Against the paralyzing sentiment of decomposition . . . I have set the thought of *Eternal Recurrence*.

(WP frag. 417, 224; trans. modified; KSA, vol. 10, 1882–1884, 661)

This thought does not assure a life to come. It affirms the life that is. This affirmation resurrects the Dionysiac wisdom of nature opposing nature (*and* decadent civilization) and perishing at the end of its course. A new justice is adumbrated that at least is not based on a lie and grasps the operation (not an imputed telos) of evolution: to produce exemplary individuals. Nietzsche's ethic works against moralities rooted in the Christian weltanschauung, proposing a different resurrection. His resurrection concretizes the tragic sense of life while holding to physiology's insight that living and dead are not antitheses but different organizations of matter. Nietzsche's resurrection takes place in a moment that interrupts the everyday as much as does Levinas's moment of interruption.

Now, it has been argued that Nietzsche undermined morality, but that does not mean that he has no ethic. His is an ethic of the friend (or enemy), approached at a respectful distance, *such that "I" might not consume him.* The famous "star-friendship" that Nietzsche describes in *Gay Science* (§279) elaborates the respect even for enemies and the distance that enacts no violence.[16] Nietzsche's thought would thus prepare us to take on those attributes of which we have deprived ourselves, having cast them onto an inscrutable god. The return to life sought to be a route toward understanding the continuity of body-psyche-cosmos in its compositional dynamism. Nietzsche's wager was that a multiperspectival love of life is the only thing that could contribute to a new understanding of justice and the sense of human becoming as innocence and self-fashioning.

In one respect, the wager succeeded. The idea of life as innocence certainly overtook visions of tainted life. Levinas himself evinces a certain ambivalence toward Nietzsche's vision, since Levinas also characterizes living as love of life, even as he interprets Heidegger's Being as an "ever-present possibility of war." What made Nietzsche the "dynamite" he knew himself to be lies in the difficulty of keeping the innocence of life close to the creativity of the child, yet away from the negating will of the lion, as "Of The Three Metamorphoses" (TZ 54–56) illustrates it. Recall that Zarathustra pronounced these metamorphoses while he was living in a city called the "Pied Cow," which is also Plato's democratic city in the *Republic*—that polychrome cloak. And, in the shifting of perspectives, one is at a loss to determine how to live the becoming-child, or how to make of one's existence a work of art. How shall we determine the *successful* colors on the cow's hide from the *failed* ones? In the uncanny crossing of triumphalist tones and the tragic sense of life, the surpassing of the Pauline heritage of sin and awaiting does not open easily to the possibility of responsibility. Yet Nietzsche knew that power lay in the ability as much to follow as to lead: "The most spiritual human beings . . . find their happiness where others would find destruction . . . in severity towards themselves. Life becomes harder . . . as it approaches the *heights* . . . the responsibility increases" (AC §57). Consciousness, fleeting and sovereign, is a responsibility for Nietzsche as also for the most spiritual beings. The thinking of forces permits us to establish a continuum between bodies and communities, the biological and the political—all of them the objects of an existential hermeneutic. But how to keep this responsibility from erupting into contemptuous laughter before the misery of the world? How to hold Nietzsche's friendship of free spirits apart from the destructive aestheticism of his great passion?

> The two doctrines that [morality] preaches with predilection are "the equality of rights" and "pity for all those who suffer." We think that we must simply *suppress* pain. . . . But . . . one is obliged to think that [the human plant] has grown in altogether contrary conditions; to prosper, it was necessary for it that peril grow to an extreme, that its force of

invention and dissimulation be affirmed beneath a protracted strain and long oppression, that its will to live be intensified into absolute will to power and supremacy; what is necessary for the exaltation of the human type is danger, harshness, violence . . . the inequality of rights. . . . (WP frag. 957, 502–3; trans. modified; KSA, vol. 11, 1884–1885, 581–2)

The Two Bodies After the Death of God

While Levinas draws rhetorical energy and grounding from embodiment, it is no longer and cannot be Nietzsche's embodiment, whose ambiguity was not without positive elements. Because Levinas eschewed the embodiment of forces by exploring sensibility's radically passive side, he could embrace the hyperbole of suffering that transforms Nietzsche's trials because Levinas's suffering is utterly unmotivated, "for nothing." Substitution opens a different set of options in Levinas's logic. Radicalizing Buber's relational thinking of "I-Thou" and "I-It," Levinas takes what may well be an ultimate step to free himself from Heidegger's ontology *and* Nietzsche's eternal recurrence, at least as Levinas interprets it.

> In speaking of the recurrence of the ego to the self [*du moi au soi*], have we been sufficiently free from the postulates of ontological thought . . . where eternal being . . . always takes up what it undergoes, and whatever be its submission, always arises anew as the principle of what happens to it? It is in this reference to a ground of an-archical passivity that the thought that names creation differs from ontological thought. *It is not here a question of justifying the theological context of ontological thought.* . . . In this context, this said is already effaced in the absolute diachrony of creation, refractory to assembling into a present and a representation.   (OB 113; AE 181; trans. modified)

Opposing ontological thought as a quest for the presencing of Being (Heidegger), and the Yes-saying that assembles the present into an affirmation of self and world or self as world (Nietzsche), Levinas sets the "movement" of substitution into a moment of pure sensibility that suffers yet affirms the relation to the other. His recurrence, unfolding in the an-archy of substitution, shares the asubjectivity of Nietzsche's body-thoughts but sets it always in a world whereby "I" come to be through relations with others.

Recall one characterization of the eternal recurrence in terms of forces in nature, but also as the semiotics of bodies—the site of the same unconscious *Zeichensprache* by which Nietzsche developed his physical-political continuum.[17] Pierre Klossowski interprets:

> Thus, in each one . . . moves an intensity whose flux and reflux form signifying or non-signifying fluctuations of thinking, *which is never the property of anyone in particular,* and without beginnings or ends. If, contrary to this flowing element [*cet élément ondoyant*], each of us forms a closed and ostensibly delimited totality, then this is by virtue of those traces of signifying fluctuations, . . . We have not the slightest idea where our own fluctuations, which allow us to signify and to speak to ourselves and to others, begin and end; we know nothing of this unless it be the case that in this code, *one* sign always responds to degrees of intensities now at their highest, now at their lowest point. Thus, the *me*, the *I,* subject of all our propositions: it is thanks to this sign, which is nevertheless nothing but a trace of an ever-variable fluctuation, that we constitute ourselves as thinking . . . even as we never rightly know if it is not others who think and continue to think in us.[18]

For Klossowski, eternal recurrence grasped at the level of thought and bodies shows the anonymity *but also the intersubjectivity* of signifying consciousness. The flowing element of which he speaks echoes numerous passages in Nietzsche, notably his "Will and Wave" (GS §310), where he addresses those "dangerous green bodies." But Nietzsche's dialogue is as much with the elements as it is with those others before whom he observes the pathos of distance. His body of forces is an anarchic arena in which it is ultimately difficult to distinguish between active and passive forces, flux and reflux. Signification makes and unmakes itself in an immanence that is either open to the point of anonymity or churning upon itself.

When Levinas takes up the notion of signifying traces, he does not emphasize the anonymity of language, which speaks or thinks *in me*. He argues that the indeterminacy of these traces *supposes* the movement between self and an other who addresses me and gives me myself. At the base of *his* flow is a self that "in recurrence" does not return fixedly to the same. From the depth of his wager, the anarchic ground that comes to pass in the diachronous instant is the *intersubjective* sensibility that escapes our grasp through sheer excess and dynamism.

The *oneself* must be thought outside of every substantial coincidence of self with self and without this coincidence becoming—as Western thought which unifies subjectivity and substantiality would have it— the norm already commanding every non-coincidence.

(OB 113–14; AE 180; trans. modified)

At this level, "A does not come back to A, as in identity, but *recoils to the in-side* of its point of departure" (OB 114; AE 180; trans. modified). Substitution is, for Levinas, the figure that allows us to unite the movement of displacement that permits (verbal) signification *and* its condition of possibility, called "sincerity." Responsibility or "Saying," before it becomes verbal address—much less thought, as in Klossowski's Nietzschean wager—is simply moving sensibility *that affects me*. This is a sensibility that flows into affect and back into sensibility (cf. OB 189n. 25; AE 65n. 2). At a more conscious level, we should speak of intersubjective ties, or spontaneous gestures like the expression, "Here I am." Levinas's wager is that this instant is so brief that it undercuts conation and intentionality. This is prior to the interpretations of positivist psychology and philosophies of the subject, a "psychism, which can signify this alterity in the same without alienation, in the guise of incarnation, *as being-in-one's-skin*, as *having-the-other-in-one's-skin*" (OB 115; AE 181; trans. modified).

Where Nietzsche found the secret of the waves, and Klossowski the chaos and conditions out of which anonymous thought crystallized, Levinas insists that discourse speaks "in us" because intersubjectivity has constituted us affectively before we began to speak. Must the other voice in the same be another *person?* Yes and no. Above all, it is the affect that accompanies human encounters and signals them. This is an enrichment of Levinas's "self . . . out of phase with itself" (OB 115; AE 181). In a surprising reversal of Nietzsche's forgetting, as sign of health, Levinas adds, "Forgetful of itself, forgetful in . . . the reference to itself which is the *gnawing away* at oneself in remorse" (OB 115; AE 182). While it is healthy to forget, our first forgetting—of ourselves in our "as for me"—is a momentary absence in which we are unable to assemble ourselves, through whatever sort of force. This displacement is caused by pain, but it also lightens the weight of our narcissism. In a move whose logic *resembles* Klossowski's characterization of the shared secret of forces or traces, which extends into the return of the same, Levinas doubles such a moment with a sensuous-affective contraction whose "subsequent" phenomenalization is responsibility. If it is facile to call this a revaluation, "the flesh made word," the overbid he proposes to Nietzschean embodiment is the circulation of signification, occasioned by the openness of the flesh to other humans: "an identity undone to the end, without remaking itself in the other, on the in-side of trans-substantiation in another avatar . . . because not *resting in the other* but remaining in one-self without rest" (OB 196n.20; AE 185n.1).

It remains undecidable which comes first, the "Saying" whose trace is encompassed in words said, or sensibility and affectivity. As the priority of word and flesh remains undecidable, the question of ontologizing Levinas's claim is suspended, much as it is absurd to ask whether Nietzsche's forces "are truly what they are." It is not possible, given the status of pre-intentional passive sensibility, to ask, "Is this a true account of the upsurge of sensibility and affectivity?" Levinas has read Nietzsche too carefully not to recognize the petrification of truth—born of commodity and use—into the fictions we call the logics of identity, adequation, and sufficient reason. An *other* conception of living bodies—less marked by physiology than was Nietzsche's, though he too recognized the moral question underlying the question of "life"[19]—is ventured by Levinas under the aegis of substitution. With substitution culminates his lifelong project of holding life, responsibility, and passivity together—*against* the chaos of forces within and without us; that "nauseating *remue-ménage* of the *il y a* recommencing [eternally] behind every negation" (OB 183; AE 280; trans. modified). This would be life before our concepts of life—religious or scientific (OB 168; AE 261)—had given it the form it took in nineteenth- and twentieth-century vitalism. By virtue of the sensibility-affectivity hermeneutic, a dimension of suffering in "life" is tied to an indeterminate memory—we might say, "of the flesh"—even to "conscience," regret, or remorse. Interpreted as moral sentiments, these resemble an eighteenth-century conception of nature. Jacob Golomb argues that Nietzsche was influenced by that century. Like him, Levinas works past its constructions: "the altruism of the subjectivity-hostage is not a tendency, is not a natural benevolence, as in the moral philosophies of feeling. It is against nature, non-voluntary . . . anarchic" (OB 197n. 27; AE 195n. 1).

After the death of a certain god, then, two wagers—both in different senses aesthetic, both suggesting an indeterminate image or ideal—arose, massively focused on embodied life. One drew from energetics and self-surpassing, exploring the question of how to take on the projections reserved for the now dead God. The other, dialogically influenced wager set its poetic and argumentative resources on the unexplored passivity in which life forces—active or reactive—spring up. These affect an X before it becomes "I." Nietzsche and Levinas approached suffering as if from two distinct perspectives; in both cases, the philosophical understanding of the body was preeminently a moral question.

NOTES

Warm thanks to Gabriel Malenfant, Université de Montreal, and to Jill Stauffer for the depth and intelligence of her comments.

1. Jacob Golomb, *Nietzsche and Zion* (Ithaca, N.Y.: Cornell University Press, 2004), 173–88. Hereafter abbreviated as NAZ.

2. See Steven E. Aschheim, "Nietzsche, Anti-Semitism, and the Holocaust" and J. Golomb, "Nietzsche and the Marginal Jews," in *Nietzsche and Jewish Culture,* ed. Jacob Golomb (London: Routledge, 1997), 3–20 and 158–92, respectively.

3. See Nitzan Lebovic's remarkable essay "The Beauty and Terror of *Lebensphilosophie,* Ludwig Klages, Walter Benjamin, and Alfred Baeumler," *South Central Review* 23, no. 1 (Spring 2006): 23–39. Lebovic's thesis is that "between Klages and Baeumler [the difference] is . . . large enough to [encompass] every twentieth-century theory of totalitarianism and fascism, but it has been neglected because of the general contempt in which postwar historians and philosophers held right-wing theories; [but] this approach *has also shaped how 'progressive' thinkers were and are being* read" (35; emphasis added).

4. Nothing unfolds in a vacuum. Heidegger also confronted this question from 1927 in *Being and Time.* Heidegger's effort to get past the logicism of Husserl's conception of the word as founded on immanent, silent signification, led Heidegger to argue that words are not surface effects or contractions of a deep layer, but rather the original unfolding of truth as the world or the "There." Levinas will modify Husserl's thought less: signification is affective *first;* it unfolds into speech *not* because the world is intrinsically signifying, as Heidegger argued in 1927, but because the other faces and addresses me.

5. Didier Franck, *Nietzsche et l'ombre de dieu* (Paris: PUF, 1998); trans. by Bettina Bergo (Northwestern University Press, forthcoming). Hereafter abbreviated in the text as NOD.

6. Friedrich Würzbach (1938) established a collection of *nachgelassene Fragmente* on the basis of the Peter Gast–Elisabeth Förster-Nietzsche collection, *Wille zur Macht. Versuch einer Umwertung aller Werte,* whose organization Walter

Kaufmann largely used, and which was available in French before Colli and Montinari's critical editions (*Kritische Studienausgabe* and the comprehensive *Kritische Gesamtausgabe: Werke*) were available in French. I cite from this: VP I Fragment 226 "Morality and Physiology," 1885, 299; in KSA, vol. 11, 1884–1885; June–July 1885, Notebook 37, 4, 576–79 "Moral und Physiologie." I cite the shorter Colli and Montinari, KSA, wherever possible.

7. Nietzsche used this expression, along with "nervous influx," see notes from 1888: "Free will or subservient will?—*There is no 'will'*; this is a simplified conception due to intelligence, like 'matter' . . . the 'goal' is but an 'internal excitation'—nothing more." In WP, 354–355; KSA, vol. 10, 1882–1884, Winter 1883–1884, Notebook 24, 32, 663. Also see Jean Starobinski's study, "Le passé de la passion: textes médicaux et commentaires," *Nouvelle Revue de Psychanalyse: La Passion*, no. 21 (Spring 1980): 51–76.

8. See Deleuze, *Nietzsche and Philosophy*, trans. Hugh Tomlinson (New York: Columbia University Press, 1983), 39–72. He observes, "What defines a body [according to Nietzsche] is this relation between dominant and dominated forces. Every relationship of forces constitutes a body—whether it is chemical, biological, social or political" (40). Also see KSA, vol. 11, 1884–1885, Notebook 25, 401, 116.

9. See Levinas, "Intentionalité et Sensation" (1965) in ED 145–62; DEH 135–50. If the originary form of consciousness is the upsurge of the instant, as some given of sensibility, and this present moment *is intentionalized,* thanks to a spontaneous synthesis, then we must assume that passive synthesis confronts activity in the upsurge of the *Urimpression.* The Urimpression is not itself a synthesis, is not passive in its incipience. But the "active" sensuous instant is itself a spontaneous beginning because it has affected something and must be preceded by a previously retained instant as it arises. Thus the spontaneity and successiveness of sensations are always accompanied by a passivity that temporalizes. The dual origin, spontaneous sensation and passive synthesis, hearken to debates in *Lebensphilosophie* concerning the body and consciousness. Nietzsche had a different answer to this, which is in some ways close to Levinas's project, insofar as it does not rule out the work of nonconscious "intelligent" forces in the body that make the simplest intentional or conscious act possible. Neither is simply vitalistic; they are two hermeneutics of the body that avoid mentalism and formalism.

10. Compare Didier Franck's critique of Husserl's phenomenology of time consciousness using Nietzsche, in *Dramatique des phénomènes* (Paris: PUF, 2001), 105–123. Hereafter cited as DDP.

11. RH 63. This essay, "Reflections on the Philosophy of Hitlerism," was first published in 1934.

12. See WP frag. 524, 284; KSA, vol. 13, 1887–1888, Notebook 11, 145, 67–68.

13. See Wilhelm Roux, *Der Kampf der Theile im Organismus* (Leipzig: Wilhelm Engelmann, 1881), 64–110.

14. See Gérard Bensussan, *Le temps messianique: Temps historique et temps vécu* (Paris: Vrin, 2002).

15. The divine qualities also entailed their directly related values, which Nietzsche enumerates in his notebooks as: "1) the 'immortal soul'; the eternal worth of the 'person'—2) the answer [*Lösung*], the orientation, the valuation of the 'Beyond'—3) the moral value as highest value, the 'salvation of the soul' as cardinal interest—4) 'sin,' 'earthly,' 'flesh,' 'pleasures' [*Lüste*]—5) stigmatized as 'world'" (WP 30; KSA, vol. 13, 1887–1888, Notebook 11, fragment 148, p. 69). To this, the attributes we should have to ascribe ourselves would include, "a great asceticism leading toward hyper strength and consciousness in reference to the forging of a strong will," but also "to learn how to obey [*gehorchen lernen*]" (WP 921; KSA, vol. 13, 1887–1888, Notebook 11, 146, p. 68).

16. For a discussion of Nietzsche's ethic, see Aïcha Messina "Levinas's Gaia Scienza" in this volume.

17. Compare what Klossowski writes with Nietzsche's fragment from 1885–1886, in which he observes: "*It is necessary to interpret all movements [of and in the body] as gestures,* as a sort of language thanks to which forces understand each other. . . . The contradiction is not between 'true' and 'false,' but between the '*abbreviations of signs*' and the signs themselves" (VP I 325; cf. WP frags. 564 and 565, 304–5).

18. Pierre Klossowski, *Nietzsche et le cercle vicieux. Essai* (Paris: Mercure, 1969), 99, my translation. In English, *Nietzsche and the Vicious Circle,* trans. Daniel Smith, (Chicago: University of Chicago Press, 1998).

19. Nietzsche, posthumous fragment from 1885 in VP I 298–99 (not in WP). "To the contrary, this prodigious synthesis of living beings and intellects that one calls 'man' can live only from the moment at which the subtle system of relations and transmission was created, and thereby the extremely rapid understanding among all these superior and inferior beings—and this, thanks to intermediaries, all of which are alive . . . this is not a problem of mechanics, it is a moral problem." Cf. WP frag. 492, 271, a contemporary (1885) fragment on physiology; also, §524, 284 and §707, 375–77, fragments dating from two years later. Also see BG §19, 25–26.

7

Nietzsche, Levinas, and the Meaning of Responsibility

ROSALYN DIPROSE

Why Responsibility Matters

"Responsibility" is usually defined in terms of the *juridical* concept of *self-*responsibility where, as Bernhard Waldenfels puts it, the "dialogical idea of giving account, inherited from the Greeks, meets the juridical idea of imputation (*imputatio*) invented by the Romans."[1] In his genealogy of responsibility, Robert Bernasconi helpfully outlines the individualism and the notion of temporality assumed in the usual definition.[2] This *legal* idea of *backward*-looking accountability (and blame), he suggests, becomes linked, in the late eighteenth century, with the *moral* idea of accountability that focuses on the agent's *forward*-looking conscious intention. While providing a means of making the individual accountable to others at a time when the radical individualism of emerging capitalism and democratic politics forced the dissolution of existing social bonds, this juridico-moral idea of personal responsibility leaves us with two problems: it fosters determinism (in demanding continuity between past and future) and undermines rather than fosters social bonds that would support justice and democratic plu- ralism. These are the problems that Levinas's revisions to the meaning of responsibility address. However, uncovering the dialogue (largely implicit) between Levinas's and Nietzsche's critiques of juridico-moral responsibility allows a fuller appreciation of why such revisions matter.[3] Such an analy- sis also provides a means of diagnosing how, in contemporary social rela- tions, a failure of political responsibility may precipitate a crisis of personal responsibility.

Before Levinas, it was Nietzsche who challenged the notions of subjec- tivity and temporality underlying the juridico-moral model of responsibility by questioning the "bad conscience" that attends it (GM 62, 84). Insofar as it is assumed that the self of juridico-moral responsibility is given, phil- osophical debates about responsibility have tended to center on whether "conscience," understood as conscious awareness of the difference between right and wrong, is driven and determined by the laws and moral norms one inherits or by an original capacity of freedom to oppose or affirm that or- der. Nietzsche, on the other hand, severs "conscience" from juridico-moral accountability *in terms of any juridico-moral code* and reinvents the self and the normative basis of conscience accordingly. This is a radical move that explains, I suggest, Levinas's rare and late explicit acknowledgement of his debt to Nietzsche: the "Nietzschean man above all was such a moment" when the "history of philosophy . . . has known this subjectivity that [by 'reversing irreversible time'] . . . breaks with essence" (OB 8). In breaking with essence, Nietzsche breaks with the determinism of conventional ma- terialism which, for Levinas, is a determinism of "war and matter" (OB 8). But Nietzsche also, by critiquing the notion of "free will," avoids a second kind of determinism: ideological or sociopolitical determinism that Levi- nas describes as a reassembling of beings "in a present that is extended, by memory and history, to a totality determined like matter" (OB 5, 8). For Nietzsche, "genuine" responsibility requires that "conscience" not be de- termined either by material forces or by a tradition enforced by either moral universalism or totalitarian government (GM 60).

The question remains though: Whence comes the criteria of conscience if not the laws and moral norms that we inherit and that, at least in part, condition us? Answering this question not only motivates Nietzsche's and Levinas's revisions to the meaning of responsibility; it also points to the relevance of this task for contemporary ethics and politics. The juridical concept of self-responsibility cannot explain, and indeed may exacerbate, an apparent crisis of conscience in some contemporary liberal democracies, where democratically elected governments initiate programs that endorse the treatment of persons in ways that are *felt* to be in direct conflict with the normative basis of the moral sensibilities of the citizenry. Under such conditions of a *failure of political responsibility* there is a tendency either to fall into step with this revised code of conduct such that personal responsibility (in the juridical sense of accountability or duty) seems to vanish, or public life descends into a blame game and responsibility (duty and blame) falls disproportionately toward women, particular racial and ethnic groups, the socially disadvantaged, and the dispossessed. What Nietzsche and Levinas together help to explain is what happens to the capacity for personal responsibility, and the normative basis of conscience, judgment, and conduct, when the laws and moral norms we supposedly embody seem to be undermined by a government that we assume is responsible for keeping them in place.

The value of Levinas's revision of responsibility is often put in different terms. There is consensus that his radical move consists in changing the referent of "for" in "that for which I am responsible" and thereby challenging the individualism that necessitates the juridical concept. For him, in being-responsible I am not first of all responsible for my self or for upholding the juridico-moral code. Rather, *I am*, most fundamentally, *responsibility for the other*. This contribution is made possible by an idea of *corporeal subjectivity* that first emerges from both Nietzsche's idea of subjectivity and his critiques of the juridical concept of responsibility

What is particularly radical about Nietzsche's approach to responsibility, and what accounts for the "reversing of irreversible time" and the "break with essence" that Levinas admires, is that Nietzsche locates the conditions of subjectivity, normativity and self-responsibility, not in free will or in the maintenance of the same self through memory but in responsiveness based on what I will call *somatic reflexivity:* a corporeal and affective self-relation that manifests as "conscience"—a futural ability to respond to circumstances in excess of existing law and custom. This is an important intervention into the meaning of being-responsible, for several reasons. First, it moves responsibility beyond the freedom-determinism debate by proposing that the relation between the self and the juridico-moral code, while constitutive, must also be excessive, self-critical, and transformative of norms. Second, in placing the highest value on the uniqueness and opacity of this somatic reflexivity, rather than on, say, "life itself" or human "dignity" based on autonomous practical reason, Nietzsche and then Levinas, more radically still, revise the very basis of normativity in ethics and politics: this corporeal reflexivity, and the uniqueness it signifies, is that through and for which we are, most fundamentally, responsible, whatever other characteristics (sex, race, religion, age) that corporeality may signify.

Where Levinas departs from Nietzsche is on the question of how this corporeal reflexivity arises and, hence, whose responsiveness takes priority: for Nietzsche it is the self's somatic reflexivity through and for which I am "genuinely" self-responsible; for Levinas, it is the other's. Examining the bases of this difference exposes the third contribution that juxtaposing their accounts might offer to a revision in the meaning of responsibility. In grounding responsibility for the other and its suffering in the opacity of the other's somatic reflexivity, Levinas challenges what Nietzsche's account of self-responsibility diagnoses but does not limit: the tendency to assume the privilege of self-responsibility that breaks with history, determinism, and the prevailing social order without assuming responsibility for the effects of that privilege on others.

Fourth, both Nietzsche's and Levinas's emphasis on the temporality of somatic reflexivity reveals what is most at risk in a crisis precipitated by a failure of political responsibility: the *body open to an undetermined future* that is a condition of conscience and hence responsibility. Drawing out the implicit "conversation" between Nietzsche and Levinas on responsibility diagnoses the impact on personal responsibility of a failure of political responsibility in some liberal democracies in the present. What I will argue is that a failure of political responsibility consists not so much in an undermining of a juridico-moral code, but more so in the futural inclination of bodies and, with this, the *normative basis* of democratic sociality that political and ethical responsibility would ordinarily share.

Nietzsche and the Making and Overcoming of Juridical Self-Responsibility

It is in the first three sections of the second essay of *On the Genealogy of Morals* that Nietzsche outlines his thesis of how self-responsibility, in the juridical sense, is made.[4] Rather than being given, this subjectivity arises through the process of "breeding an animal with the right to make promises" (GM 58–59). The promise is of interest to Nietzsche not only as the basis of a sociality governed by contract of which he is critical but also for exemplifying, in its structure, the temporality of the self central to self-responsibility in general: a *body*, not only open to the past but also to the future. Contrary to the model of self upon which the juridical concept is based, Nietzsche's genealogy suggests that what I have called *somatic reflexivity*, rather than the faculty of reflection, is the primary condition of agency, conscience, and self-responsibility. And he shows how both somatic reflexivity and memory arise through the imposition of a juridico-moral code through what I will call the *force of law*.

He proposes that we are by nature creatures governed not by self-consciousness and memory but by forgetting. This forgetting is not passive—in us forgetting "represents a force" (GM 57–58). While forgetting does constitute the present (by "having done" with an impression), this is not enough for juridical self-responsibility, which requires that experience assume a significance sufficient to register in present consciousness as one's own and sufficient to be recalled in the future and attributed to the same self retrospectively. As Levinas will later confirm, for subjectivity, "time is needed"; there must be a "getting out of phase with the instant"; a "divergence of the identical from itself," a divergence of the present from the past and the future (OB 28). For Nietzsche, it is the codification of experience via a juridico-moral code that temporalizes the self in a way that counters forgetting. But to counter the force of forgetting, the juridico-moral code has to be attached to some intensity and it must act on the same material of forgetting. The intensity, the force, is provided by affect, pain, and also pleasure, so that, to be a force, this law must join forces with those of the body. As Nietzsche puts it in *Twilight of the Idols:* culture is inaugurated, "*not* in the 'soul'" or through a disciplining of thoughts; "one must first persuade the *body*" (TL 101). So, self-responsibility originates with the creation of a "real *memory of the will*": a "morality of mores" in concert with the "mnemotechnics" of pain orders events and their meaning, opens a gap between the decision ("I will") and the future discharge of the will (the act), and opens the ability to anticipate a future and, through a selective memory, to recoup in the future a past that is now present (GM 58). The body is disciplined in line with prevailing norms, and some events and their meaning become both conscious and "unforgettable" (GM 61).

This social disciplining of the body is not itself a problem for Nietzsche—it is how we come not only to embody a juridico-moral code, but also to have an affective, self-reflexive, and self-critical *relation* to it (see also BG 30). This is not the reflex action of conventional materialism: in its reflexivity, the body attempts to enhance pleasure and move beyond pain, but, as pleasure and pain, along with "everything of which we become conscious" are already codified, "interpreted through and through" (WP 263–64), somatic reflexivity involves contestation and transformation in the meaning of experience, of effects and their relations. Somatic reflexivity then is the basis of "will to power" (GM 77). The self, for Nietzsche, is the body divided and doubled by the force of law: accompanying habitual evaluative action, normalized according to convention, are both affect *and* the force of reevaluation and futurity beyond mere affect. This responsive self is the self that Nietzsche considers of supreme value.

Levinas, from his earliest work in 1934, sees merit in the "importance attributed to this feeling for the body . . . [as] the basis of a new conception of man" (RH 69), although there he seems reluctant to attribute its positive conception to Nietzsche. He locates the appearance of this new materialism (as opposed to "popular materialism") in nineteenth-century Marxism, associating Nietzsche's philosophy with its corruption by National Socialism. Shortly after, in his 1935 paper *On Escape*, Levinas clarifies what he meant by "this feeling for the body": the feeling of being "riveted" to a body *and* the feeling of escape (OE 52–53)—not escape from the body, nor from "social convention," but "escape" as the futural experience of "going somewhere" (OE 53). The value Levinas finds in this "new conception of man" is that it avoids the "ideological expansion" implied in idealism's and liberalism's conceptions of the subject as "absolutely free" and above the historicity of concrete embodied existence; and it avoids, at least in the first instance, the determinism of biologism and conventional materialism (RH 64–65, 69). While Levinas drops the terminology of "feeling for a body" and "escape" in his later formulations of subjectivity in terms of the ethical relation to alterity, he arguably never abandons this self, conceived in terms of corporeal reflexivity, even if he moves beyond it with his notion of sensibility. It is, therefore, Nietzsche's idea of the self as affect and a futural responsive movement beyond mere affect and traditional meaning that attracts Levinas's later praise in *Otherwise Than Being*: this is the subjectivity that "breaks with essence" (OB 8). It is also this conception of "the Nietzschean man" that reverses "irreversible time": he stands at the "gateway" called "the moment" in Nietzsche's most considered account of eternal recurrence (TZ 267–72). Here, Zarathustra, in a critique of both cyclic time and linear, historical time, describes the present moment as a kind of existential knot of becoming from which a path extends eternally to the past and a contradictory path extends eternally toward the future: in this "moment" of recurrence the self is stretched between a past and an undeterminable future.

Somatic reflexivity, therefore, is also the primary condition of critical "re-valuation of value," and it is a condition of, but not reducible to, thought and reflection: "the whole somber thing called reflection" is no more than further "mastery over the affects" (GM 62) and to "think" is to envisage how pain might be avoided and pleasure repeated in the future (TZ 147). And it is this responsiveness, given by somatic reflexivity, that is the condition of *one kind of conscience*—"bad conscience" informed by discipline according to prevailing norms. But with this comes a *second "conscience"* that renews the world through reflexivity—"conscience" as a responsive relation to oneself and to the norms that the self embodies and that guide its action, and as a temporality open to a past that is "owned" in the present but under the compulsion of an undetermined future opened in advance.

This idea of conscience helps to explain a crisis of conscience precipitated by what I referred to in the beginning as a failure of political responsibility. The "real problem regarding man," for Nietzsche (GM 57), and, I suggest, for us in the present, is that this body in its responsiveness and futurity is at risk, most notably from the ideal of juridical responsibility that governs it. A condition of somatic reflexivity is that a *relation* to both the juridi-co-moral code and the future be maintained, not that the self is entirely engulfed by either. In assuming responsibility for itself, the self risks itself for an unknown future; the self "goes under" as Nietzsche puts it (e.g., TZ 126–28). But the ideal of juridical self-responsibility would remove this risk: it assumes the endurance of a preordained image of the self as the faithful embodiment of the prevailing juridico-moral code. That is, the temporal structure of the promise and of accountability assumes the ability to commit the self to a *particular* future and, through a selective memory, to recoup in that future a past self, word, or deed that is now present. According to Levinas, such a responsible "will" would require the impossible: a memory or "temporality of time [that] makes possible . . . a recuperation in which nothing is lost" (OB 28–29). Moreover, for Nietzsche, to the extent that a particular future is ordained in advance by the juridico-moral idea of responsibility in concert with totalitarian, nationalistic, or utilitarian government, this is at the expense of futurity per se and therefore at the expense of somatic reflexivity and hence responsibility.

With regard to this overarching concern for the body's reflexivity and futurity, Nietzsche has three related criticisms of juridical self-responsibility. First, insofar as the constitution of the responsive self is normalizing, any responsibility the individual assumes for such action is not genuine (GM 59; HA 74). This is the paradox that arguably still ails us: responsibility cannot rest on blind obedience to the law and norms one inherits rather than chooses. Second, and conversely, Nietzsche is critical of the "fable" of responsibility insofar as it rests on the illusion of free will (HA 43). Two aspects of his critique of free will are relevant here. One is that the illusion of free will carries with it the illusion that we can choose and predict the future in advance (HA 73). The other is Nietzsche's claim that the individual is not responsible for anything arising from his "nature" because his "nature" is not freely chosen; it is to some extent inherited—"an outgrowth of the elements and influences of past and present things" (HA 43; see also GM 44–45). While, for Nietzsche, we cannot choose the future or our inheritance, we can, through somatic reflexivity, transform our inheritance and so keep the future open.

Nietzsche's third criticism of juridical self-responsibility is the one I wish to emphasize: in preempting a particular future, juridical self-responsibility closes down "the reversal of irreversible time," responsiveness and futurity. Insofar as the "last man," for example, is the embodiment of a socially prescribed good, in him the future, ordained in advance, is actualized (EH 328–30; TZ 128–30). But such individuals would be "unable to *create*" (EH 330). They would be unable to respond to "elements and influences" of historical existence (HA 43) in a way that, without escaping the body and therefore the norms one has inherited, keeps the body open to the undetermined future and affects open to the transformation of meaning. Those who embody the juridico-moral code they have inherited so extensively that they merely repeat it with resignation, in sacrificing "the future to *themselves*—they sacrifice all man's future" (EH 330). The "last man" is the end of history, the end of spatio-temporalization and so would be as "dyspeptic" as the self for whom the force of forgetting is dysfunctional— "he cannot 'have done' with anything" (GM 58). He would have the "conscience" of a machine.

"Genuine" Responsibility and Levinas's Provisional Critique

Nietzsche has a solution of sorts to these paradoxes of juridical responsibility and to the closure of responsiveness and futurity it fosters. But with this solution, he and Levinas part company. In section 2 of the second essay of *On the Genealogy of Morals*, Nietzsche welcomes the possibility that a genuinely responsible "sovereign," "noble" individual may emerge from this regime of accountability, punishment, and blame. Without explaining how this might happen, Nietzsche describes the sovereign individual as unique ("like only to himself"), having his own measure of value, and thus "liberated again from the morality of custom," and in whom a consciousness of this power and freedom has "become flesh" (GM 59). This "proud awareness of the extraordinary privilege of *responsibility*, the consciousness of this rare freedom . . . this sovereign man calls . . . his *conscience*" (GM 60).

Conscience? Nietzsche cannot mean the conscience of the liberal individual whose free will, as Levinas puts it, arises from "outside the brutal world and the implacable history of concrete existence" (RH 66) and, while appearing to break with determinism, actually, "by memory and history," reassembles the present into a totality "without fissures or surprises" (OB 5). There are two other ways to interpret Nietzsche's picture of genuine conscience and responsibility. First, he could be suggesting that the sovereign individual ordains his future in advance insofar as his or her *self-legislated* meanings and values have become flesh. But such a self would be little different from the "last man" or a thing in one crucial respect: such an individual would be a body reduced to and coincident with a fixed form and meaning with no excess, no affect, no somatic reflexivity, no ability to respond creatively. As with those who embody the ascetic ideal that Nietzsche discusses in the third essay (GM 103–8, 162), "a few ideas are to be rendered indistinguishable, ever-present, unforgettable, 'fixed,' with the aim of hypnotising the entire nervous and intellectual system" (GM 61). Any set of ideas or "legal order thought of as sovereign and universal . . . would be a principle hostile to life, an agent of the dissolution and destruction of man, an attempt to assassinate the future of man" (GM 76).

Nevertheless, this seems to be how Levinas interprets Nietzsche's materialism in his early discussion of the philosophy of "Hitlerism."[5] Conceptions of the self as adhering to a body become a problem, for Levinas, if the reflexive futural aspect of the body is denied. The body is then governed by the law of its inheritance: "The mysterious urgings of the blood, the appeals of heredity and the past for which the body serves as an enigmatic vehicle, lose the character of being problems that are subject to a solution put forward by a sovereignly free Self" (RH 69). With this, says Levinas, "if race does not exist, one has to invent it" (RH 69). The danger of this materialism is that it harbors a philosophy of expansion for which everyone denies responsibility. This is not the "ideological expansion" of idealism but a material expansion of one's own biological or inherited truth through "war and conquest" (RH 70–71). While Levinas attributes this principle to the rediscovery and glorification of "Nietzsche's will to power" (RH 71; EN 97), this, as the analysis above suggests, is not Nietzsche's materialism. It is true that he says, in *Beyond Good and Evil,* that no education or critical revaluation of affects can completely eradicate from the body the cultural "qualities and preferences" of one's "forefathers" (BG 184). This "constitutes the problem of race" (by which Nietzsche means cultural rather than biological race). But there is a difference between living through the "qualities" one has inherited and being determined by those "qualities." Hence, Nietzsche objects to the kind of transnational politics that, while transnational, evokes the "storm and stress of 'national feeling'" involving the adaptation of everyone toward one ideal identity (BG 153–54). By cutting the individual off from the material and cultural traditions that condition her and from the undetermined future that her reflexivity would open, such totalizing politics thereby turns everyone into a slave of the State. This is "*slavery* in the subtlest sense," and "is at the same time an involuntary arrangement for the breeding of *tyrants*" (BG 154).

The second and most likely interpretation of Nietzsche's picture of genuine self-responsibility, more consistent with Levinas's admiration in *Otherwise Than Being,* is of an individual for whom a future is open because the revaluation of value, one's own *force* of law, has become flesh. Genuine self-responsibility makes the most of the force of forgetfulness, of contradictory forces of somatic reflexivity, thereby interrupting and transforming the work of law and morality and its imposition of a few "demands of social existence as *present realities* upon these slaves of momentary affect" (GM 61). Put in the best possible light, the conscience of "genuine" self-responsibility is given by an aesthetics of self and a critical politics. This sovereign individual is irresponsible in the sense that she is not accountable in terms of—and will not necessarily uphold—the juridico-moral code that would shape her. But she is responsible in the sense that, in responding to and either affirming or contesting those norms, she sacrifices an enduring image of herself to keep the future open. This is the prereflective moment of "conscience" that "reverses irreversible time." In this contradictory recurring knot of existence, the past, including the juridico-moral code one has inherited, is neither forgotten nor entirely recuperated through memory: it is revised and either affirmed or contested through transforming the "it was" into thus "I willed it" (TZ 251–3). Thereby the self "goes under" while taking responsibility for her "destiny."

While the idea of somatic reflexivity, as the condition of conscience, is helpful for understanding the material impact of too much juridico-moral government, there is a problem with Nietzsche's solution—the only criterion of conscience, of critical revaluation, and "judging" the right thing to do, seems to be the maintenance of the *self*'s responsiveness and hence uniqueness. There is no internal *limit* to the creative forces that accompany this expression of freedom. While I accept the reading of "will to power" as enhancement of a "feeling of power" from the discharge of creative forces of reevaluation of value, rather than a will to domination, there is nevertheless an imperialism that haunts Nietzsche's picture of genuine self-responsibility.[6] This is not because "will to power" is driven blindly by meanings it has inherited in the way Levinas suggests in his analysis of Hitlerism: as I have argued, "will to power," as a manifestation of corporeal reflexivity, consists in a break with such determinism. Rather, the problem is that the "will to power" of genuine responsibility and "great politics" operates as a *force*, the expression of which is both inevitable and usually aggressive (e.g., BG 174–75; GM 77; EH 327). This is partly because Nietzsche formulates the forgetting that governs the presocial self in terms of force such that memory techniques and other means of enculturation are understood in terms of counterforces that "will to power" then opposes. But also, more fundamentally, the imperialism apparent in his descriptions of "will to power" arises from the individualism he espouses.

This individualism appears when Nietzsche forgets his own genealogy of genuine self-responsibility, where somatic reflexivity, conscience, and responsibility are born of *relation* with others (and not just with those who enforce prevailing laws through a punitive disciplinary system). If the relations that constitute and maintain the individual are denied, *relation will break through from within* in the form of a combative discharge of force. Even when Nietzsche admits the interdependence of self-responsibility, there is this confrontational element. He suggests in *Twilight of the Idols* that freedom, as the "will to assume responsibility for oneself," is not autonomous in the sense of being separated from its effects but is measured "by the re-sistance which has to be overcome . . . to remain on top" (TL 542). Hence, others are perceived as competing for sovereignty or as a potential threat to one's territorial integrity maintained through one's own force of law. In discharging its creative forces of reevaluation, the self-responsible self transgresses the unique value of the other's somatic reflexivity and extraterritoriality and is absolved of responsibility for the effects of its freedom on the suffering of others.

If prolonging or enhancing the other's suffering is an inevitable con-sequence of genuine self-responsibility, that model of responsibility would be subject to the same charge that Nietzsche levels at juridical self-responsibility: genuine self-responsibility would foreclose the responsive-ness that reverses irreversible time and hence it would foreclose futurity, perhaps not in oneself, at least not initially, but certainly in others. Inso-far as the State or individual relinquishes this responsibility for keeping the future open, by preempting the future, by imposing an image of the fu-ture self on everyone, these bodies can be undone, rendered senseless, and barred from a future. This is one meaning of suffering and terror: the pain of *passive suffering,* arising from the dissolution of the self into the absolute present (the "last man"), into the timeless flux of affect, or into the linear progressive or cyclic time of biological destiny or automatism. Nietzsche puts the highest value on the *active suffering* of the self-responsible self who suffers from an excess of creative force, and therefore from the problem of meaning (e.g., GM 162; BG 136). But, by not conceiving of a limit to the discharge of critical evaluative forces accompanying "genuine" self-respon-sibility, Nietzsche would preserve this kind of active suffering for the self by the proliferation of passive suffering in others, albeit in a blundering, nondeliberate way. While Nietzsche does allow that a genuinely sovereign individual or State will respond to others who are different (or who in some other way challenge its force of law) with generosity, mercy, and compas-sion (GM 72–73), this external limit to the imperialistic effects of will to power is too dependent on the arbitrary whim of sovereignty to be more than a fortuitous virtue.[7] On the basis of this "multiplicity in pure indiffer-ence" that Levinas finds in phenomenology (CPP 89) but that also accom-panies Nietzsche's sovereign self-responsibility, Nietzsche says in *Human, All Too Human:* "we feel toward [the neighbor] as free and irresponsible as toward plants and stones. That the other suffers *must be learned;* and it can never be learned completely" (HA 70).

Levinas, Responsibility for the Other, and Beyond

Levinas would agree with Nietzsche that the suffering of others, whether passive (the result of external force) or active (responsiveness as the expression of uniqueness), is learned. But the other's suffering is learned as it is felt in the very process by which the responsiveness of somatic reflexivity and self-responsibility arises. Hence, in contrast to Nietzsche and by going further into the preconditions of responsiveness and responsibility, Levinas argues that "the condition for, or the unconditionality of, the self does not begin in the auto-affection of a sovereign ego that would be, after the event, 'compassionate' for another" or resentful of another or just indifferent (OB 123). "Quite the contrary": the self begins in "compassion" or responsibility for the other, in response to the other's alterity that breaks through the other's (cultural) form (CPP 96). So, while Levinas agrees with Nietzsche that the break with determinism is prior to the distinction between "free" and "un-free" will (BG 32–33) and that the criteria of conscience (the "norms of morality") are "not embarked in history and culture" (CPP 101), the "finite" freedom of self-responsibility that Nietzsche describes is neither original nor unlimited (OB 122–23). Levinas's claim that uniqueness and autonomy arise through interdependence points to four departures from Nietzsche's account of the prehistory of somatic reflexivity, responsiveness and therefore responsibility.

First, for Levinas, responsiveness, as a condition of responsibility, does not arise by way of *force,* whether an "original" force of forgetting, a counterforce of law, or a force of revaluation that arises in the reflexivity resulting from the relation between the other two. Rather, the intensity or "inspiration" necessary to move the self beyond itself comes from the other, "over and beyond the logos of response" and as a condition of sociality, normativity, the juridico-moral code, and the affective powers of one's creative relation to that code (OB 102). And this provocation of the other is pacific rather than hostile (OB 139). This is to take the condition of responsibility beyond essence caught in an ontology of war and "rational peace" to a "forgetting" and "ignorance of what is not noble" (OB 177). Levinas's forgetting shares synergies with Nietzsche's but is not a force in opposition to memory. Rather, forgetting lies beyond "the bipolarity of essence, between being and nothingness" and is "absolutely opposed to oppression" (OB 177).

Hence, and second, it is the other's alterity that introduces "a lapse of time" inaugurating the "getting out of phase of the instant," the temporalization of *time* that would constitute a self who would be self-responsible (OB 51; CPP 105). This being affected by alterity affects me beyond and as a condition of the "moment" of recurrence that Nietzsche describes. For Levinas, in this knot of recurrence the self does not return to itself the same, not because it remakes the world all by itself (by reversing time in transforming "it was" into "thus I willed it") but because this "is a recurrence to oneself out of an irrecusable exigency of the other" that puts into question all "self-affirmation" and all "egoism born again in this recurrence" (OB 109, 111). Still, following Nietzsche, the place of this temporalization is the body: "recurrence is incarnation" (OB 109). But it is the felt strangeness of others, the extraterritoriality of a (no)place unconstituted by me, that constitutes the uniqueness of the self signified as corporeal reflexivity or the "non-coincidence with oneself" (OB 56). Respons-ability is *sensibility* that exceeds but also is a condition of somatic reflexivity, a responsive body with meaningful projects open to a future, and to a critical relation with the juridico-moral code.

Third, while building on the value Nietzsche attributes to the futurity of the body's reflexivity, Levinas rejects any implication that maintaining the self's responsiveness (through an aesthetics of self-overcoming or a critical politics) is the primary normative basis of "conscience." He follows Nietzsche's conviction that conscience is not about accountability with reference to cultural convention. But Levinas locates "responsibility for the other" beyond the condition of "good" or "bad conscience" such that this responsibility is dedicated to the other "before being dedicated to myself" (EN 169–70). This inclination toward the corporeal expression of the other's alterity disrupts moral norms while providing the basis of all normativity: it says "thou shalt not kill," and this unique sense puts existence on a human and moral plane and introduces value and "meaning into being" (Levinas OB 128; CPP 88–89, 92, 95–96). As a nonvolitional, affective "response" to the other, I am therefore responsible for the other's responsiveness: "I have to answer for [the other's] very responsibility" (OB 84) and "defend the rights of the other man" (OS 125). As it is through and for the futurity of the *other*'s body that I am responsible, it is this, rather than preservation of my own reflexivity, that is the normative basis of "conscience"—that felt conviction about what is right and wrong "beyond convention" (OB 88).

Finally, contrary to Nietzsche, that I am responsibility for the other implies an internal limit to the creative forces of self-responsibility: responsibility for the other puts into question the freedom of the ego and "its pride and the dominating imperialism characteristic of it" by limiting my freedom to possess, kill, or in any way negate the other's uniqueness (OB 110). More positively, this responsibility is "responsibility for the freedom of the others" (OB 109), and, as responsibility for the other, the subject "frees itself from its 'return to self'" (OS 125), from "enchainment to itself" (OB 124).

The value of these interventions into the meaning of responsibility does not lie most fundamentally in promoting tolerance and multiculturalism. They support such a cause, but one could equally rely on the pluralism inherent in Nietzsche's ontology for that. More valuable I think is that Levinas's idea of responsibility for others, juxtaposed with Nietzsche's "genuine" self-responsibility, pinpoints what would precipitate a crisis of responsibility in a liberal democracy of the kind with which I began. Political attempts to secure a particular future for the nation or for oneself, through reasserting the borders of one's sovereign territory, by imposing one's will upon the world, or through racism and other exercises in political determinism, consist in evasion of responsibility for others. Evasion of political responsibility (for the preservation of the responsiveness of all others) would not just affect the others who are targeted by enhancing their suffering in Nietzsche's "passive" sense—that undergone as a dissolution of the spatio-temporality of subjectivity. Evading responsibility for the futurity of others would also enhance the suffering of those *within* the political community that practices such imperialism by destroying the "source" of the break with determinism (the other) that is a condition of responsiveness, *self*-responsibility and openness to an undetermined future.

This conclusion about the impact of the evasion of political responsibility on the corporeal reflexivity of both self-responsibility and responsibility for others cannot be easily derived from either Nietzsche or Levinas alone—partly because they both neglect politics—but also because they both view "useless" suffering (meaningless, unwitnessed, for no purpose) as both what we deem "evil" and that which is to some extent "congenital" (GM 67–69; EN 92–93). What is not clear is how much they thereby condone the passivity *and* dissolution of subjectivity (and hence loss of responsiveness) that is characteristic of such suffering. Nietzsche seems to build passive suffering inflicted on others into "great politics" itself as a by-product of the "deification of cruelty" in the figure of the sovereign individual (GM 65–67). Levinas, however, insists that suffering inflicted by such sovereign forces is neither congenital nor inevitable: this is "suffering and evil inflicted deliberately . . . in a manner . . . of a reason become political and detached from all ethics" (EN 97). This "degrades human beings by affecting their freedom" and reducing them to "the identity of a mere thing" (EN 92). Even if the other's suffering is not my own doing, the non-indifference of responsibility for others demands that we not "abandon the world to useless suffering, leaving it to the political fatality—or drifting—of blind forces" (EN 99–100).

On the other hand, for Levinas, the suffering that is "congenital" is that of responsibility for the other: "the just suffering in me for the unjustifiable suffering of the other" (EN 94). While this does not promote politics detached from ethics that would abandon the other, it could imply an abandonment of the self—a dissolution of self, the undoing of the lived place and time of the body into affectivity and sensation without sense, a utopia of no-place, no-time, and no-meaning. It is Nietzsche who reminds us of the consequences, for responsiveness and futurity, of such pure passivity and receptivity. Added to this is a second possible problem in accounting for the impact of the evasion of political responsibility on responsiveness: not only does Levinas's account of responsibility for others not suggest anything concrete for politics; he holds that any actual response to others (including politics), by imposing conditions, evaluations, and judgments, consists in a withdrawal from responsibility for others (e.g., TI 64).[8]

However, through occasional qualification, by way of the notion of the "Third Party," Levinas, particularly in his later work, points to an internal limit to this apparently unlimited, unconditional responsibility for the other. And this is where ethics meets political responsibility. The limit comes not from specific moral or juridical laws that would give one reciprocal rights against the other but from the concern for *all* others, including one's self, that *underlies* the egalitarian principles of justice in liberal democracies. This "concern for justice" arises from and is justified by sensibility as responsibility for the other (OB 128). It also limits the unconditional and asymmetrical dimensions of responsibility for the other in that, "from the first" the other for whom I am responsible is always also a Third Party with respect to another and, while no one can substitute for my responsibility, "I am another for the others" (OB 158). As responsibility for the other, I do not get reduced to pure passivity or to a thing because the uniqueness expressed in my corporeal reflexivity emerges through and is supported by the welcome of other others who are responsible for me. This idea of the Third Party also suggests that the "concern for justice" arising from but "spreading around" responsibility for the other is what Levinas would understand by the normative basis of political responsibility in liberal democracies. Indeed, he suggests in an interview in 1988 that the "very excellence of democracy" lies in the attempt, through "legislation, always unfinished," to be open to the better expression of "justice . . . in the name of responsibility for the other" (EN 229–30).

If Levinas is right that this concern for justice based on responsibility for the other is what underscores the "conscience" of political responsibility, and if Nietzsche is right that we embody some of those norms of the juridico-moral code that emerges from this concern for justice, as well as a reflexive relation to that code, then an evasion of political responsibility would manifest in a dissolution of the limits that keep operative sociality as giving to and inclination toward the uniqueness and alterity of all others. Keeping a check on the dissolution of the self implied in the passive suffering of both responsibility for others and that inflicted by the sovereign forces of self-responsibility would require a chiasmic, rather than asymmetrical, relation between ethics and a critical politics, between responsibility for others and self-responsibility. Nietzsche and Levinas's idea of the body in its futurity as the expression of the highest value provides the ground for a link between the two. This is the body understood in terms of somatic reflexivity or sensibility, the body that breaks with determinism but that is thus enabled because it is affected by the other and is compassion for the other. These bodies are at risk under present conditions not from the suffering for others of somatic reflexivity or from the insecurity of an unknown future, but from either an ethics detached from politics or from a politics detached from ethics. Nietzsche and Levinas are at their best when they see the two, ethics and politics, as interdependent. What would reattach ethics and politics is a critical politics that mobilizes the revaluation of value of "genuine" self-responsibility—but in a way that preserves the independence of the self's reflexive and therefore critical powers by assuming responsibility for the preservation of the independence and unique value of the other's responsiveness and responsibility. This is a concept of responsibility that Nietzsche and Levinas together may have envisaged for our time.

NOTES

1.   Bernhard Waldenfels, "Response and Responsibility in Levinas," in *Ethics as First Philosophy: The Significance of Emmanuel Levinas for Philosophy,*

Literature, and Religion, ed. Adriaan T. Peperzak (New York: Routledge, 1995), 46.

2. Robert Bernasconi, "Before Whom and For What? Accountability and the Invention of Ministerial, Hyperbolic, and Infinite Responsibility," in *Difficulties of Ethical Life,* ed. Shannon Sullivan and Denis Schmidt (New York: Fordham University Press, 2008)

3. For an alternative analysis of the relation between Nietzsche's and Levinas's approaches to responsibility see Judith Butler, "Giving an Account of Oneself," *Diacritics* 31, no.4 (Winter 2001): 22–40, revised in *Giving an Account of Oneself* (New York: Fordham University Press, 2005), chapter 1.

4. I have borrowed some of my analysis of Nietzsche from another paper: Rosalyn Diprose, "Arendt and Nietzsche on Responsibility and Futurity," *Philosophy and Social Criticism* 34, no. 6 (2008): 617–42. The research for both papers was supported by an Australian Research Council Discovery Project grant.

5. For a more detailed discussion of Levinas's essay "Reflections on The Philosophy of Hitlerism" in relation to Heidegger's philosophy, see Tina Chanter, "Neither Materialism nor Idealism: Levinas' Third Way," in *Postmodernism and the Holocaust,* ed. Alan Milchman (Amsterdam: Rodopi, 1998), 137–54.

6. For a comprehensive analysis of various meanings of "will to power," see Mark Warren, *Nietzsche and Political Thought* (Cambridge, Mass.: MIT Press, 1988), chapter 4; for a comparison of Nietzsche's idea that will to power is about increased "feeling of power" with that of Hobbes, see Paul Patton, "Nietzsche and Hobbes," *International Studies in Philosophy* 33, no. 3 (2001): 99–116.

7. For an account of why this volitional generosity is an insufficient guarantee against the imperialism of sovereign "will to power," see Rosalyn Diprose, *Corporeal Generosity: On Giving with Nietzsche, Merleau-Ponty, and Levinas* (Albany: State University of New York Press, 2002), chapter 1.

8. His most explicit statement to the effect that politics closes down the ethical relation to the other can be found in an interview, "Dialogue with Emmanuel Levinas," in *Face to Face with Levinas,* ed. Richard A. Cohen (Albany: State University of New York Press, 1986), 29.

8

Beginning's Abyss

On Solitude in Nietzsche and Levinas

JOHN DRABINSKI

The origin, perhaps, will only be the burn of its erasure.
—Edmond Jabès

ETHICS OR *the anti-moralist.* What more is there to say? Either moral consciousness reflects the degeneration and death of a dancing star or ethics is first philosophy. That is, there is either Nietzsche or Levinas.

Yet there is always more to say. How are we to say more? To what end? Where might we locate a conversation between Nietzsche and Levinas? These are our first and most crucial questions. Location is of course everything, and location is especially difficult in this conversation. Levinas has had little to say about Nietzsche; even treating those scattered evocative and provocative statements, a reader of Levinas has little with which to work. If there is little with which to work, then any conversation is imaginary—and therefore bears within it so much possibility. This contested and conjoined space of philosophical imagination can no doubt say more than any text, which is especially important given that Levinas is typically a poor reader of historical figures. That is to say, if we are not simply bound by Levinas's comments on Nietzsche, few as they are, then a conversation must root itself in and depart from *die Sachen* of philosophy. This root is all the more potent given each thinker's insistence that *die Sachen* of philosophy are the fractured expanse of life at the moment of its break with history. That is, and this is my central claim here, each is engaged in a certain kind of phenomenology conceived at the limit of historical experience. *Life, even in its separation(s) from history, gives itself to thinking.* The conversation, then, must address itself to what is given to thinking rather than to what is said first (in this case, by Levinas) and then said again in commentary on that. The location of thinking Nietzsche and Levinas together, that site in which philosophy begins as a mutual saying, motivates conversation. What, then, is the *philosophical* motivation for putting Levinas before Nietzsche, Nietzsche before Levinas?

———

I would like to begin my reflections with a slightly different motif in order to attend again to *die Sachen* of the present inquiry. I am struck by an initially *rhetorical* location: at the very moment that everything is evacuated, and so the moment in which everything is at stake, both Nietzsche and Levinas produce a melancholic discourse. It is melancholic insofar as it lacks an object to mourn, lacks an attachment or alternative catharsis and is at the same time affectively saturated with pain and loss. The evacuation for both Nietzsche and Levinas is the vacating of an illusion, a lie that has come to dominate the West. Nietzsche and Levinas lose that illusion and are left with nothing. All idols are dead. Whatever the pleasures in what is possible after the illusion vacates, there is also pain. First and irreducibly, there is pain.

Now, one might immediately (and not unjustifiably) object that Nietzsche's work is playful and animated by that spirit throughout and that Levinas's work—especially in *Totality and Infinity*—is full of a voluptuousness that exceeds any pull of the melancholic. There is real justification in this claim, especially in the case of Nietzsche. Zarathustra's playfulness, nearly to the point of suggesting that the task of self-overcoming is a game, hardly seems melancholic. Levinas's identification of the ethical break with history in the prophetic ought to celebrate the death of the tyranny of politics. Are Nietzsche and Levinas not plainly ecstatic, albeit in structurally opposite directions, in this evacuation of the tradition? Without a doubt. Yet I want to insist that melancholy is also always central to how each engages philosophy in its rhetorical dimension. Nietzsche and Levinas suffer losses as the precondition of their work. Nietzsche's Zarathustra is drenched in lonely sadness, Dionysus writhes in pain, and the Madman is mad with anxious despair. The frantic, shifting character of each figure suggests as much misery as joy. In his 1881 postcard to Overbeck, Nietzsche identifies with Spinoza (who is "closest to me") as the "most unusual and loneliest thinker."[1] Indeed, at the very moment that self-overcoming is glimpsed as an opening to ecstasy, there is the despondency of loss. Ecstasy is wrenched from pain. Whatever his pleasures, Zarathustra (like Dionysus) is born of pain and loss, betrayal and fragmentation. This bears out in Nietzsche's opening narrative to all four parts of *Thus Spoke Zarathustra*. Zarathustra is lonely and restless. While this may be read as a literary device employed to motivate Zarathustra's coming failures, such a reading misses the melancholy of his journey—one already fated to failure. Zarathustra's departure from solitude collapses the ground underneath him. "Yesterday, in the stillest hour," Zarathustra tells us, "the ground gave under me, the dream began. The hand moved, the clock of my life drew a breath; never had I heard such stillness around me: my heart took fright" (TZ 257): fear as the groundlessness of life, which is, at the same time, life's liberation from the tradition.

In the case of Levinas, *Otherwise Than Being* is noteworthy for its conceptual and rhetorical austerity. Even in *Totality and Infinity,* though more promising in light of its emphasis on excess and surplus, Levinas's work presents us with an authentic disconnection. On the one hand, there is the hope and promise of peace against history's long story of war that commences his reflections. On the other hand, there is the asceticism and even hopelessness of Levinas's descriptions. Our hands are emptied by the Other, and my voice is always already violence. *Otherwise Than Being* only repeats this shift, bringing even more rhetorical force to the starkness and sobriety of a life born of absence before absence, a life borne by an exposed subject. From the glory of the Infinite to persecution to obsession. Consider this passage from the fourth chapter of *Otherwise Than Being,* where Levinas writes of how we are so radically overturned by loss:

> Obsession is irreducible to consciousness, even if it overwhelms it. In consciousness it is betrayed, but thematized by a said in which it is manifested. Obsession traverses consciousness countercurrentwise, is inscribed in consciousness as something foreign, a disequilibrium, a delirium.   (OB 101)

Without the tradition, there is the complete disorientation of subjectivity. There is no footing or ground on which subjectivity might gather itself or make sense of the world.

Nietzsche and Levinas evacuate completely not only the closure constitutive of the tradition but also any sense of nostalgia (not all loss is rooted
in nostalgia, after all). Still, we are left with a disconnection between what
such an evacuation promises—another beginning, another future—and the
affect that saturates the life given after the tradition exits: melancholy. Neither Nietzsche nor Levinas mourn the tradition. To do so would repeat the
violence against which both labor so intensively. Rather, the parricide—as
Levinas famously puts it in *Time and the Other*—leaves no object in its wake
but only the lingering, haunting affects of trembling fear and melancholy.

What are we to make of this disconnection? What happens if we take disconnection seriously, not just as a rhetorical surface but rather as crucial—
perhaps even to the point of reading such disconnections as performatives—
to the task of understanding Nietzsche and Levinas philosophically? If rhetoric crosses so decisively with philosophical meaning and sense, then we
can and must proceed with the melancholic character in Nietzsche's and
Levinas's work in constant view, reading sensitively for its haunting presence even at moments of transformation and release. Their work is melancholic because of this very disconnection; indeed, what marks melancholia
as melancholia is the refusal of a connection between what is lost and what
remains. Mourning, on the other hand, is that relation in which what is
lost remains connected to the subject. Mourning puts a broken subjectivity
back together in the process of working through traumatic events that have
wreaked havoc on one's life. The catastrophic despair of the melancholic,
however, begins in the loss of that very connection, and therefore the loss
of the possibility of repair. If nowhere else, we encounter Nietzsche and
Levinas in that space of non-reparative thinking.

Why this evacuation? What catastrophe empties everything from philosophy? And where are we left *after* catastrophe, evacuation, and the emptying
of what *might have* given something to thinking? That is, in and through
what abyss might we locate a conversation between Nietzsche and Levinas
about the problem of beginning? In raising and addressing these questions,
I do not hope to discover new connections or obscure passages but rather
to open an urgent philosophical space in which these two thinkers might
resonate: the abyssal space of beginning.

———

What does it mean to begin? Beginning is work, a production from a certain kind of labor. I am drawn to Heidegger's conception of work in "The

Origin of the Work of Art," where he writes that "to work-being, there belongs the setting up of a world [*Werksein heißt: eine Welt aufstellen*]."[2] But Heidegger is attentive to how this setting up of a world risks a failure to gather, whether in the moment of manifestation or in a future. Consider what Heidegger famously says about the encounter with the ancient Greek temple: "The temple, in its standing there, first gives to things their look and to men their outlook on themselves. This remains open as long as the work is a work, as long as the god has not fled from it."[3] If the god remains, gathering before the encounter with the temple, then everything is given to thinking. Philosophy is its own kind of work, and so its own kind of gathering with a certain kind of god or gods in the antechamber of thinking. As with the temple, so tragic in Heidegger's encounter, we can ask: Have the gods fled philosophy? If so, how are we to begin the task of thinking?

The experience of the long twentieth century has been an experience of catastrophe. Whatever our pretensions, this long century has been defined by trauma and loss. Yet philosophy has largely been deaf to this experience—and historical experience in general, one could argue—and so the question remains: What happens to philosophy's beginning if we take catastrophe seriously?

En route to Nietzsche and Levinas, I would like to detour through Benjamin's "Theses on the Philosophy of History." Benjamin's theses address the problem of beginning through *an other* encounter with history. This other encounter both begins and sits patiently with the unredeemed violence constitutive of history's movement. The master narrative, on Benjamin's treatment, gives way to trauma and loss, and so those slain on Hegel's famous slaughter-bench of history recover voice and force. But we cannot register that voice and force if our relation to history is guided by an epic narrative. Such narratives redeem violence in the story of history's meaning and significance. Redeemed violence is therefore located in and by a citable history. Citability recalls to us Benjamin's figure of the chronicler. Benjamin writes:

A chronicler who recites events without distinguishing between major and minor ones acts in accordance with the following truth: nothing that has ever happened should be regarded as lost for history. To be sure, only a redeemed mankind receives the fullness of its past—which is to say, only for a redeemed mankind has its past become citable in all its moments.[4]

The citability of history draws on a vision of redemption. Epic narrative overrides and neutralizes loss and trauma in order to make sense of history's movement. On this rendering, the corpse of Hegel's slaughter-bench is muted—muted, not mute. Epic narrative acts and intervenes in the very materiality out of which history is formed *as* citable history. The corpse is acted upon, not described. Muting and muted, then, with the *verbal* sense in the first position rather than the adjectival or nominal. As victim, the corpse retains its rights to question us.

Citable history assembles a redeemed event or series of events. Yet, the chronicler interrupts his narrative by folding major and minor events into historical significance. The corpse on Hegel's slaughter-bench here shows its face. What, then, can and must be said about violence as such, this violence here, and so of catastrophe *before* the neutralizing epic narrative? This question prompts the famous reading of Klee's *Angelus Novus*. What does Klee's angel say to history? Benjamin writes:

> This is how one pictures the angel of history. His face is turned toward the past. Where we perceive a chain of events, he sees one single catastrophe which keeps piling wreckage upon wreckage and hurls it in front of his feet. The angel would like to stay, awaken the dead, and make whole what has been smashed. But a storm is blowing from Paradise; it has got caught in his wings with such violence that the angel can no longer close them. This storm irresistibly propels him into the future to which his back is turned, while the pile of debris before him grows skyward. This storm is what we call progress.[5]

Klee's angel sees the "materialism" of history, of loss, corpses as the wreckage of history's catastrophe(s). This is *an other* encounter with history, made other by way of its interruption of the predominance of epic in conceiving not only historical events, but also our relation to history's significance. Klee's angel disconcerts historical experience as the slaughter-bench accuses.

The slaughter-bench of history accuses in the recurrence of the *human problematic*, a recurrence in which Nietzsche and Levinas have decisive interventions. This problematic counters the cost of catastrophe with the question of beginning. For the angel does not see only catastrophe. He is also propelled into the future. And so historical experience is a movement into the past while that very movement both conditions and is conditioned by a simultaneous move into the future. The angel, then, is a figure of both catastrophe *and* the interval between past and future. That is, the angel is a figure of beginning.

Benjamin brings us to the historical experience of loss. What is this loss? Toward what beginning? What sort of catastrophe haunts the work of Nietzsche and Levinas?

————

Klee's angel puts philosophy's work in question. The temple fails to gather the gods, but we should not hear the resonance of Heidegger in this. Rather, we should hear Heidegger's first moment of absence. In the erasure of a lingering origin, we can make a sort of anti-pilgrimage to the abandoned temple with Klee's angel. No gods gather. Therein lies the force of catastrophe. What sort of catastrophe haunts the work of Nietzsche and Levinas?

Let me begin with Levinas. I do not think that the Shoah functions as a motivation for the melancholic character of Levinas's work. Whatever the shadow it casts for Levinas, I have always thought his address was to another sort of condition in history: totality as the project of traditional metaphysics *and* antimetaphysics. The dedication to *Otherwise Than Being* is to the six million dead, of course, but also and at the same time to victims of the *same* anti-Semitism, the *same* hatred of the other man. This *sameness* of anti-Semitism lodges the specificity of the Shoah within a wider claim about (Western) history. The Shoah is yet another—and exceedingly graphic— upsurge of what has always defined the West's intellectual and cultural trajectory. Totalitarianism is not a politics. Totalitarianism animates Western thinking, tradition. So, when what animates thought becomes manifest, defining the actual character of a *politics*, we would be mistaken to identify the genesis of catastrophic violence in the moment of social organization. When Levinas begins *Totality and Infinity* with the famed juxtaposition of war and the ethical, he does not draw us back into the very immediate disaster. This is not an evocation of the Shoah. Rather, Levinas is drawing us too far back, drowning us in the enormity of his claim. *The entirety of the West is a story about totalitarianism and the calculus of war.* In a very real sense, then, the West is a theorizing and cultural practice of a voracious, eliminationist subjectivity.

This first moment of catastrophe haunts Levinas's work, a catastrophe of nonlocalizable yet constantly present violence. It is a catastrophe that works very much like the vision of Klee's angel: he sees a series of disasters in the history of thought. For this very reason, the preface to *Totality and Infinity* begins with such ridiculously high stakes. There is either war or peace. History tells us that there is nothing but war, that violence is the rule, and that the struggle to dominate is inherent in social existence. To this, ethics is posed as a challenge. But herein lies a second catastrophe, one that comes *after* the angel's vision. For it is not enough to say that war and violence have dominated Western history in thought and politics. The story is neither so bleak nor so alien, even if it is one from which Levinas will never retreat. We must also say that we have made our home in this particular sense of place. Totality is where I find comforts and the satisfaction of my needs, where desire does not vanish the "I" and always returns the "I" to itself full and content. This is a doubled second catastrophe. First, it is so intimate. My home lies at the center of the logic of violence; Levinas's repeated appeal to Pascal's musings about the usurpation of the world should register this real loss. Second, though we are putatively transformed into the possibility of peace, the abandonment of history leaves us with nothing and takes leave of what *had* defined life: the pleasures of need, knowledge, and so many other forms of autoerotics.

It is in this second sense of catastrophe that we catch sight of Nietzsche. Whatever the wandering character of his work, Nietzsche returns, every time, to the motif of the degeneration of life. The Apollonian motif of bringing to light, reconciliation, and even redemption comes to dominate—even simply define—the West. A certain god stands in for the shifting and varying set of crimes against life, from despising the body to the last temptations of pleasure and happiness. The death of God is therefore never about the passing of a belief or an institution, but rather the vanishing of the very idea of belief, the very idea of an institution. This is why Nietzsche is so blunt in *The Gay Science:* God's death provokes us to bid farewell to "all that was built upon it, leaned on it, grew into it; for example, our whole European morality" (GS 279) "Morality" here of course points to the collapse of the very meaning of otherworldly infused worldly life—a meaning that Nietzsche convincingly identified as nihilism.

Again, at the very moment we glimpse our (possible) liberation from the degeneration of life, we must also register the loss of what has for so long been our home: home as what heals and redeems, a site of comfort and contentment. Indeed, insofar as Nietzsche's moment of beginning again—which is actually a *first* beginning—leaps over the abyss and into the

Dionysian, beginning is possible only as repudiation and slaying of Apollo. John Sallis's account of Apollo in *Crossings* establishes precisely what is lost in this murderous repudiation: brilliant radiances, the commanding distance of the god, and, in (the) light of both, the power to heal and redeem pain.[6] In a word, and to say it directly, with Apollo also goes *beauty*. With beauty also goes an important series of conceptions, meanings, and roots of life: wisdom, virtue, obligation, consolation, redemption, happiness, contentedness. Nietzsche rightly celebrates the possibilities of a future untethered to such conceptions, meanings, and roots, but there is also the now ever more insistently present ghost of a new abyss. The terror of the new is where the sense of loss resonates—in the intellect, stuttering speech, and trembling hands.

The melancholic thread in Nietzsche and Levinas is therefore to be expected. The degeneration and degradation of what is *best* about the human—the Dionysian, the ethical—is catastrophic. That we find ourselves at home in that degeneration and degradation only doubles the sense of loss when it becomes clear that it is all just so untenable. When the trajectory of the West is flattened by the wave of excess—be that the excess of the Dionysian or the ethical—we gain something, however little. We gain very little, perhaps only a promise whose fulfillment is indefinitely (infinitely?) postponed, deferred. But we lose everything.

———

The catastrophic is a twofold moment for both Nietzsche and Levinas. First, it is the cessation of tradition. Tradition is destroyed. In that destruction, out of that nothing, in the burn of erasure (and so not in its ruins) we begin. As we have seen, arrival at this space of conversation is at once a story about pain and loss *and* relief and ecstasy at the vanishing of our being-at-home in the tradition. Second, and older than this first implication of catastrophe, the burning erasure of the tradition reveals what sustained Western thinking as the anti- and ante-tradition. This sustenance is the root-which-is-not-one, this something before and always an excessive remainder to what *had been* given to thinking. For Levinas, the face initiates language in the solicitation of response and sociality. The violence of propositions always presupposes this initiation. For Nietzsche, as he has it in *Thus Spoke Zarathustra*, one must *still* have chaos in one's self to give birth to a dancing star (TZ 17). Indeed, we *still do* have that chaos in us, no matter the millennia of degenerative labor we call "our history."

One might be tempted to think this "before" as an origin; the term certainly captures the notion of something that sustains and predates. But "origin" is of course itself a word born of the totalitarian trajectory of the West and so warrants some pause. The measure of what sustained the West, if it is taken as other than and radically outside of that trajectory, cannot be measured in relation. As well, what is given to thought after the catastrophe of the tradition's collapse is itself the erasure of any arch(a)ic sense of origin: the abyss. Indeed, the very phrase "abyssal origin" collapses into itself. Nietzsche's famous figuring in the first part of *Thus Spoke Zarathustra* of the human person as a rope over an abyss, between beast and Overman (TZ 126), is instructive. The abyss is what consumes the beast and the merely human, leaving only the terror of the absolutely groundless and new. An abyssal "origin," wholly preoriginal, is given to thought as thinking begins again, perhaps for the first time, only after the evacuation of the tradition—and without originating anything other than loss. The temporal fracture here is real; there is no past toward which one might look for grounding. The backward glance submits to the abyss and the losses it initiates and seals, yet we are not this past. We always meet a future, become a(nother) beginning.

Benjamin's profound meditation on catastrophe attunes us to a different sense of futurity. The angel of history is propelled into the future. The corpses of history compel the angel toward and with the past at the very moment he is blown into a future. Historical experience, in this sense, need not be like the historian in *Twilight of the Idols,* who, always looking backward in his "searching out origins," becomes a crab, coming eventually to *believe* backward (TL 470). The posture of Benjamin's angel is everything: the pile grows *before him,* which means the disaster of history fixes and rivets the gaze. Yet we always become a(nother) beginning. The future is therefore a necessity after disaster, rather than a possibility. What is this space of necessity?

The collapse of what was foundational—the vanishing of all that might make life readily intelligible—changes everything. The question of beginning again is therefore not, as it was for Heidegger in relation to the Greeks, a matter of reactivation. The gods have fled the tradition's temple—or, perhaps better, have all been dissolved as illusions. After this collapse, this dissolution, we are left with the kind of consuming nothing captured in Nietzsche's notion of abyss. It is important here to remember that the abyss belongs to beginning, forestructuring what it means to begin. That is, the abyss is not produced by my own lack, my melancholy, my disappointment, or my despair. The abyss is not measured as abyssal in my approach, and so not in relation to finitude, which is to say that we've moved into that space predating economies of knowing and being. Indeed, this is why it is so difficult to read Nietzsche and Levinas: the abyss belongs to beginning, so the language of philosophy must be transformed into a response to rather than an articulation of the immeasurable chasm from which thinking is born—and which it must always bear. Theirs is a community with nothing in common—to borrow a title from Lingis,[7] perhaps our most important reader of Nietzsche *and* Levinas. The nothing in common is this abyssal space of beginning, this location of a conversation without proceeding from community or shared space. At the abyss of beginning, the common is evacuated. Non-site par excellence.

Nietzsche's operative concept of loss is rooted in exactly this sense of debt to the abyssal. Indeed, much of Nietzsche's articulation of the process of self-overcoming is suspended over the abyss, which is, perhaps, what maddens the madman. In his account of the rendering of the world as illusion in *Twilight of the Idols*, Nietzsche opens us into the space of beginning. Whatever the rhetorical flourishes of his retelling, the story is fundamentally a sad one. After all, it is a story of how we fell in love with what would slowly kill us, and how we made our home in what was only degeneration. Let's face it: *this is epic self-sabotage*. As well, there is Nietzsche's trepidation before the decision about the future, asking, at the close of "How the 'True World' Became a Fable," "what has remained?" (TL 486) The apparent and the true vanish, of course, and we are left with nothing except the ambiguous though celebratory shout. INCIPIT ZARATHUSTRA.

We begin with Zarathustra. It is here, as well, that Zarathustra *can* enter and begin to make sense as the one who does not unmake sense but rather, as Sallis puts it, "twists free into the exorbitant, the immeasurable, the boundless—in a word: *das Masslose*."[8] In *The Gay Science* Nietzsche writes with both anxiety and cheerfulness about the sea lying before us after the death of God.

> At last the horizon appears free again to us, even granted that it is not bright; at last our ships may venture out again, venture out to face any danger; all the daring of the lover of knowledge is permitted again; the sea, *our* sea, lies open again; perhaps there has never yet been such an "open sea." (GS 280)

The free, the open, the sea, daring, and dangerous—these figures and motifs gather together Nietzsche's transformation of the Dionysian. If, as Sloterdijk argues, Nietzsche's break with the Apollonian is a direct break with Enlightenment notions of autonomy,[9] then our assessment of Nietzsche's beginning must attend to this "venturing out" as a movement without foundation or return. That is, movement from the abyss into a space unconstrained by the real world or its fables—a space outside metaphysics, otherwise than being, and beyond essence—in which identity itself is submitted to the abyss.[10] Sloterdijk is instructive here when he remarks that the specifically Dionysian break with the Apollonian—Nietzsche's loss of the tradition and beginning's abyss—marks an aesthetic of life *without* redemption of that aesthetic;[11] hence the radical break with the (vo)luminous healing power of Apollo noted above. Having gazed into the abyss and refused the seductions of pessimism, beginning is properly Dionysian when it exchanges redemption for danger, becoming *this* wanderer at *this very (historical) moment.* Beginning again is always hard.

Just as we say that Zarathustra can only make sense out of the collapse of the apparent and the true into the abyss, we can also say that ethical subjectivity only makes sense after the collapse of totality. Economies and logics of sense making and manifestation pervert, to the point of rendering unrecognizable, the subject subjected to the Other. Thus, responsible subjectivity emerges out of the ruins of a collapsed tradition of knowing and being. In *Otherwise Than Being,* Levinas's language is more emphatically attuned to this collapse. That is, it is unclear in *Totality and Infinity* whether the prophetic character of ethical subjectivity is prior to what eclipses its sense or whether it is, rather, always in an interruptive relation to history, totality, and violence. The meditation on identity in *Otherwise Than Being,* worked through a newly central notion of diachronic time, is unambiguous, sealing ethical subjectivity in that which *was,* which, in an important twist, becomes that which *could never have been:* the immemorial as otherwise than being, where being itself is configured (then punctured) as time. Once subjectivity is sealed in this temporal anti- and ante-sequentiality, we can only understand Levinas after all context for understanding collapses—*neither totality nor the interruption of totality.*

With what are we left? Again, the abyss belongs to beginning, which in *Otherwise Than Being* is found in the consequences of eliminating the reciprocity of the saying and the said. Whereas in *Totality and Infinity* one meets the other with full hands, and so begins in that relation-without-relation with *something,* Levinas's retreat from language in *Otherwise Than Being* is devastating. And therein lies beginning's abyss, where we begin having already failed, having seen our will and effort consumed by the abyssal distance between the original said and the preoriginal saying. I can only render a said to the Other, yet the Other's saying initiates my subjectivity. To begin with this Other, to begin as a response to a saying which has already vanished at the moment of its manifestation—"at the price of betrayal" (OB 6), Levinas writes—is to begin, fated to failure. The ground gives, as it did for Zarathustra, and any beginning-as-response is a movement into the finite open of the possible, commanded and structured by the infinity of the necessary.

Here Levinas meets Nietzsche in the space of beginning with nothing, in a space bordered by the abyss, and so at a moment of (in their peculiar sense) the historical experience of catastrophe. The collapse of what, in all of its pretensions, might have promised to give necessity to the open possibility and impose a finitude on the commanding necessary, sets us adrift. That sense of being adrift is a site of conversation, though this is a wholly different kind of conversation for philosophy. Indeed, this is a conversation with the shared resignation to—even embrace of—the fact that there will be no redemption for the aesthetics of life and response. Rather, this is a conversation about how to live with the impossible, how to remember always that the catastrophe has given birth to who and what we are, and that beginning's abyss twists us free in order that we may wander without a purpose, without a sense of the good or right outside of fidelity to the rights of loss over us and the mixture of sadness and ecstasy that comes with being submitted to those rights as the precondition of an open future. This is a conversation under the watchful, melancholic, and even hopeful eye of their distinctive angel of history.

———

As abyss belongs to beginning, we are projected by the abyss into a future and given the abyss for thinking. Ecstasy and the ethical, with all of their melancholic shading, emerge nonetheless as a sense of possibility and perhaps even hope. Benjamin's rendering of Klee's angel of history is thereby transformed from the one who gazes at corpses—both literal and figurative, in the cases of Nietzsche and Levinas—into the one who imagines the new future. Indeed, beginning and beginning's abyss attend to the complex folding of the angel's backward glance at history's catastrophe into his propulsion forward.

And, further, it is here that Nietzsche's and Levinas's meditations on beginning become important for theorizing what it means for human communities to begin again after historical disasters. This might seem an abrupt shift of focus, from high theory to urgent practice, except that Nietzsche's and Levinas's great gift to the problem of beginning lies in thinking from the most disastrous sense of abyss. So this hyperbole prepares the ground for thinking about what it means to respond to the catastrophe of human violence. Traditions collapse for philosophers in the transformation of thought. Traditions also collapse for communities in disastrous internal violence. In cases of overwhelming state violence, for example, a community is left with very little, almost nothing with which to begin claiming meaning. This nothing might be the literal collapse of the prior state or the moment in which the state reckons with an untenable, unworkable model of the past in order to conceive a wholly different future. In both cases, the collapse of political life leaves two options in its ruins: a return to the old order or the forging of something altogether new. While neither Nietzsche nor Levinas pose their work in such complex terms of transformation, the possession of beginning by the abyss catches sight of the same site: beginning as utterly ungrounded, beginning as burdened by memory of pain, beginning as the wholly new and unprecedented.

By way of conclusion, then, I want to ask a question about the gravity of thinking. Whatever Nietzsche's playfulness and gaming, whatever Levinas's disinterestedness and earnestness, both are joined in the gravity of the task of beginning. The gravity of the task of beginning initiates the metanarrative against the metanarrative, the grand countertellings that go by the names self-overcoming and the ethical. Everything is at stake, and the discourses of both Nietzsche and Levinas match that sense of stake. In that sense, the lack of a vision of the future is appropriately attuned to the abyss that belongs to beginning: total evacuation, total indeterminacy, indefiniteness, and perhaps for both, infinity.

At this point, however, I'm drawn back to a pair of scenes from Abbas Kiarostami's 1991 semi-documentary *Life and Nothing More*. In this film, the second in his *Earthquake Trilogy*, Kiarostami explores the aftereffects of a catastrophic earthquake in rural Iran. The lead character, a filmmaker, travels a devastated series of highways and side roads through equally devastated towns. In other words, it is a film about traumatic pain and its aftermath, in this case the traumatic pain of natural catastrophe. We might expect Kiarostami's lead character to meet with townspeople telling tales of the unspeakable experience of mass destruction. Indeed, the fixed, lingering shots that structure the film suggest just such trauma. The trauma is there, without a doubt. But what is not there is the gravity of thought in response to such devastation. Rather, the filmmaker meets and talks first with a man carrying a toilet seat. Then an extended conversation with a young man who was just married in the ruins—quite literally on top of the rubble—of his community. What are we to make of Kiarostami's witnesses to catastrophe? Are they inauthentically attuned to what has happened and how nothing can be the same afterward? Or do we theorists (of which Kiarostami may have been one) infuse such catastrophes with a gravity of thought that eclipses the mundanity of life when life not only *does* go on, but *must* go on? After all, the evacuation of one's home and place does not mean one is also alleviated of the need to sit comfortably, in privacy, and, well, "to evacuate" oneself—or marry one's beloved and begin the mundane domestic life the young male character embodies.

What kind of space of conversation might this mundanity of life open when life goes on? How are we to register the gravity of thinking after the abyss in that mundanity? How, indeed, are we to begin accounting for a conversation between the one who clings to the toilet seat and the one who proclaims the Overman or the ethical? This is an important conversation, for both the mundanity and the gravity of thinking after disaster belong to the same community of those who have nothing. And both belong to beginning's abyss.

NOTES

1. Friedrich Nietzsche, "Postcard to Overbeck" (1881), in *The Portable Nietzsche*, trans. Walter Kaufmann (New York: Viking, 1968), 92.
2. Martin Heidegger, "The Origin of the Work of Art," in *Basic Writings*, ed. David Farrell Krell (New York: HarperCollins, 1993), 171.
3. Heidegger, "The Origin of the Work of Art," 168.
4. Walter Benjamin, "Theses on the Philosophy of History," trans. Harry Zohn, in *Illuminations* (New York: Schocken, 1991), 254.
5. Benjamin, "Theses," 258.

6. John Sallis, *Crossings: Nietzsche and the Space of Tragedy* (Chicago: University of Chicago Press, 1991), 23–25.

7. Alphonso Lingis, *The Community of Those Who Have Nothing in Common* (Bloomington: Indiana University Press, 1994).

8. Sallis, *Crossings*, 2.

9. See Peter Sloterdijk, *Thinker on Stage: Nietzsche's Materialism*, trans. Jamie Owen Daniel (Minneapolis: University of Minnesota Press, 1989), 83.

10. Sallis, *Crossings*, 52.

11. Sloterdijk, *Thinker on Stage*, 79.

9

Beyond Suffering I Have No Alibi

DAVID BOOTHROYD

> To see somebody suffer is nice, to make somebody suffer even nicer—that is a hard proposition, but an ancient, powerful human-all-too-human proposition. . . . No cruelty, no feast: that is what the oldest and longest period in human history teaches us.
> —Nietzsche, *On the Genealogy of Morals*

> For pure suffering, which is intrinsically meaningless and condemned to itself without exit, a beyond takes shape in the inter-human.
> —Levinas, *Useless Suffering*

Levinas *and* Nietzsche?

Suffering and vulnerability to the cruelty of violence constitute the contexts of Nietzsche's and Levinas's accounts of morality and moral value. Suffering, moreover, is central for both of them to the formation of moral selfhood. For Nietzsche, it is through the refusal of the meanings attributed to suffering by the herd that the sovereign noble both differentiates himself from the herd and contemplates a reversal of the will, which has become mired in forms of ascetic idealism that are "hostile to life." For Levinas, ethical responsibility is premised on the radical differentiation of suffering in me from the suffering of the other, such that the ethical subject can be open to the approach of the other. A principal focus of this chapter will be the significance attached by each of them to the materiality of sensation and embodiment in their accounts of subjectivity. For both philosophers, I shall argue, however different the destinations of their thinking, the passage of thought "beyond suffering" is crucial—for Nietzsche to what he refers to as "the affirmation of life," for Levinas to the claims he makes concerning "infinite responsibility."

Richard Cohen has written, in his admirable book *Ethics, Exegesis, and Philosophy,* that Nietzsche was "troubled" by the "'meaninglessness of suffering'" and that he "rejects all interpretations whatsoever for suffering," finally offering only a "brave but fantastic heralding of the heralding of yet another messiah: Zarathustra, heralding the Overman."[1] I want to begin by recalling, however, that it is only from the perspective of herd morality that the "meaninglessness" of suffering is an issue, according to Nietzsche; only the "lower type" of human being suffers from the "meaninglessness of suffering"—by bringing it upon themselves. Of course, this entire discourse might be judged highly objectionable, even protofascistic nonsense, were it not for the simple fact that the noble and the herd are also to be understood as aspects of every one of us. And, for that reason, everywhere there is tension and loathing between these "two" in Nietzsche's genealogical account, we are effectively referred back to the internal struggle between them. Nietzsche's analysis of morality in the *Genealogy* goes hand in hand with the critique of antithetical thinking per se.

Suffering, I want to suggest, is a point of condensation for Nietzsche's and Levinas's respective philosophical positions tout court. It is fundamental for Nietzsche's project, expressed in such terms as "becoming," "overcoming," and "the affirmation of life," and for Levinas's project of ethics, expressed in terms of the "humanism of the other" and "transcendence." Both of them articulate responses to the problem of "the meaninglessness of suffering" from *within* suffering itself. My own questions in this context concern the sense in which Nietzschean affirmation and Levinasian responsibility are accessible only "beyond suffering." Are these notions of affirmation and responsibility complementary or mutually exclusive alternatives, and what is at stake in deciding between them?

There is, of course, no denying that these thinkers generally present us with radically differing perspectives on suffering. In Nietzsche we read:

> You want if possible—and there is no madder "if possible"—*to abolish suffering;* and we?—it really does seem that *we* would rather increase it and make it worse than it ever has been! . . . And do you understand . . . that *your* pity is for the "creature in man," for that which has to be formed, broken, forged, torn, burned, annealed, refined—that which has to *suffer* and *should* suffer?   (BG §225)

And in Levinas we read:

> The vortex—suffering of the other, my pity for his suffering, his pain
> over my pity, my pain over his pain, etc.—stops at me. The I is what
> involves one movement more in this iteration. My suffering is the cy-
> nosure of all the sufferings—and all the faults, even of the fault of my
> persecutors, which amounts to suffering the ultimate persecution, suf-
> fering absolutely.   (LR 122n 20)

This juxtaposition is illustrative of the inescapable difficulty of trying to
think with Nietzsche *and* Levinas on suffering: the strategic and fictitious
"we," the voice of Nietzsche's aristocratic noble at pains to differentiate itself from the "you" of the herd, cannot strictly be compared to the actuality
of the inclusive Levinasian "me"—which includes Levinas himself, me, you,
and every other singular "me" for whom, on the matter of the responsibility for suffering, Levinas's last word will always be "the buck stops here."
The initial difficulty I identify, then, concerns the matter of the "who" or
"what" of suffering, and this in turn directs us to a set of questions concerning various relationships: for instance, the relationship between the self
and suffering—both myself in relation to my suffering and my relation to
the other in his or her suffering, and not forgetting the other's relation to
me in my suffering. The way I shall approach these relationships now is
along the lines of connection they suggest between Nietzsche's and Levinas's thinking of "individuation" and "separation," respectively, and the
roles they play in their discourses on pain.

Pain and Individuation

One of Nietzsche's earliest and most abstract figures of suffering can be
found in his early work, *The Birth of Tragedy,* in the sufferings of the God
Dionysus. As Keith Ansell-Pearson notes, Dionysus experiences the sufferings *of individuation* as such, adding:

> This gives us a profound and pessimistic way of looking at the world:
> what exists is a unity and primordial oneness; individuation is mere ap-
> pearance and is the primal source of all evil; art offers the joyous hope
> that the spell of individuation can be broken and unity restored. We

suffer from life because we are individuals alienated from nature and because consciousness of this separation afflicts us.[2]

If we let this stand as an early sketch of the Nietzschean project of thinking, then we can say it is generally aimed at producing a reversal of this metaphysics of individuation and at a re-aestheticization of life. In contrast to such a reorientation of thought toward the restoration of "unity," the orientation of thought "beyond being" in Levinas's work is actually premised on an account of individuation as the "substantive" subject's separation from being: separation is established as the fundamental condition of possibility of the orientation of the "I" toward the Other (*l'Autrui*) by way of my relationship to the face of the other person whose separate existence is secured. Separation is accomplished, for Levinas, in the "upsurge" of the existent, which sustains itself through "nourishment," "labor," and "enjoyment" in relation to "the element" that it inhabits; the existent is born of "effort" and it can collapse in "fatigue" (as the phenomenological studies in *Existence and Existents* and *Totality and Infinity* claim to show). Such an existent can suffer, but its life is happiness and enjoyment in the first instance: "suffering is the failing of happiness; it is not correct to say that happiness is an absence of suffering" (TI 115). Phenomenological descriptions such as these offered by Levinas do not refer to any consciousness; they are rather presented as descriptions of moments (or "instants") of the existent's life.

The achievement of aestheticized life in its highest form for Nietzsche is premised on a prior accomplishment of a certain *dis*-individuation rather than an individuation, whereas the "substantivity" of the subject for Levinas is premised on the individuation (separation) of the existent from existence in general (or impersonal being—the "*il y a*"). Levinas's account of the existent explicitly aims to *counter* the characteristic forms of the "dissolution of subject" (TI 298) that he identifies with much of modern philosophy—especially that of Heidegger and, perhaps less obviously, Nietzsche. Where these two accounts of suffering touch, I suggest, is in terms of a suffering that causes, or threatens to cause, the *failure* of a certain projected fulfillment—for Levinas that of the "satisfaction of needs" of the existent, for Nietzsche life's quest for "unity" as the reunification with nature. Though Nietzsche equates Dionysian "joy" with such *dis*-individuation, and "enjoyment" is said to secure separation for Levinas, and though Nietzsche valorizes a return to "unity," whereas "ipseity" is the condition for transcendence for Levinas, with suffering, in both cases, we are in the presence of a certain less-than-wholly-individualized subject; a subject that is either halfway to coming into being or halfway to becoming unified—depending on the "direction" one supposes. In both accounts the suffering of such a subject threatens to forestall the process at hand, and what is called for is the unblocking of its movement.

One way to approach the relationship between the two philosophers, then, is to consider how they each understand the relationship between suffering and what lies "beyond suffering." Intriguingly, both philosophers address the problem of the "meaninglessness of suffering," but neither supposes the "abolition of suffering" to be a meaningful goal: suffering is approached by both, rather, as a feature of the human condition. Any justification of suffering, or theodicy, is impossible not only because of the disproportionate degree of suffering in the world (the paradigm of which, today, is the excess of suffering represented by the Holocaust),[3] but just as much because of the lateness of the justification, in the sense that it comes always "after the fact" of suffering and hence always deals with its representation. Having rejected theodicy from their differing perspectives, Nietzsche and Levinas both direct their thought to the question of how we might *live* our proximity to suffering.

Suffering and the Body

Even though *The Birth of Tragedy* presents an abstract image of suffering, one apparently far removed from the suffering experienced in the body and the banality of physical pain, it is important to remember that such "high-mindedness" is grounded in the materiality of sensation. In a note at the end of the first essay of the *Genealogy*, Nietzsche says: "Every table of values, every 'thou shalt' known to history or the study of ethnology, needs first and foremost a *physiological* elucidation; rather than a psychological one" (GM 37). And at the root of the second essay's account of how modern moral indignation over suffering is aimed not "at suffering itself, but at the meaninglessness of suffering" (GM 48) is a recollection of how historical punishment in the form of the infliction of bodily pain in torture was through and through a "physiological" matter. The cultures of antiquity, such as the Greeks, Romans, Egyptians, and more recently even the medieval Germans, Nietzsche notes, lived by penal codes that were practiced quite literally on the body of the miscreant (GM 42). By showing how such corporal punishments were, in fact, entirely "meaningful" practices within certain cultures, Nietzsche presents his evidence that "meaningless suffering" is actually a recent invention. In his genealogy of the concept of "suffering as meaningful," he locates such punishments "half way" (in the sense I indicated earlier and corresponding to a particular stage of individuation) between the characterization of a relation to suffering as pure "joy" and "festivity" and the transformation of the concept of debt (*Schuld*) into that of guilt (*Schulden*). Punishments are indicative of a point where "compensation is made up of a warrant for and entitlement to cruelty" (GM 88–90). There is no need here to recall the full trajectory of Nietzsche's account of how the "negative" value assigned to suffering emerges through various stages of the reversal of its origin in "the joyous life," culminating in Christianity's seeking to abolish suffering altogether. I wish only to recall at this point how the "superior type," the noble, accomplishes individuation in the form of his or her *response* to the suffering of *pain*. Nietzsche's texts frequently invoke examples of the life subjected to extreme suffering, in the pains of torture and punishment or in those of illness. In each case, the suffering of pain forces the sufferer into the sensual dimension of bodily existence, a force against which the body itself can offer no resistance. It can do nothing (other than suffer), and its becoming thus falters in such pure suffering. However, Nietzsche views such a condition of life positively, as the occasion for a revaluation of suffering, and thereby of life itself.

In their thinking on suffering, Nietzsche and Levinas overlap most significantly, I suggest, in their respective accounts of the formation of morality as it emerges from the experience of the body. Nietzsche emphasizes this in many places, for example, in Zarathustra's "I am body and nothing beside" (TZ 61; a sentence uncannily echoed in Levinas's remark that I am "entrails in a skin" [TI 77]), and, for instance in the following late remark from *Will to Power:* "Our most sacred convictions, the unchanging elements in our supreme values, are judgments of our muscles" (WP 173). Similarly, the suffering of the "I" for each of them, as noted above, is an "undergoing" rather than *conatus essendi*. The meaning of suffering, as such, has its origin in the *response* to pain undergone at the level of sensation. The manner in which they each articulate their thinking on this point may differ, but the rootedness of the pained subject in material life, approached by way of the theme of embodiment, is crucial to both. In neither case, let us be clear, are we referred to the body as it is objectified in the sciences of biology, physiology, and anatomy, all of which deal with *representations* of the body: both thinkers direct us, rather, to the not-yet-represented materiality of sensation. For Nietzsche, the sensibility of the body is the origin of "our most sacred convictions," and the suffering body signals the possibility of overcoming the individuation it suffers in its very suffering of extreme pain. Even Christ himself, in the most painful moment of his suffering on the cross, Nietzsche speculates, may have discovered the "complete disillusionment and enlightenment in regard to the deceptions of life" and thereby "insight into himself." This is perhaps evident, suggests Nietzsche, if the words "'My God, why hast thou forsaken me!'" are understood in their "ultimate significance" (DB 114). Extreme pain, for Nietzsche, is the occasion for self-mastery and self-insight, the production of something new, growth and the affirmation of life. It is because of the transformative power of sensate suffering that suffering is deemed to be necessary—and desirable. The difference between aristocratic and ascetic sensibilities is that the former appropriates and directs the energies of suffering "inward," using them to reinvent the self, whereas the latter directs them "outward" in a gesture of pity for all those whom it recognizes to be *the same* as itself—to all "humanity." Pain thus places the sufferer in a situation where "it could go either way."

That Levinas also directs us to this same point of "decision" is most clearly to be seen in his account of ethical subjectivity, where he speaks of the "subject" in terms of its being a "being-in-a-skin," as he does throughout *Otherwise Than Being*.[4] In his account of ethical subjectivity, the skin is said to be "a modality of the subjective" (OB 26) —a nonphilosophical, unthematized actuality, no less. And yet this "actual" should not be misconstrued as the *physical* skin—which is indeed only "known" by way of its conceptualization in the natural sciences. It is discussed, rather, as the as-yet *undecided*, as *both* vulnerability and absolute passivity: "exposure to the other is at one and the same time the surface of all possible 'contact' and the exposedness to injury, wounding and violence—and physical pain itself. As a passivity, in the paining of the pain felt, sensibility is a vulnerability" (OB 55).

Levinas holds fast to this moment of the undecidedness of pain in his phenomenological discourse in order to reveal the manner in which "the possibility in suffering of suffering for nothing prevents the passivity in it from *reverting into an act*" (OB 74; emphasis mine). Where Nietzsche's thinking goes outward from pain in the direction of *dis*-individuated "unity," Levinas's thinking goes toward what he calls the superindividuation of the substantive subject as a being-in-a-skin: "The individuation, or superindividuation, of the ego (*le Moi*) consists in being itself, in its skin," but, take note, this is "without sharing the *conatus essendi* of all beings which are beings in themselves" (OB 118). Is it not possible to say here that Nietzschean *dis*-individuation directed at the accomplishment of "unity" and Levinasian "superindividuation" of the substantive "being-in-a-skin" directed at the openness to alterity share a common starting point, if we understand this starting point to be the rejection of a certain egological interiority? In other words, both Nietzsche's and Levinas's projects are premised on a certain notion of "dis-individuation," if one understands that as a refusal of the naturalness of the psychological notion of "the ego" or "self." For Levinas, this is the moment in which there is an "ambiguity" of which the "body is the very articulation," in which "it frees itself from all the weight of the world, from immediate and incessant contacts" and is "at a distance" (TI 116). All of this pertains to the "I" viewed from the perspective of the "I." In Nietzsche it corresponds to a point at which there is a tentative balance of the forces that are given the names "noble" and "herd": the herd becomes, so to speak, self-obsessed, and its pity (*Mitleid*) for the suffering of the other is simply an inversion of self-pity as it turns outward. The noble is presented as the disruption of this equilibrium through the articulation of its contempt for the herd as it turns inward. And just as these two perspectives are in reality aspects of a play of forces at work within one individual, Levinas's "I" emerges through a process of differentiation from what is other (*autre*), played out through the satiation of its material needs (for example, in the satisfaction of the hunger it suffers). This accomplishment of independent existence—interiority or ipseity—which, I am suggesting, could just as well be called the "becoming I," is the necessary precondition of such an ethical subject's orientation toward an alterity beyond being.

The significant *difference* between Nietzsche and Levinas, which we must pursue further, concerns what happens next.

Meaningless Suffering and Useless Suffering

For Nietzsche the theological conundrum of the "meaninglessness" of suffering, in response to which the herd resorts to theodicy, marks the point of its entrapment in a cycle of bad repetition; it is, in other words, a figure of the "eternal return of same," but a negative one, one that can be discerned in the structure of the *Mitleid,* which is redoubled in the pity expressed *for* suffering and multiplied further in the pity for that pity. The herd is thus caught in a downward spiral of pity. It wills suffering upon itself in order to indulge itself further; it embraces, even celebrates its victimhood and becomes a neutered will to impotence. It would be only too easy (and shortsighted) to view Levinas's discursive deployment of the biblical figures of "the widow, the orphan and the stranger" in his articulation of responsibility for the other human being—and especially his suggestion that the other person is "a value"[5]—as the insignia of Nietzsche's ascetic priest. But to do so would be to disregard the manner in which "what happens next" comes after his account of the substantive subject by means of a certain phenomenology.

If we accept the discoveries of this phenomenology, worked through in extraordinary detail throughout Levinas's writings and culminating in his claim that "suffering sensibility . . . is an ordeal more passive than experience,"[6] then we have to accept that the suffering that is a pure "undergoing" (of pain) is of a radically distinct order from "suffering as meaningful." Meaningful suffering is but the reflection of suffering in conceptual thought. It is on the basis of his phenomenological studies that Levinas can insist on this splitting of suffering into two as an irreducible fact and mark "meaningless suffering" as a simple tautology: it has the descriptive value of "suffering suffers." Nietzsche's discourse misses this discovery, not only because he has no recourse to phenomenology but because he is preoccupied with the struggle between two impersonal perspectives on suffering occurring within *the same* individual, whose ideal resolution (in both senses of "whose") he conceives of as a re-turn toward primordial unity. Levinas's description of the suffering of pain as "unassumable" by the subject is of the pain which "results from an excess, a 'too much' which is inscribed in *sensorial content*" (US 156). As such, it neither lacks nor awaits *a meaning;* it is said, rather, to "penetrate" the dimension of meaning, which is "grafted on to it." He continues:

> What counts in the non-freedom of the undergoing of suffering is the concreteness of the *not* looming as a hurt more negative than an apophantic not. This negativity of evil is, probably, the source or kernel of any apophantic negation. The *not* of evil is negative right up to nonsense. All evil refers to suffering. It is the *impasse* of life and being. The

evil of pain, the harm itself, is the explosion and most profound articulation of absurdity.   (US 157)

This could perhaps be viewed mistakenly as an *identification* of suffering with evil (*mal*), and hence as making an error comparable to that made by Nietzsche's herd, were it not for the fact that this does not amount to the same thing as the identification of the *meaning* of suffering with evil. The coincidence of evil and absurdity in suffering means, rather, that suffering is "for nothing." There is nothing to be said about suffering qua suffering. By itself suffering is without any moral implication. However, Levinas's "positive" thesis is that for

> pure suffering, which is intrinsically meaningless [i.e., useless] and condemned to itself without exit, a beyond takes shape in the inter-human . . . the suffering of suffering, the suffering for the useless suffering of the other person, the just suffering in me for the unjustifiable suffering of the Other, opens upon suffering the ethical perspective of the inter-human. . . . Properly speaking, the inter-human lies in the non-indifference of one to another, in a responsibility of one for another.
> (US 158–65)

The brazen "no cruelty, no feast" of Nietzsche's noble is effectively challenged, though obliquely, by Levinas's "no suffering, no ethics." Levinas's ethical perspective, that of responsibility, is no more assumable, to use his word, *by me* than is my own suffering, and to be ethical is not *my* decision: it is not a matter of my good character or my personal qualities but rather of what intransitively articulates my very existence, my entry into existence as such.

As it is made clear repeatedly in *Otherwise Than Being*, my responsibility for the suffering of the Other is a matter of *accusation*. It comes to me prior to any subjective interpretation I may place upon it: I may regard it as a matter of my shame, guilt, or conscience; I may "walk away" in fear, but this does not diminish its objective ethical implication for me. That such an "absolute alterity" and "ethical objectivity" remained invisible to Nietzsche is illustrated well by the following passage:

> If we love, honour, admire someone [who] . . . is suffering . . . our feeling of love, reverence and admiration changes in an essential respect: it grows *tenderer;* that is, the gulf between us and him seems to be

bridged. . . . We try to divine what it is that eases his pain, and we give it to him . . . but, above all, if he wants us to *suffer* at his suffering, we give ourselves out to be *suffering;* in all this, however, we have the *enjoyment of active gratitude*—which, in short, is benevolent revenge.[7]

(DB 138–39)

Nietzsche here views tenderness toward the suffering of the other as an inverted form of self-interest, and the scene of suffering as the continuation of a struggle of wills. The Levinasian notion of the Other's "absolute otherness" (*Autrui*)—the coincidence of the Good beyond being and the other person who suffers—remains undiscovered by Nietzsche. This is not, however, the consequence of a truly vengeful, malevolent, or sadistic philosophy of suffering; it is, rather, a consequence of Nietzsche's *theoretical* insistence on the other as an individual who *always calculates* his or her own interests, even in his or her moment of suffering. Levinas's phenomenology of suffering shows to the contrary that in moments of extreme suffering the "I" can no longer even constitute itself so as to be so self-pitying: hence his idea of an infinite responsibility that is "all mine," with no scope for "pretence" on either side. In contrast to Nietzsche's thought in the above citation, the "tenderness" of my proximity to the Other in his or her suffering is expressed in terms of the "tenderness of skin," which "*is* the very gap between approach and approached, a disparity, a non-intentionality, a non-teleology," and "I can enjoy and suffer . . . because contact with skin is still proximity of a face" (OB 90). We might therefore say that Nietzsche's account of "tenderness" is of the psychological "tenderness of the heart," whereas Levinas's "tenderness of the skin" points to the precedence of my ethical obligation.

Pity, Compassion, and the Ambiguity of Language

The Judeo-Christian discourse of pity (*Mitleid*) is so dominant that Nietzsche's rejection of it must struggle against the determining force of language itself, which forces us to speak in its terms—as must Nietzsche in order to get through to his audience. This situation is compounded somewhat further by the fact that the term "*Mitleid*" in German expresses both "pity" and "compassion." In *Beyond Good and Evil* he unravels the structure of *Mitleid* so as to distinguish between the pitying of the pitiful (essentially for themselves and their kind) and the pity the strong feel *for* the piteous attitude of the weak toward the world while at the same time blaming the weak for infecting the strong with such piteousness:

> Anyone conscious of creative powers and an artist's conscience will look down on [the herd] with derision, though not without pity. Pity for *you!* That to be sure is not pity for "social distress," for "society" and its sick and unfortunate, for the vicious and broken from the start who lie all around us; even less is it pity for the grumbling, oppressed, rebellious slave classes who aspire after domination—they call it "freedom." *Our* pity is a more elevated, more far-sighted pity—we see how *man* is diminishing himself, how *you* are diminishing him!   (BG §225).

This is just one of Nietzsche's many attempts to distinguish noble and herd understandings of *Mitleid*. Noble *Mitleid* amounts to saying "I do feel 'sorry' for you, but above all in that you feel sorry for yourselves." Characteristically, he expresses contempt (*Veracht*) for this wallowing in the reciprocity of piteous sympathy for the suffering of the herd. Elsewhere he says that what the herd cannot appreciate is that "to offer pity is as good as to offer contempt" (DB 135). All of this is articulated within a *discourse of antithesis* forced, as it were, upon the noble (and Nietzsche), who responds to *the concept* of pity by stridently calling for an *intensification of suffering* as an antidote to the sentiment ultimately directed at its elimination. Why? Because unopposed pity does not merely serve to define the moral identity or value system of the herd. If that were all it did, it would be safe to let the herd go off on its self-piteous, suffering way. Pity signifies a threat to the health of the noble—it is a contagion, and the sick are viewed as the greatest threat to the strong, who must, therefore, guard against the corrosive effects of pity.

Nietzsche's legitimate critical concern—"beyond suffering" and the form of *Mitleid* that suffering demands in all of this—is clearly with the fate of culture as a whole. It is not with the relationship between anyone in particular and any particular other. Levinas's thinking "beyond suffering," on the other hand, returns us to the primal scene of a certain "intimacy"; something that cannot be "given as an example" of some greater whole (such as culture) "or be narrated as an edifying discourse" (US 163).

I now want to look more closely at the suggestion—voiced by Richard Cohen, for example—that Levinas takes up, specifically, "Nietzsche's challenge" (EEP 270), which I take to refer generally to the problem of moral value after the "death of God." Bearing in mind the discussion so far, I want to return briefly to their overlapping interpretations of the *ambiguity* of the other's suffering in its relation to the perspectivist strategies of each philosopher. First, there is a sense in which they each *refuse* the suffering of the other, albeit for different reasons. For Nietzsche it is because suffering signifies a manipulative demand for pity; for Levinas it is because the "I" cannot literally suffer the other's suffering any more than it can *be* the other. The other's suffering is ambiguous for Nietzsche because the other (the herd, for example) prevails within me, it is in fact a part of me, and without this other's suffering "in me" I could not contemplate the prospect of overcoming the self that I already am. The Other's suffering is ambiguous in Levinas because the Other is the one who "obliges" me *to be* responsible and calls me to my responsibility, such that responsibility may be said to be the very modality of my subjectivity. In both cases, ambiguity is a matter of the coarticulation of (their respective senses of) self and other. In Nietzsche's work this takes the form of the play of opposing forces "present within one soul," and for Levinas this corresponds to the precedence of the ethical obligation to the other person over the egological relation of the self (*le soi*) to itself. Second, it is now clear that the ambiguity of suffering is a matter also of the ambiguity of language and, specifically, related to the limitations imposed by the subject/predicate structure of language. In their philosophical responses to this, both Nietzsche and Levinas use perspectivism in formulating *theories* of value. This is evident in Nietzsche's *Genealogy* as a whole being forced to express itself in the language of the herd while simultaneously asserting the noble's "seigneurial privilege of giving names" (GM 13). It is precisely because of this "privilege" that one can only too easily read Nietzsche as an enemy of "compassion" (*Mitleid*) in his critique of "pity" (*Mitleid*). But his negative account of "pity" does not imply a negative account of, or for that matter even an insensitivity on his part to, the value of and need for what is ordinarily called "compassion" in the face of actual suffering. All one can say is that the danger Nietzsche highlights is that of "over-identifying" with the suffering of the other, which leads to deleterious effects on oneself. The dead God of salvation, let us recall, died "of his pity for Man" (TZ 114).

The ambiguity of language in Levinas's ethics comes to the fore in his attempts to articulate the difference and the asymmetry of the I-Other conjuncture and to give expression to the *unthematized* situation of suffering. It is evident in every attempt he makes at "unsaying" (*dédire*) the objectification effectuated by "the said" (*le dit*). Turning once again to how this plays out in Levinas's account of suffering: in the instant of physical pain, the very ex-istence of the "I" "merges with the impossibility of detaching oneself from suffering" (TO 69). Such pain is, "in its undiluted malignity," described as "useless" and "for nothing" (US 163). And, as he says elsewhere of the skin—Levinas's trope of unthematized sensibility— the suffering of it might also be described as "wholly sign, signifyingness itself" (OB 26). The Levinasian "I," which is "being-in-a-skin," exists as pure sensation. Richard Cohen in his summary of Levinas on this point says, "Just as a bodily being enjoys enjoying, it suffers suffering. The unwanted and at the same time inescapable character of pained corporeal reflexivity is what distinguishes the phenomenon of suffering: one suffers from suffering itself" (EEP 272). The "reflexivity" of the substantive "I" in its suffering is, emphatically, "bodily" rather than of consciousness. In speaking to us from within the discourse of phenomenology, of the pain lived by "me" from the perspective of the pain of the other person considered as *a* "me," this voice has to express such a "saying" in defiance of the subject/predicate structure of language. While "compassion" is perhaps the word that in its ordinary usage is best suited to express what I "feel" for the suffering other—and Cohen uses this word to name what Levinas calls "the only meaning to which suffering is susceptible"—Levinas's discourse of obligation and my being "hostage" to the Other, in *Otherwise Than Being*, emphasizes better the absence of any volition on my part with respect to what he calls my responsibility for the Other's suffering. From a transcendent perspective, there is the sense in which I and the other person are united in his or her suffering, but the term "united" here refers always to *relatio* rather than *res*. It is, as he says of it at one point, a "relation without relata" (TI xxx). Perspective, for both Nietzsche and Levinas, is always a matter of *relatio* rather than *res*. As far as my relation to the suffering of the other is concerned, then, this means that I do not, indeed cannot, suffer the other's suffering for him or her but, without ever willing it, I suffer *for* the other's suffering in me:

> In this perspective a radical difference develops between suffering in the Other, which for me is unpardonable and solicits me and calls me, and suffering in me, my own adventure of suffering, whose constitutional and congenital uselessness can take on a meaning, the only meaning to which suffering is susceptible, in becoming a suffering for the suffering—be it inexorable—of someone else. (US 159)

Despite its explicit origins in the physiology of the body and its experience of pain, one wonders whether Nietzsche's diagnosis of the general health of culture could ever be united with the reality of *individual suffering*. In contrast to the remoteness of the everyday to the Nietzschean project of "revaluation of all values," Levinas's ethics can be seen as move toward a certain kind of ethical realism or even an empiricism of suffering (notwithstanding all the caveats that apply to Levinas's own use of that term). The Other's suffering, his or her "pure pain," directs me to "the problem which pain poses 'for nothing': the inevitable and pre-emptory ethical problem of the medication which is my duty" (US 158). This particular formulation may be awkwardly Kantian rather than Levinasian, but "duty" is the way we tend to *think* and *represent* to ourselves the obligation that the suffering Other brings to me by virtue of his or her "absolute alterity." Hence, according to Levinas, I have no excuse and no alibi: *after* the death of the God of salvation, waiting any longer for His saving actions is "impossible without degradation" (US 159).

NOTES

1. Richard A. Cohen, *Ethics, Exegesis, and Philosophy* (Cambridge: Cambridge University Press, 2001), 270–71. Hereafter abbreviated EEP.
2. Keith Ansell-Pearson, *How to Read Nietzsche* (London: Granta, 2005), 12.
3. See EEP chap. 8 for a detailed discussion of this aspect of Levinas's account of suffering.
4. See my "Skin-Nihilism Now: Flaying the Face and Refiguring the Skin," in *Nihilism Now! Monsters of Energy,* ed. Keith Ansell-Pearson and Diane Morgan (London: Macmillan, 2000).
5. Emmanuel Levinas, "The Contemporary Criticism of the Idea of Value and the Prospects for Humanism" in *Value and Values in Evolution,* ed. E.A. Mariaz (New York: Gordon and Breach, 1979), 187.
6. Emmanuel Levinas, "Useless Suffering," trans. R. Cohen, in *The Provocation of Levinas,* ed. D. Wood and R. Bernasconi (London: Routledge, 1988), 157. Hereafter abbreviated US.
7. For further discussion of the relationship between love and contempt in Nietzsche's *Genealogy* and *Zarathustra,* also see my "Levinas and Nietzsche: In-between Love and Contempt," *Philosophy Today* 39, no. 4 (1995): 345–57.

10

Levinas, Spinozism, Nietzsche, and the Body

RICHARD A. COHEN

LEVINAS'S REJECTION of "Spinozism" means far more than a rejection of the philosophy of Baruch Spinoza. Spinozism certainly includes the philosophy of Spinoza, but it also includes the thought of such apparently disparate figures as Hegel, Marx, Freud, Heidegger, and, as I shall argue, Nietzsche. What then does Levinas mean by "Spinozism"? What is his argument against it? And how does Spinozism—and hence Levinas's radical opposition to it—manifest itself in Nietzsche's philosophy? These questions guide the present inquiry.

Levinas's Rejection of Spinozism

Levinas's opposition to Spinozism and his reasons for it are summed up in the final sentence of the first part—entitled "Separation and Absoluteness"—of *Totality and Infinity:* "Thought and freedom come to us from separation and from the consideration of the Other [*Autrui*]—this thesis is at the antipodes of Spinozism" (TI 105).

Spinozism denies the *transcendence* of thought and freedom because, *first,* it denies "separation," the independence of the human subject. It is thus "monist" or "pantheist," a philosophy of "immanence" and "totality." Ethics, in contrast, is based on separation, the "autonomy" of the "subject," and out of this independence of one subject from another it is based on "the consideration of the Other." For Levinas the irreducibility of the human and, based on this, the inter-human, constitutes the very "humanity of the human." Spinozism denies the legitimacy of the independence of these dimensions of signification. It denies freedom and humanity in the name of a greater totality. It is precisely this denial that prevails in the thought of Friedrich Nietzsche, though by embracing the body in contrast to the mind it takes a new and distinctive form beyond the Spinozism of Spinoza.

By *separation* Levinas means the independence of the human subject's interiority from both the amorphous anonymity of what Levinas calls the "there is" ("*il y a*"), an *apeiron* of be-ing, which threatens the subject's distinctiveness with dissolution from below, as it were; and the radical transcendence of the other person, which calls to and calls forth the subject from above, from moral obligation. But inwardness must not be understood in an ethereal sense, as self-consciousness, say, or as an act of representational or judgmental negation. Levinas speaks of human subjectivity as "created," not in the credulous religious sense of a miraculous existence posited ex nihilo but rather as embodiment beginning in the primitive "reflexivity" of self-sensing. The originary base of initiative, agency, and free will, then, occurs from out of an original circuit of sensing and sensations. "For an existent is an existent," Levinas writes in the paragraph before the one in which he announces his opposition to Spinozism, "only in the measure that it is free, that is, outside of any system, which implies dependence" (TI 104). Separation, then, means "unconditioned," an absolute, but an absolute that is nevertheless an embodiment and vulnerability whose contours are uncovered through phenomenological investigation.

Second, by "consideration of the Other" Levinas refers to another human being whose alterity is encountered only in the transcendence of moral obligations, that is, as moral imperative, from "above," in an "asymmetrical" relation with a "you" who disturbs the self-enclosure or complacency of the "I," giving rise to the responsible self, the self for-the-other. It is important to keep in mind that this structure emerges because the other person, too, is a separate being. And it is from the other's separation, from the other's independence, that the other transcends and "reconditions" the self.

The *relation* between these two terms, the independent subject and the transcendent other, occurs precisely and only as a moral relation, for it is only as a moral relation that radically separate selves can both be respected in their independence from one another and yet for all that also be in genuine proximity. The moral relation *as moral* cannot be looked at from the outside, however, but is a relationality within which human subjects are always already implicated—commanded—in the first-person singular. These two aspects, morality and singularity, are indeed the central "theses" of Levinas's entire philosophy, and they are central not as theses or themes but as impositions, provocations, imperatives. "Here," Levinas writes, "the relation connects not terms that complete one another and consequently are reciprocally lacking to one another, but terms that suffice to themselves" (TI 103). As we shall see, this means that Levinas's opposition to Nietzsche is based not on some a priori or idealist metaphysics, as one might imagine, but rather on a different conception of the nature and meaning of the human body and embodied sociality. Unlike Levinas's opposition to Spinoza's Spinozism, then, which is an opposition to an abstract or intellectualist rationalism, Levinas's opposition to Nietzsche's Spinozism meets Nietzsche on his own grounds, on the terrain of the body.

Spinozism, in any case, is constituted by the rejection of both points: separation and transcendence. It does this in one fell swoop by affirming the primacy and totality of context over terms—in Spinoza's case the systematic universal and necessary knowledge of modern science, and in Nietzsche's case the differential play of will to power. Here lies the meaning of Spinoza's famous refusal in his *Ethics* "to conceive man in nature as a kingdom within a kingdom."[1] Spinoza will treat humans as he treats everything: as objects subject to a strict "geometrical" logic. To deny that humanity is a kingdom within a kingdom, Spinoza must and does at once deny the independence of the self and the transcendence of the other. In other words, he denies the reality, as opposed to the ignorant person's illusory or imaginary belief, of both free will and morality. Heir to the rationalist tradition of Western thought, Spinoza bases his denial on the root affirmation that "Will and intellect are one and the same thing" (E 2: "Proposition, Corollary" 49, 96). For Nietzsche, as we know, the independence of the subject, its alleged freedom, is an untruth, an error, a "seduction of language" (GM 1: §13, 45).

How does Levinas respond to such thought? The crux of Levinas's argument depends, contrary to what many commentators have suggested, not on the transcendence or infinity of the other person but rather on the independence of the self—a self that in the other person is indeed encountered as transcendence. How, then, without arbitrary fiat, does Levinas defend the all-important notion of the subject's independence?

Self-Sensing

That subjectivity emerges as self-sensing, as an embodied way of being both engaged and disengaged in elemental sensations, is perhaps the earliest theme of Levinas's own thought. It appears already in 1935 in his article "On Escape," when Levinas was fresh from his training in Husserlian and Heideggerian phenomenology. There Levinas speaks of the existent's embodiment in terms of the unity of a dual movement or restlessness, at once, on the one hand, entrapment, enclosure, and self-compression, freighted with its own materiality and backed up against being, and, on the other hand, rebellion, a desire to escape, an urge to get out of this circuit of its own immanence. "The necessity of fleeing," he writes, "is put in check by the impossibility of fleeing oneself . . . precisely the fact of being riveted to oneself, the radical impossibility of fleeing oneself to hide from oneself, the unalterably binding presence of the I to itself" (OE 64). "In nausea," he continues, "which amounts to an impossibility of being what one is—we are at the same time riveted to ourselves, enclosed in a tight circle that smothers" (OE 66). In critical contrast to the Heideggerian analysis of Dasein opened up by and to being in an "ecstatic" subjectivity anxious before its own death and as such already a form of self-understanding as the revelation of being, for Levinas it is precisely the unbearable but inescapable self-compression of embodiment that "*is the very experience of pure being*" (OE 67).

After the war, Levinas will again return to this theme, the "solitude" of the self unhappily trapped in itself, extending his reflection with more precise phenomenological analyses that are found in his first two books, *Existence and Existents* and *Time and the Other*, both published in 1947. In *Existence and Existents* he will speak of the self's embodied self-enclosure as "fatigue and indolence" (EE 24): "There exists a weariness," he writes, "which is a weariness of everything and everyone, and above all a weariness of oneself" (EE 24). "Indolence makes one prostrate, idleness weighs us down, afflicts us with boredom" (EE 28). Or writing in a more traditional philosophical language: "There is a duality in existence, an essential lack of simplicity. The ego has a self, in which it is not only reflected, but with which it is involved like a companion or a partner; this relationship is what is called inwardness" (EE 28). This book goes on to describe the efforts of such a self to escape itself into the world through the ecstatic time (projective and retentive)—"temporality"—of labor, action, and representation, and finally, successfully, in the transcendent time of sociality. *Time and the Other* covers this same ground, ending also in the liberation afforded from immanence—whether of embodiment or worldliness or knowledge—by the only relation whose transcendence breaks being's adhesion to itself: the transcendence of the other person.

It is only after these careful phenomenological studies that in Levinas's masterwork, *Totality and Infinity*, the transcendence of the other receives its full articulation beyond the epistemological confines of phenomenology, as an ethical transcendence. Yet here, too, the entire second part, "Interiority and Economy," is devoted to what are now even more careful, closer, and more precise phenomenological analyses of the self as embodied and of the embodied self's futile efforts to escape its self-enclosure, its immanence, through the world, through labor, activity, and representational consciousness. After once again having laid the groundwork of the independence and solitude of the embodied self, Levinas *then* turns to consider "Exteriority and the Face" (title of section 3), that is, the transcendence of the other person encountered as moral imperative.

Levinas's second major work, *Otherwise Than Being; Or, Beyond Essence*, also returns to the embodied self, but this time to examine and elaborate its new way of being—shamed and responsible—responding to and suffering for the other. Thus the deepening or refinement of Levinas's thought follows the progression of ethics itself: beginning in embodied solitude, jolted by the face or transcendence of the other, and responding as an embodied responsibility for-the-other before itself. It is not a chronological movement, to be sure, but rather one of conditioned and conditioning, where the unconditioned solitary self is "re-conditioned," or decommissioned, *per impossibile* for rational thought, by the noncondition of the other person. Here, too, in the moral structure of being for-the-other, the language and impact of embodiment remains: the self is "turned inside out" by and for the other, "as though its very skin were still a way to shelter itself in being, exposed to wounds and outrage, emptying itself in a no-grounds, to the point of substituting itself for the other, holding on to itself only as it were in the trace of its exile" (OB 138). The passivity of the body is not surpassed or overcome, but now as responsibility the self is a body responsive to—because "pierced" by—the imperatives of the other, in a "suffering for the other" that holds a place higher than the self-initiated freedom of activity and reflection (Sartre) or the other-initiated freedom of being (Heidegger) or nature (Jonas). Such is the moral elevation Levinas calls the "humanity of the human," a life nobly lived, "loving the neighbor as oneself." Morality is not enacted as a disembodied spirituality but as a giving, and first, prior to a giving of things, it is a giving of oneself to the other.

The True and the Good: "Dangerous Life"

The true self, for Levinas, is therefore not literally true, a function of knowing, but good. By "good" Levinas does not mean an innate inclination, a predilection, or a graced disposition, which certain philosophers and theologians have posited but never proven and which certain horrible events of the last century and our own clearly belie. Rather, the good is the self's responsiveness to others, its interpersonal and social responsibility. "No one," Levinas has written, "is good voluntarily" (OB 11). One's nobler self is good, a being for-the-other more deeply—higher—than its ownmost being-for-itself. At the same time, it is by means of the self's goodness understood in these terms, and only by means of its goodness, that there is access to and, indeed, demand for the true, that is, for knowledge. The issue of the relation of the good to the true is complex, and all of its nuances cannot be presented here, but because it is important in terms of Levinas's critique of Spinozism generally and to Nietzsche's reevaluation of the value of knowledge, the following brief remarks must suffice to indicate the relation of the true to the good.

Truth, in contrast to opinion, is justified knowledge, propositions supported by appropriate and sufficient evidence. Beyond the confines of coherence and correspondence theories of truth, proposition candidates for truth must be validated by an intersubjective community. Levinas draws our attention to the fact that statements neither come out of the sky nor are confined to "minds." Whether they are proposed as truths or intended for different purposes, statements are first of all *enunciations,* significations said by persons to other persons. There is a *saying* that underlies and charges the *said.* It is to the ethical character of this order that Levinas calls attention. Enunciation or saying, the discursive character of speech as communication—what Levinas calls its "accusative" dimension—is the source of what is said, even if it does not appear as a thesis or theme within what is said. The inaccessibility of saying, which always transcends and yet brings forth the said, functions therefore as a sort of "paralogism," to use Kant's term, except that its orientation is not logical or epistemological but moral, a matter of ethics, of the other's elevation and the self's ennoblement. That the "saying" that is absent from the "said" is not and cannot become a theme is certainly a difficulty for philosophical reflection and perhaps explains its neglect, but this difficulty in no way justifies the exclusion or occlusion of its primacy in the upsurge of meaning.

Communication is not, however, simply a matter of making private thoughts public, as if everything is already accomplished within the confines of one's mind and then empirically made public to another. Enunciation is elicited. Why speak at all if everything is really said and done within one's own mind? Communication, in other words, is not simply added to signification. I will cite Levinas at some length on this point because it is both subtle and crucial if we are to understand how ethics is "first philosophy" and the source of truth.

> Those who wish to found on dialogue and on an original *we* the upsurge of egos, refer to an original communication behind the *de facto* communication (but without giving this original communication any sense other than the empirical sense of a dialogue or a *manifestation* of one to the other—which is to presuppose that *we* that is to be founded), and reduce the problem of communication to the problem of its certainty. In opposition to that, we suppose that there is in the transcendence involved in language a relationship that is not an empirical speech, but responsibility. . . . Communication with the other can be transcendence only as a dangerous life, a fine risk to be run. . . . Here there is proximity and not truth about proximity, not certainty about the presence of the other, but responsibility for him without deliberation, and without the compulsion of truths in which commitments arise, without certainty. . . . The trace in which a face is ordered is not reducible to a sign. . . .

> To thematize this relation is already to lose it, to leave the absolute pas-
> sivity of the self.   (OB 119–20)

The other as other, an alterity beyond what is said, signifies prior to empirical speech, solicits our saying, which is also beyond what is said, in a
communication that leaps, as it were, "as a dangerous life," to use Levinas's formula (one frontally challenging Nietzsche's "live dangerously"),
from one interiority to another, a communication in which one responds
to another prior to the certainties of truth, responds to the other as other,
that is, takes responsibility for the other first. It is in the risk of this moral
responsibility—solicitation and response, the "saying of the said"—wherein
lies the source of signification, including the rigorously controlled significations that constitute truth, and as such are demanded by the larger project
of human justice.

Nietzsche's Spinozism

It is profoundly revealing that Nietzsche, despite his fundamental criticisms
of Spinoza's rationalism, enthusiastically embraces Spinoza as his "precursor." This self-declared genealogy finds its clearest and fullest articulation
in a postcard of July 30, 1881, that Nietzsche wrote to his close friend and
former colleague at Basel, Professor Franz Overbeck. Here is the postcard
in full:

> I am utterly amazed, utterly enchanted. I have a *precursor,* and what a
> precursor! I hardly knew Spinoza: that I should have turned to him just
> *now,* was inspired by "instinct." Not only is his over-all tendency like
> mine—making knowledge the *most powerful* affect—but in five main
> points of his doctrine I recognize myself: this most unusual and loneli-
> est thinker is closest to me precisely in these matters: he denies the free-
> dom of the will, teleology, the moral world order, the unegoistic, and
> evil. Even though the divergences are admittedly tremendous, they are
> due more to the difference in time, culture, and science. *In summa:* my
> lonesomeness, which, as on very high mountains, often made it hard for
> me to breathe and made my blood rush out, is now at least a twosome-
> ness. Strange.[2]

The five points of agreement Nietzsche names can be summed up in one: a denial of the metaphysical underpinnings of morality. It is morality, of course, that requires a human will or agency that can be evaluated, that is to say, a will or decision-making process in some significant sense free, unconditioned, uncompelled. And it is morality, too, that affirms purpose, the aim of doing good rather than evil, opposing evil, promoting goodness and justice, and toward this end it is morality that exhorts the superiority of selflessness to selfishness. In his *Ethics* Spinoza had clearly argued for the falseness, indeed the illusoriness of all the metaphysical notions upon which morality is based. In his epistemology they are the product of imagination, not reason. They are unscientific, subjective rather than objective, and only hold sway for the ignorant masses driven by their passions, their bodily desires. But they have no truth-value for the few, the scientists and philosophers who know better, who, driven by their intellects (*amor intellectualis*), know scientifically (*ratio* and *scientia intuitiva*) the truth that the universe unfolds by strict and unbreakable necessity. A decade and many books after his postcard, in *Twilight of the Idols,* published just weeks after his own mental breakdown in early January 1889, hence in one of his last and one of his most unrestrained (if not exaggerated) books, Nietzsche formulates in his own name, and as his own, Spinoza's position as follows:

> One knows my demand of philosophers that they place themselves *beyond* good and evil—that they have the illusion of moral judgment *beneath* them. This demand follows from an insight first formulated by me: *that there are no moral facts whatever.* Moral judgment has this in common with religious judgment that it believes in realities which do not exist. Morality is only an interpretation of certain phenomena, more precisely a *mis*interpretation. Moral judgment belongs, as does religious judgment, to a level of ignorance at which even the concept of the real, the distinction between the real and the imaginary, is lacking: that at such a level 'truth' denotes nothing but things which we today call 'imaginings.'   (TL 55)

While still agreeing with Spinoza's writings of more than two centuries earlier, Nietzsche has here conveniently forgotten his name. Of course, in a few days Nietzsche will also forget his own name, or rather, famously, he will embrace "every name in history."[3]

Nietzsche's Differences from Spinoza

Keeping in mind their fundamental agreement to reject the several metaphysical principles that underlie morality (and religion), it is time to look more closely at the divergences of Nietzsche's Spinozism from Spinoza's. In this we are again guided by Nietzsche's postcard: "Even though the divergences are admittedly tremendous, they are due more to the difference in time, culture, and science." Though there are many divergences in this regard, here I have space enough only to mention two, namely, the shift from a theological world to a secular world and the rise of scientific historiography and historical consciousness, in order to more closely examine the third, which is also the most decisive, namely, the shift from a mechanistic to a vitalist model in the modern scientific worldview. Indeed, Nietzsche's much vaunted appreciation for historical consciousness is itself oriented by this third shift, as one sees already in the title and content of his early "untimely" study of history, *On the Use and Abuse of History for Life*—history, like everything else, is of value to Nietzsche only to the extent that it serves *life*.

From Mechanism to Vitalism

Darwin's *On the Origin of Species by Means of Natural Selection* was published in 1859, and *The Descent of Man* in 1871. The influence of these books, not simply their theses regarding the origin of humanity and the development of species—Nietzsche never accepted Darwin's doctrine of natural selection and considered it slavish, relying as it did on a quantitative rather than a qualitative standard of success—but their general outlook, their biological rather than mechanistic perspective, had the profoundest influence on the spiritual life of Europe in general and on Nietzsche's thought in particular. Despite his specific rejection of Darwin, there is no question that it is now biology and more specifically physiology that provide the dominant medium of Nietzsche's thought.

Nietzsche insists repeatedly that in contrast to the deathless abstract ideas of previous philosophers, his own thought is a "philosophy of life." In *The Gay Science*, for instance, he writes the following against Spinoza:

> These old philosophers were heartless; philosophizing was always a kind of vampirism. Looking at these figures, even Spinoza, don't you have a

sense of something profoundly enigmatic and uncanny . . . mere bones, mere clatter . . . I mean categories, formulas, *words* (for, forgive me, what was left of Spinoza, *amor intellectualis dei,* is mere clatter and no more than that: What is *amor,* what is *deus,* if there is not a drop of blood in them?).   (GS 333)

Nietzsche's thought is from the start and throughout always and self-consciously a philosophy of *life,* of health and sickness, strength and weakness, growth and decline, self-preservation and disintegration, a thought of instincts and organisms.

Spinoza and Nietzsche are both elitists, dividing humanity between the approved few and the disparaged many. Given his commitment to science, for Spinoza the few are those for whom the mind is primary, hence those who are intellectually active, who know the truth and conform to it, while the many are those for whom the body is primary, hence are passive, driven by their emotions and faulty imaginations. Nietzsche will both reverse this priority, recognizing the body as the genealogy of the mind, and alter the meaning both of the mind, now a derivative function, and the body, no longer an abstract mechanism but a vital multiplicity of forces in contention. Thus Nietzsche's decisive evaluation of humanity is no longer determined by mathematics but by biology—or more precisely by "life"—as a contest between strength and weakness, health and sickness: "Everywhere," he writes, "the struggle of the sick against the healthy" (GS 3: §14, 123).

While he often characterized himself as a *psychologist* to distance himself from what he took to be the ersatz objectivity of previous philosophers, his thought is more profoundly—and Nietzsche explicitly recognized this—that of a *physiologist,* a knowledge piercing and breaking up the surface of cognition and consciousness to uncover the underlying but ruling drives of the body. This reversal and revaluation of the mind-body relation accounts for Nietzsche's high-spirited style, his dashes, his exclamation points, his ego, and his tempo—what Nietzsche calls "dancing." He wants the body to speak or to sing. It is no accident, then, that while for Spinoza, with his mechanistic model, the basic character of all things is "*conatus essendi,*" perseverance in being, inertia, for Nietzsche, in contrast, the basic character of all things is "will to power," a dynamic, aggrandizing play of forces. It is on this basis, making the will primary and interpreting the will as will to power, that Nietzsche criticizes Spinoza (and Darwin). In *The Gay Science* he writes:

The wish to preserve oneself is the symptom of a condition of distress, of a limitation of the really fundamental instinct of life which aims at *the expansion of power* and, wishing for that, frequently risks and even sacrifices self-preservation. It should be considered symptomatic when some philosophers—for example, Spinoza who was consumptive—considered the instinct of self-preservation decisive and *had* to see it that way; for they were individuals in conditions of distress.

That our modern natural sciences have become so thoroughly entangled in this Spinozistic dogma (most recently and worst of all, Darwinism with its incomprehensible one-sided doctrine of the "struggle for existence") is probably due to the origins of most natural scientists. . . . The struggle for existence is only an *exception,* a temporary restriction of the will to life. The great and small struggle always revolves around superiority, around growth and expansion, around power—in accordance with the will to power which is the will to life.

(GS 5: §349, 292)

We see in this citation the grounding of Nietzsche's thought in life, life interpreted as will to power, as will to expansion, and its contrast to both Darwin's survival of the fittest and Spinoza's *conatus essendi,* both of which Nietzsche critically reinterprets accordingly as expressions of will to power, namely, as expressions of a physiology declining and distressed.

Will, for Nietzsche, is the universal character of all things, organic and inorganic. And this is why Nietzsche remains, no doubt despite himself, a metaphysician. He claims to know and evaluate the whole, even if, unlike Kant and Schopenhauer, and contradicting himself, he explicitly denies the possibility of such a claim and evaluation. His affirmations nevertheless betray him. Everything for Nietzsche is a gigantic struggle, an ever-changing provisional arrangement of striving forces, "individuals" (at whatever level) being but temporary nodes of power relations, temporary configurations of multiple forces in passing differential relations of dominance and submission (in contrast to Spinoza's mechanistic characterization of individuals as ratios of motion and rest). How Nietzsche knows this one cannot say, but it is what he repeatedly claims—or rather proclaims.

Nietzsche does not ask *what* morality or politics or religion or philosophy is, but rather *who* believes this or that. The strong believe one thing, the weak another. Nietzsche's well-commented-upon "perspectivism," then, must be understood not simply as the claim that truth is the expression of a finite point of view, a claim made by many philosophers before and after Nietzsche, but also, more profoundly and in a more Nietzschean vein, the claim that perspective follows physiology, that perspective is the conscious expression of a certain biological state of health or sickness, strength or weakness. Nietzsche's attacks upon Christianity, science, morality, and so much else in high European culture are at bottom a rebellion against the asceticism that protects and preserves an "*impoverishment of life*" (GM 3: §25, 154). In contrast to all asceticism, Nietzsche demands greatness: "*great health*" in individuals and "grand politics" for nations. Nietzsche's philosophy is therefore an *aesthetics:* a philosophy of the body, and on top of this it is a pagan or Greek aesthetics: the celebration of victory, superiority, domination—hegemony as greatness.

And this is why Nietzsche supports art, the artistic life, with its "will to lie," against religion, morality, and science. As early as 1872, in an unpublished work entitled "The Philosopher: Reflections on the Struggle Between Art and Knowledge," he had written: "History and the natural sciences were necessary to combat the middle ages: knowledge versus faith. We now oppose knowledge with *art;* return to life."[4] The artistic life, the willful lie, the display, the show, is closest to the will to power, and this is why Nietzsche affirms it.

A question arises: By affirming the artistic life does not Nietzsche also affirm a freedom of will? Would not such an assertion conflict with his fundamental agreement with Spinoza that there is no free will, that free will is a lie that only the ignorant and deluded masses believe or, in Nietzsche's case, that only the weak and sick masses believe? It is a tricky question and is perhaps without a fully satisfactory answer because both Nietzsche and Spinoza are caught in a bind when they deny free will and yet *recommend* that others *should* deny it also. In what, after all, lies the superiority of Spinoza's scientists over the ignorant masses? All one can say, perhaps, is that knowing is *less painful* than ignorance. Spinoza promises "beatitude" to the man of science. Nietzsche resorts to the same justification. To discover that all is will to power, that consciousness itself is simply an aftereffect of will to power, is to discover the necessity of the universe, even if that necessity is no longer the causal or deductive necessity of Spinoza's rationalism—and such a discovery, so Nietzsche asserts repeatedly, is "joyful."

Nietzsche thus mimics Spinoza's recommendation regarding causality and deduction: one must conform to its necessity. Freedom lies in conformity. Freedom is necessity—again, philosophy's oldest conceit. To discover will to power is to embrace necessity, but now as what Nietzsche calls *amor fati*, "love of fate"—to the point that one accepts one's life without moral or metaphysical judgment, to the point that one accepts one's life and all of reality even if it were to recur eternally. "My formula for greatness in a human being is *amor fati*," Nietzsche writes in *Ecce Homo*, "that one wants nothing to be different, not forward, not backward, not in all eternity" (EH 258). Again, Spinoza: eternity, but now the eternity of the ephemeral! Again, too, the promise of pleasure. Here is Nietzsche's highest desire and highest joy: "to will eternity." "Joy," his Zarathustra declares, "does not want heirs, or children—joy wants itself, wants eternity, wants recurrence, wants everything eternally the same" (TZ 4:434).

A life of complete conformity to will to power, without judgment, without regret, willing all and everything to the point that one would will it to recur again eternally, such is the life of the Overman, "beyond good and evil," beyond the history of ascetic humanity and its antinatural ideals. "Joy wants the eternity of *all* things, *wants deep, wants deep eternity*" (TZ 4:436). In contrast to the conformity recommended by Spinoza's Spinozism of the mind and intellect, grounded upon and bound within substantial being, Nietzsche's brand of Spinozism demands a conformity of the body to the body, and hence exalts imagination, which is a closer expression of the body than rationality, "liberated" to the nonprinciple of multiplicity, the production of masks of masks without end.

Levinas Contra Nietzsche's Spinozism

It goes without saying that regarding the points upon which Nietzsche and Spinoza agree, their mutual denial of "freedom of the will, teleology, the moral world order, the unegoistic, and evil," Levinas stands at their antipodes. The new question before us is whether Nietzsche's divergences from Spinoza deriving from changes in "time, culture and science" introduce differences that somehow buttress and justify Spinozism in Nietzsche's case and enable Nietzsche to succeed, vis-à-vis Levinas's opposition to Spinozism, where Spinoza's Spinozism failed. Does Nietzsche's biological-physiological model deriving from the body succeed in creating a new form of amoralist naturalism impervious to Levinas's ethical challenge? The confrontation is important not simply as a scholarly exercise but because Levinas and Nietzsche are both philosophers of embodiment and as such square off against each other at close quarters and as our contemporaries, rather than across the mind-body divide that separates Spinoza's idealism from them both and no doubt from us all.

Responsible Body

Just as Nietzsche's adoption of the body in its vitality—interpreted as will to power and multiplicity, in contrast to Spinoza's attachment to the mind and its representation of the world in terms of substantial being and *conatus essendi*—stands as the greatest difference separating Nietzsche's Spinozism from Spinoza's, so, too, Levinas's notion of the obligated body elevated by moral responsibilities stands at the farthest antipode challenging the hegemony of the Nietzschean body.

Starting with the body, Nietzsche uncovers a philosophy of fragmentation, of various forces each pulling in its own direction to establish provisional moments of stasis, reflected as symptoms—ideas, images, or desires—in consciousness. The imperative of his philosophy is to continually pass beyond such derivative unities by opening up and accepting the creative, form-giving play of the forces that temporarily sustain them. "The whole surface of consciousness—consciousness *is* a surface—must be kept clear of all great imperatives" (EH 254). To "love one's fate" is to give oneself over to the evanescent play of will to power, whose mobility is the becoming of what is. The Nietzschean self is thus constantly reinventing itself, releasing new energy configurations. Its "overcoming" is a constant shattering of the "idols" of pretended unity. It is in this sense that Nietzsche famously labels himself "dynamite" and "philosophizes with a hammer"—to undo the lies of consciousness, its denial of its physiological roots, to be sure, but more deeply to undo the lie of consciousness itself, to break up a surface that is always only a prison. Thus for Nietzsche the philosopher is "a terrible explosive, endangering everything" (EH 281). Nietzsche thus does not aim for progress in the Enlightenment sense of the term, as a cumulative movement toward greater self-consciousness with an attendant increasing responsibility in the face of greater self-knowledge, but rather provokes a release of the body into its own vital dynamism as an open and endless play of possibilities that consciousness can only grasp retrospectively—always too late—as a "schizoid" activity (to use Deleuze's felicitous term). "The last thing *I* should promise," Nietzsche writes in *Ecce Homo*, "would be to 'improve' mankind. No new idols are erected by me. . . . *Overthrowing idols* (my word for 'ideals')—that comes closer to being part of my craft" (EH 217–18).

But Levinas, too, is a philosopher of the body. As we have seen, his philosophy begins with the emergence of the existent from anonymous existence as an "enjoyment," a "self-sensing," a sphere of immanent sensations content with themselves and "bathing" in an elemental sensuousness. Such a description is true to the phenomenological origin of selfhood as independent being, and Levinas's philosophy remains faithful to the findings of his phenomenological investigations. He avoids, as Spinoza and Nietzsche do not, importing theoretical constructions—presuppositions, really—such as "substance" or "will to power" into his analyses. Levinas detects within the body's self-sensing not only enjoyment and contentment but dissatisfaction, disturbance, desire for *escape*. Levinas discovers that nothing bodily or worldly liberates the self from its own self-enchainment—not labor, not representation, not even being-toward-death. The only "answer" to this aspect of its desire must come from an outside truly exterior, beyond itself and beyond its worldliness, whether practical or theoretical. That exteriority, as we know, arrives with the face of the other person. Not the face as phenomenon, however, but as "enigma," an absolute transcendence sustained in its exteriority as moral imperative.

We should not forget, then, that the moral encounter with the other, the famous Levinasian "face to face," is not some idealist or ethereal revelation. It is a bodily event: an internalization of the suffering, needs, and destitution of the other person. It is the "other in me," to use Levinas's formula, or the self "for the other." This transformation of the immanent body, the spontaneous body, the body as a play of vital forces, into the body for-the-other is, as I have indicated, the central topic of Levinas's second major work, *Otherwise Than Being; Or, Beyond Essence*. In *Totality and Infinity* Levinas had focused primarily on the otherness of the other person, on the absolute transcendence of the other as moral imperative. In *Otherwise Than Being*, in contrast, his primary goal is to show that and how such otherness "transubstantiates" or "de-nucleates" the embodied subject into responsible being—responsible body.

Levinas's language, even when speaking about morality, indeed, especially when speaking about morality, therefore remains visceral. In *Otherwise Than Being*, for example, he writes:

The tenderness of skin is the very gap between approach and approached, a disparity, a non-intentionality, a non-teleology. . . . Proximity, immediacy, is to enjoy and to suffer by the other. But I can enjoy and suffer by the other only because I am-for-the-other, am signification, because the contact with skin is still a proximity of a face, a responsibility, an obsession with the other, being-one-for-the-other.

(OB 90)

And:

It is the passivity of being-for-another, which is possible only in the form of giving the very bread I eat. But for this one has to first enjoy one's bread, not in order to have the merit of giving it, but in order to give it with one's heart, to give oneself in giving it.   (OB 72)

And thus, too, when speaking of moral subjectivity Levinas invokes the image of the "skin turned inside out" for-the-other. The responsibility of the responsible self, the responsive self, too bodily, too passive to evade responsibility, lies in "its vulnerability, its exposedness to the other" (OB 74). Morality is carnal rather than ethereal being-for-the-other. The other's requirements make the self suffer. One does not approach the other with empty hands. In this way Levinas is certainly free of a Nietzschean charge that might apply to Spinoza, to have overvalued the mind, the intellect, "ideals," at the expense of the body. But of course, too, Levinas sees in responsiveness the true *greatness*—the glory—of humanity, whereas Nietzsche detects only weakness, sickness, hypersensitivity, and the inability not to respond.

But what does it mean when Nietzsche criticizes pity? What is the significance of demeaning moral responsibility for one's neighbor and the ceaseless sacrifice of creating a just world? Is a "revaluation of all values" really accomplished in the destruction of all values for the sake of a private self-glorification absorbed in and reflecting a multiverse of will to power and more power? Why call this "revaluation"? Where is the "value"? By what imperative should human beings become events of nature? Is this not once again to be caught in the abstractions of rationalism and its partner materialism, even if now energized by siding with the body instead of the mind? Is not "revaluation of all values" rather found, as Levinas teaches, in the never-fulfilled and hence never-ending task of uplifting values to their proper height, incarnating and institutionalizing them? Who can say that humanity has accomplished the values Nietzsche wants already to destroy? Who, in the face of constant outrages, has the temerity to say that our world is just or that justice is not worth valuing?

Is it not rather the case that Levinas is right about our noblest task? Do we really need to be nudged, no less harangued, toward our animal natures, toward more selfishness? Nietzsche was certainly right that we must not flee the body and desire. But he was wrong about shame and the alleged desirability of a "new innocence." We are not innocent. Shamelessness requires no additional advertising from philosophers. Levinas is far more right that we must not lose sight of—must not lose heart for—what is most desirable, that our real nobility lies in the most "difficult freedom," that in the risks of embodying moral responsibilities, in compassion for others, in daily acts of kindness, and by embracing all others by struggling for a just world here and now, in these great risks lies the true revaluation of all values.

NOTES

1. Baruch Spinoza, *The Ethics,* trans. Samuel Shirley (Indianapolis, Ind.: Hackett, 1992), vol. 3, preface, 102. Henceforth cited as E.

2. Nietzsche, "Postcard to Overbeck" (1881), in *The Portable Nietzsche,* ed. and trans. Walter Kaufmann (New York: Viking Press, 1954), 92.

3. Nietzsche, letter to Jacob Burckhardt, January 6, 1889, in *The Portable Nietzsche,* 684.

4. Nietzsche, *Philosophy and Truth: Selections from Nietzsche's Notebooks of the Early 1870s,* ed. and trans. Daniel Breazeale (Atlantic Highlands, N.J.: Humanities Press, 1979), 14.

III

——

Heteronomy
and Ubiquity

God in Philosophy

II

Suffering Redeemable and Irredeemable

JOHN LLEWELYN

Levinas is thus at once quite close and quite far from Nietzsche.
—Jacques Derrida, *Writing and Difference*

I

Absolute responsibility is significance as my signifying to another my always-already, a priori having answered yes to another's always-already having required of me that I be not violent to him or her. My affirmation is a priori in that it precedes my having heard another human being's words— "You shall not kill"—words that may be understood, consistent with what Levinas writes, as a prohibition of any deed that diminishes the duration or quality of the life of another, diminishes his or her well-being. The responsibility thus affirmed is absolute because it is a necessary condition of responsibilities constituted by moral laws or contingent circumstances. It is absolute through being that which prevents obligations defined by law from being the violence of responding to another only as a case subsumed under a law. This particular violence, though not necessarily all violence, is prevented by the dissymmetry of my being face to face with the other. Not all violence is excluded thereby, not, for example, the violence of injustice relative to specific laws. But such relative injustice assumes that the unjust deed is done to one who is not merely a case. A case is symmetrical with another case. This holds when one of the cases is myself. In the plane geometry of cases, the subject makes both of itself and of others an object of consciousness. In the alternative geometry of myself facing and being faced by another addressing to me the command "You shall not kill," my "experience" is not measurable according to any metric available to perceptual or conceptual consciousness, that is to say, consciousness defined as consciousness of an intentional object. Levinas sometimes writes of a consciousness that is other than intentional. He sometimes writes of a consciousness whose intentionality is inverted. It is intentional consciousness that he means when he opposes consciousness to absolute ethical responsibility. Absolute responsibility is not perceptually or conceptually representative. Although in the light of the ambiguity of the French word for "consciousness," it is permissible to think of absolute consciousness as absolute conscience, it is not permissible to think of it as a *scientia*. Nor, strictly, is it a *cum-scientia*, a knowledge-with. Being *with* the other, *Mitsein*, is a possibility only thanks to being *for* the other. Being for the other is not a possibility but an impossibility or an unpossibility in that it is prior to any "I can."

So is what Levinas understands by absolute responsibility logically prior to the relative responsibilities for which holds, according to Kant, the principle that "I ought" presupposes "I can"? Yes and no, depending on whether "logically" is understood in terms of the logic of what is said or in terms of Saying. According to the first way of understanding logic, Levinasian absolute responsibility is logically prior not only to relative responsibilities but also to the Kantian absolute moral law and therefore to the feeling of respect experienced as a categorical imperative by human beings. This feeling for a rational object, here for universal practical reason as such, would not be an ethical feeling, according to Levinas, unless it were supplemented by an "experience" of responsibility toward another singular human being. How does Levinas escape the risk of the sentimentalism that Kant would consider to be incurred through focusing upon particularity? By doubling the focus. It is in terms of their sentiments, likes, and taste that one human being is distinguished from another, according to Kant. If we took this analysis of particularity as a guide to what Levinas understands by singularity, we would be in danger of interpreting his account of ethicality as one more sentimentalist account among those of Hutcheson, Hume, and Adam Smith, to which Kant wished to present a rationalist alternative.

We would be confusing the "Desire" that Levinas usually spells with an up-percase initial and "desire" sometimes spelled by him with a lowercase ini-tial. Now particularity is in the same logical category as universality insofar as it is a determination of a concept. And conceptual thinking falls under the principle of noncontradiction. How can singularity fail to fall under that principle, too? By not allowing the principle of contradiction that de-fines the logic of the conceptual sense or form of what is said to be divorced from the nonformal logic of saying. Otherwise put, the third personality of logical form and dialectical conceptuality does not stand alone in a space of its own. Its logic and the principle of noncontradiction is an abstraction removed from the concrete settings in which the third-person-ness of the "he" or the "she" or the "they" can be traced back to an "I" or a "me" faced by a "you."

When Levinas invites his readers to interpret this facing before casing as saying, he is not referring to the utterance or hearing of empirical words. Saying, "*Dire,*" as spelled sometimes but not always by Levinas with an up-percase initial, is the silent testimony that precedes and makes possible the distinction between saying as vocal utterance and the content that may be said by an indefinite number of speakers. Therefore it is an oversimplifica-tion to treat Saying as an act of speech, *parole,* as contrasted by Saussure with language as *langue.* It is also an oversimplification to read what Levi-nas writes about Saying as a variation on what John Austin writes about speech-acts. Saying as "*Dire*" is not speech as vocalization. And it is not an act. Further, to repeat a point already made, its passivity is prior to the passivity usually attributed to hearing in opposition to speaking. It is more passive than "*entendre*" understood as hearing. Its passivity is more like that of "*entendre*" understood as understanding and as understanding under-stood as what is "understood," *sous-entendu,* as what goes without saying. Its being more passive than the passivity of sensing by the ear or any other sensory organ is at least in part its being more passed, more *passé,* than any passedness that may characterize such sensing or the act of uttering or writing words, for instance, words by the speaking of which one per-forms the deed of entering into a contract. The passedness of Saying is not a passedness of something that was once present. It is exterior and anterior to any experience that is integrated into the transcendental unity of apper-ception. Therefore, when in an essay entitled "Language and Proximity" Levinas refers to Saying, *Dire,* as a contact, the "-tact" cannot be empirical touch and the "con-" (*cum*) cannot mean the linguistic com-munication of information. When it is called communication by Levinas, it is qualified as "pure" (CPP 119; ED 228). And it is language as in the French *langage,* interpreted as addressing not a message to another but as addressing oneself to another, which Levinas singles out as the "*signifiance*" that would be expressed in the words "Here I am" or "I hear you" or "Contact." When Levinas writes of "langage originel, sans mots ni propositions, pure communication," he does not mean that this pure original language can happen without something being said. He means that language as the medium in which something is said (affirmed, asked, commanded, etc.), *langue* in which a linguistic sign signifies something, presupposes *langage d'avant la langue* (CPP 122; ED 232), addressing in which someone is herself or himself a sign to the other and indeed assigned as for that other, as responsive to that other—as sensitive to the other.

II

Levinas's teaching of passivity more passive than the passivity traditionally contrasted with activity is a reworking of what Husserl writes about passive synthesis in the context of the question of intersubjectivity in the fifth of the *Cartesian Meditations.* In the lectures and other writings published under the title *Analyses Concerning Passive and Active Synthesis,*[1] active synthesis is the association of data for which the ego's intentional acts are responsible, "act" having the wide connotation that *actus* has in Scholastic philosophy. Husserl writes also of a "passive intentionality," of an attraction (*Reiz*) and of "affective rays" projected by the object itself toward the subject. His reference to this as a self-giving on the part of the object, as though the object were in its own right a subject, might well have suggested to Levinas an extension of such passive intentionality from the field of sensation that is Husserl's chief topic here—though Husserl himself treats also of axiological and practical applications—to the self as the self of another human being. Again, it is as though Husserl's analyses of association in the context of sensation and more generally consciousness (the *bewusstseinsmässig*) are extended by Levinas via Husserl's reflections in the fifth of the *Cartesian Meditations* to the primary *socius,* the society of the first-person singular and another human being, initially a you, in the horizonless, contextless context of ethical responsibility.

In what way is this context contextless? Is Levinas here challenging Derrida's assertion that there is no contextlessness, *Il n'y a pas de hors-texte?*[2] This is a question again about the *cum*, and the answer is the same as was given when it arose earlier in relation to Levinas's references to consciousness, contact, and communication. In the symmetry of the "with" of consciousness construed as a subject *with* an intentional object or *with* another subject, *con-scientia*, persists the dissymmetry of my not being equal with another because equality assumes a point of view outside the other and myself, whereas in my facing the other nothing is visible. I do not see my seeing. I do not see the other's looking. I address my regard to the other and the other addresses her or his look to me. We can call this a context provided that the "con-" is not construed as the "com-" of comparison. The relation or quasi relation of address, whether it be looks or words that are addressed, or words through looks, is not effected from any temporal zero point of Olympian survey *sub specie aeternitatis*. This is a kind of context. It is the context of all contexts in that without it no other context is possible. One could call it the *contexte d'avant le contexte*, where the "con-" of the latter "context" connotes the lateral togetherness of semantic signifiers with what is signified and of human signifiers and signs with one another. The laterality of the latter relationship could be contrasted with what one might characterize as the verticality of my facing another human being—or my facing God, as would be said by Kierkegaard, and is said by Levinas when, in the last words of "Language and Proximity," he says of the first saying, *le premier dire*, that it is indeed only a word, *n'est certes qu'un mot*, but that this word is "God." He does not say "the word 'God'" or "God." No quotation marks are used. To put God in inverted commas would be to convert God into a named being imagined and perhaps imaged as either a part of our world, and thereby profaned, or as an entity above the world, looking down on it and us as his (or His or Her or Its) creatures. This would be to take "the smooth path by which pious thinking too swiftly deduces theological realities" (CPP 124; ED 234). That mistake is avoided, Levinas emphasizes, only if the only way toward God is through the instant in which one human being—Emmanuel (God-be-with-me) Levinas or someone else—addresses the word "*hineni*," "Hear me here at your service," to another human being: a "Hebrew" word that breaks open the smooth surface of the "Greek" *logos* (CPP 126; ED 236), disrupting the togetherness of the syntax of the context formed by the formality of what is said, deconstruing its construed synthesizing structure. By following Levinas along this rough path, we not only learn why Judaism is difficult. We learn also why the madman of Nietzsche's *Thus Spoke Zarathustra* shouts that God is dead.

III

Nietzsche's first doctrine of redemption is a doctrine of redemption through art. But when he attended some of the first performances of Wagner's music at Bayreuth in 1876 he was appalled to discover that the audience was more interested in the food, the drink, the chit-chat, and being seen than they were in the music. This raised doubts in him about the viability of what he calls his metaphysics of art. But metaphysics itself was abandoned once he came to have doubts about the tenability of Schopenhauer's post-Kantian belief in an independent reality antithetically opposed to appearance. In the conversation he has with himself in the "Attempt at Self-Criticism" added in the edition of *The Birth of Tragedy* published in 1886, he judges the book to be badly written, clumsy, sentimental, so sugary as to be well-nigh effeminate—and romantic. He condemns it for being as romantic as by this time he finds the work of the person with whom he imagined himself to be having a conversation in the book itself, his erstwhile friend Richard Wagner. Why romantic? Because behind the Schopenhauerian pessimism of the book lurks an optimistic longing for an otherworldly metaphysical consolation before "*the* old God." This old God is the God of Christianity. Despite the honor the book seems to pay to ancient Greece, he now deems the book to be anti-Hellenic. It is anti-Hellenic because it is pro-Helenic, Helen being she for whom Goethe's Faust yearned, she whom Nietzsche now sees as a metaphor for the metaphysical, for what is beyond the physical, beyond the natural.

Nietzsche now endeavors to forge a nonmetaphysical or what he will call a physiological idiom that negotiates a path between Darwin and the old God of Christendom whom Darwin had killed. He will eventually discover a principle of selection that is an alternative to Darwinian natural selection yet that is natural in the sense of a "second nature": not the supernatural second nature of which St. Paul speaks, but a second nature incorporating a culture that, instead of distinguishing humanity from animality, distinguishes certain select human beings from the rest of humanity. This alternative both to Darwindom and to Christendom will show more respect for Jesus than had been shown in *The Life of Jesus,* whose author, David Strauss, is the topic of an essay published first in 1873 and later included in Nietzsche's *Untimely Meditations.* Strauss, failing to recognize that his "scientific faith" is a contradiction in terms, is in too great a hurry to preach Darwinian scientism as the new faith, replacing the old faith of Christianity. Nietzsche finds in this scientism a symptom of a European nihilism, which is as unacceptable as what he considers to be the Indian nihilism of Buddha. European nihilism is the disappointment that follows from loss of the belief that the universe has a goal or any other unifying principle such as that of the Pauline and Lutheran Christianity preached by Nietzsche's father, founded on the proposition that redemption turns solely on faith in the Resurrection. Nietzsche will say toward the end of his writing career that with this "*impudent* doctrine of personal immortality" regarded by Paul as a reward, "the entire concept of 'blessedness,' the whole and sole reality of the Evangel, is juggled away—for the benefit of a state *after* death!" (AC §41:154). Love is another name for the whole and sole reality practiced by "the noblest human being,"[3] variously named Jesus, Christ, and the Redeemer. It is worth bearing in mind that Dionysus, too, is called the Redeemer (in Greek "*lysios,*" in German "*Erlöser*") and that he was born (at least twice) of a divine father and an earthly mother. Moreover, it will be to a certain non-Christian conception of love that Nietzsche will turn when, like Plato calling upon Socrates, he finally calls upon Zarathustra, the "soothlaugher" who pronounces laughter holy, to teach an art that will redeem the suffering of this world now that the art of aesthetic illusion taught in *The Birth of Tragedy* has proved to be itself an illusion. Disappointed in his hope of finding this redemption by way of art, he goes on to seek it by way of a doctrine of eternal return.

IV

Despite the emphasis put on difference in artistic creativity, the teaching of eternal return makes much of sameness, if "same" is an allowable translation here of Nietzsche's word "*gleich,*" which can also mean equal or like. There is a conservatism about the doctrine of the eternal return of the same. This is what makes it, as Nietzsche says, the most abyssal or unfathomable (*abgründlichste*) idea. For this doctrine, introduced in *The Gay Science* and further articulated in *Thus Spoke Zarathustra* and *The Will to Power,* challenges us to utter a tremendous, unbounded, and joyful Yes "to all things," to say Amen therefore to what is painful and as mean as the all too human morality of the slave. This affirmation is Dionysian in a sense that perhaps picks up the careless or careful remark made in his first book that, while the main characteristic of Apollonian music is rhythm, what is proper to Dionysian music is harmony. In any case, the Dionysian is no longer opposed to the Apollonian because to the proliferating differences of images, perspectives, and the "mobile army of metaphors" in terms of which truth is analyzed in the essay "On Truth and Lying in an Extra-Moral Sense" (1873), is added the sameness constituted by the eternal repetition that the overman not only accepts but rejoices in and loves.

According to Nietzsche's teaching of eternal return, suffering is not redeemed by a hoped-for goal. That would be to give priority to a state of being. The "same" of the eternal return of the same is not a same *to* which a return is made. It is the same *of* the eternal return itself as such. If there is anything for the sake of which the return is made, it is the circling of the return itself. The only unity affirmed by the Dionysian Amen is the unity of this circling, not an aimed-at unity or community. So, despite what was said above about the conservatism of Nietzsche's doctrine, it must be said now that this is not incompatible with experimentalism, such experimentalism as one expects of the great artist. The doctrine itself is a thought experiment, an appeal to imagine what will appear unimaginable to the all too human person referred to in *Thus Spoke Zarathustra* as "the last man."

What the last man finds unimaginable is that he should want the eternal repetition not only of his own suffering or that of others, but "all the woe of the world together" (BG §30:43). He either does not understand or does not accept what Zarathustra says when the latter asks, "Did you ever say Yes to one joy?" and then adds, "O my friends, then you said Yes to all woe as well. All things are chained and entwined together, all things are in love" (TZ §10 "The Intoxicated Song": 331–32). This is an elaboration of a doctrine espoused by some of the pre-Socratic thinkers of whom Nietzsche writes in his early essay "Philosophy in the Tragic Age of the Greeks" (1873), for instance, Empedocles, where an antithetical opposition between love and strife is questioned the moment one asks whether the relation between love and strife is one of love or of strife. In Heraclitus, to whom Empedocles may have been indebted, love as harmony enters on the scene as that which gets expressed in the idea of a friendly struggle (*polemos*) that is said to go on among all things. The friendliness of that struggle may appear to get overlooked in those places where Nietzsche's overman is said to be a friend of war and of malice. Zarathustra declares in the section of *Ecce Homo* devoted to *Thus Spoke Zarathustra:* "I should like to rob those to whom I give; thus do I hunger for malice." *Thus Spoke Zarathustra* is a parody of the Bible. The title *Ecce Homo,* "Behold the Man," is an echo of what Pilate is reported to have said in that book (John 19:5). Thus spoke Pilate. And when Zarathustra speaks about giving, what he says is meant to bring out the way giving may be a way of achieving mastery over the recipient. Hence instead of holding that it is more blessed to give than to receive, Zarathustra dreams that it is more blessed to steal than to give.

So can one say of the values of the new Nietzschean man what Levinas says of the essence beyond essence of the ethical, that they are beyond *intéressement?* They are beyond this according to Levinas in two ways. They are beyond *esse,* beyond being. And they are beyond the *inter* in so far as this means a reciprocity. Thus far Nietzsche, too, would seem able to go. The revaluation of values returns value to becoming. And the priority of becoming excludes such a reciprocity as definitively as it is excluded from what Levinas means by the face to face. There is hierarchy in both the Nietzschean and the Levinasian doctrines at this point. In the Levinasian doctrine the hierarchy is not one of power. When Levinas insists on this he may well be thinking that he is wanting to distinguish himself from the philosopher of the will to power. But even the latter, although he distinguishes what he calls the morality of the herd from a new master morality of the hard, does not appeal to a neutral third morality in terms of which to grade the master morality above the morality of the herd. And in the morality of the master, the mastery sought is primarily mastery over oneself and over the residue in oneself of human nature as conceived according to the old tablets of law.

Sometimes when Nietzsche writes that the new philosopher must do his work with a hammer, the work must be understand on analogy with the way a physician might tap gently on a part of the body to detect whether there is a weakness hidden beneath, so that if one wished to call this work deconstruction this should not be equated with destruction. But Nietzsche's new Dionysian philosopher has a second hammer in his kit, or he uses the first one in a different way. It is sometimes wielded in order to destroy. "Among the conditions for a Dionysian task are, in a decisive way, the hardness of the hammer, the *joy even in destroying*" (EH §8 "Thus Spoke Zarathustra": 309). The overman *is* his own hammer. What he destroys is the tablet of the old law. On the new tablet that replaces it is written—with hammer and chisel—"Become hard." By the norms of the old law this will be judged an evil prescription, but that can be an objection to it only if we can make out a case for rejecting Nietzsche's genealogy of morals and the revaluation of all values that it entails. Among the laws the new law replaces is "Love thy neighbor," if by neighbor is meant any other human being whomsoever. For not only, as we have seen, are the duties prescribed by the new table of law not duties *for* everyone; they are also not duties *toward* everyone. But Nietzsche writes: "The philosopher as *we* understand him, we free spirits—as the man of the most comprehensive responsibility . . . has the conscience for the collective evolution of mankind" (BG §61:67–8). That conscience will require of *us,* us free spirits, the new Dionysian philosophers, "not to want to relinquish or share our own responsibilities; to count our privileges and exercising of them among our *duties*" (BG §272:191). That is to say, the yet to be continued list of new commands bears a parodic relation to the old ones to the extent that the command to love one's neighbor returns in the new tablet and in the *amor fati* that inspires it, and to the extent that one's neighbor means those who come after us. It is primarily for their sake that Zarathustra descends to preach his sermon at the foot of his mount. But does not the doctrine of eternal return imply that future mankind has already existed? If so, the duty of love and the love of duty comprised in *amor fati* is directed also to that segment of mankind of which one says "it was" and "it is." Does this mean that it is still only toward the future of the past, present and future mankind that this love is addressed? Not if we take seriously Nietzsche's doctrine that everything is connected with everything not only in our mental life where, he maintains, willing is a complication of sensing, feeling, and thinking and thinking is a relatedness of desires, but also in the physical world and between those whom we meet there and ourselves. Given the combination of that doctrine with the doctrine of *amor fati,* the commandment to love one's neighbor would appear to figure on the new tablet, too. Even if this inference is denied, there is no denying that the higher man, the highest man, and the overman are moved by love of others.

That is to say, even with regard to the relation of the old to the new tablets of law Nietzsche displays his distaste for antithetical opposition. And, in line with the unsettling thought that the nature of humanity remains unsettled, the new tablet of laws is fated to remain incomplete. According to the first law that Nietzsche holds to be inscribed on this, greater love hath no overman than to cry out in the face of this incompleteness not "Thy will be done," for there no longer is or ever was a personal Thou to carry this "Thy," but, impersonally and joyfully, "So be it," over and over and over.

Nietzsche once wrote, and he was still quite sane when he did so: "A certain emperor always bore in mind the transitoriness of all things so as not to take them too seriously and to live at peace among them. To me, on the contrary, everything seems far too valuable to be fleeting: I seek an eternity for everything." Nietzsche's greater love is such that by it, after all, almost *everything, almost* everything, gets saved. Perhaps even God gets saved provided a distinction be made between the God of ontotheology and the God of which Levinas says that it is the first saying.

V

One of the most noteworthy respects in which, in their vis-à-vis, Nietzsche and Levinas might be supposed to be most distant from each other is that while Nietzsche teaches will to power, Levinas teaches passivity. The seeming opposition marked here has already been qualified by recognition that, in will to power as manifest by the overman and the man in his service, will to power is turned upon one's own will. It must now be acknowledged also that although Levinas tells us that the center of gravity of our world is the other human being, the weight is borne by what he refers to as the "*Moi*," the "I" construed as me in the accusative and accused by the other human being, pursued as hostage and persecuted by the other human being without possibility of evasion: without that possibility, but not without power. His word is "*pouvoir*" (CPP 123; ED 233). It is not possible that that *pouvoir* is the possibility of the "I can," the "I can" of the free will as understood by Kant. That freedom is a conditioned freedom, conditioned, Levinas maintains, by absolute passivity. It is therefore in the power of that passivity, the power of a certain impower that cannot be identified with weakness or unfreedom. In saying this he is again saying something that brings him into proximity with Nietzsche when the latter, on analogy with his statement in the second section of the *Twilight of the Idols* that if you destroy the true world you destroy the apparent one, too, criticizes the metaphysical concept of free will endorsed by Schopenhauer and says that with the dismantling of the idea of a human or divine free will alleged to be *causa sui*, the antithetically opposed idea of an unfree will is dismantled as well (BG §21:33).

Perhaps the deepest difference between Nietzsche's doctrine and Levinas's is the former's obsession by redemption. Levinas is obsessed, but he is not obsessed by redemption. He is obsessed by obsession, a state of siege from which there is no escape. The inescapability is analogous to that of a Greek tragedy such as that through which Nietzsche first sought escape and redemption, where there is an irreconcilable conflict between two principles. The analogy, however, is one that straddles the difference between the logos of conceptual contradiction of things said and the logos of saying. We have seen that Levinas distinguishes the latter from matters of interest, *intéressement*. We have also seen that Nietzsche's aristocrat holds himself aloof from the indulgence of such interests in achieving happiness and escaping pain as shape the morality of the herd. It is important to say *such* interests. For Nietzsche has another interest, an interest that is "higher" or "nobler" than the interest in avoiding suffering: an interest in redeeming suffering. In this he is closer to Kierkegaard than to Levinas, who, when he writes of interest, may have Kierkegaard, but also Kant, in mind.

Kierkegaard distinguishes God's interest from human interests. The latter include the "worldly" interest in happiness and its ostensible opposite. But the singular individual's interest is not one that is shared with other human beings. It is one that turns on a secret between, *inter,* the singular human being and God. Kierkegaard gives to interest a special force in which it relates to the interim of transition from one stage to another, from the aesthetic to ethical generality or from the latter to the religious. It would be interesting to consider how with this force it might be extended to the transitions beyond slave morality as man becomes overman in the scheme of Nietzsche and his pseudonymous Zarathustra. This would be interesting in the less special sense in which Kierkegaard also uses the word in which it is assimilated to what he defines as the aesthetic.

Interest, according to Kant, is either a desire whose object is happiness or, in the case of an interest in duty, an interest in an action and its law itself. The ultimate law for the human being defined as a rational animal is a teleological principle directed at the highest good. This last is for Kant a totality of virtue and commensurate happiness. The good beyond being as defined by Levinas is not a telos. If we say that it is an end in itself, we are saying something that may remind us of our earlier denial that suffering is redeemed, according to Nietzsche, by a hoped-for goal and that the "same" of the eternal return of the same is a same *to* which a return is made. It is, we have said, the same *of* the eternal return itself as such. If there is anything for the sake of which the return is made, it is the circling of the return itself. This gives us a for-its-own-sake that may be seen as Nietzsche's alternative to the for-its-own-sake Kant attributes to deeds done out of respect for the moral law. But Nietzsche's doctrine of eternal return is a this-worldly mimicry of the doctrine of an immortal afterlife that is an article of faith for Christianity and Kant. And it inherits that doctrine's pattern of theodicy, albeit in an atheistic form. It is a doctrine of justification, whether we conceive it as justification by works or as justification by faith or, forcing a little bit Kierkegaard's reading of Luther, justification by a little bit of both.

Now, following Nietzsche, in *Totality and Infinity* and *Otherwise Than Being* Levinas wants to tell a this-worldly story. He wants to do that by not following Kant: by not restricting the for-its-own-sake to rationality as defined by the principle of noncontradiction and the moral law. He would have us believe that rationality thus conceived is immoral unless supplemented by a nonprinciple of contradiction, the contra-Diction, *contre-Dire*, of a singular you, as it were, saying to a singular me, "You shall not kill," "Let me not suffer," a noncategorizing categorical imperative to which I will have always already responded by saying, as it were, "I have heard." But others, each and every one of them, address their commands to me not only on behalf of themselves. They address me also on behalf of other others. This is what it is to touch and be touched by another. It implies a dissymmetry like that of which Husserl and Merleau-Ponty write when they show (a showing that sheds some light on the "problem of other minds" treated in the fifth Cartesian Meditation) how the experience of touching with my finger another of my fingers or some other part of my own body or the skin of another fails to coalesce with and can only alternate with the experience of being touched. Touching teaches us something of what Levinas means by the immediacy of the contact of that other form or rather unform of rationality that he calls "*langage*." This contact is trauma, the "immediate experience," the *donnée immédiate* of the contact of the fact that in the language Kant uses of the "experience" of obligation, we could call the undeniable *Faktum*, recorded in the lines etched on your brow, that I can never redeem either the suffering arising from the neglect entailed by my coming to your assistance rather than to theirs or my suffering from that suffering. This suffering from suffering is a suffering from the wound of love. This is why Levinas links it to glory and joy. But when he does this he cannot mean that the joy and the glory have the power to redeem the suffering. That would be to undermine his affirmation that responsibility suffered for you is suffered for nothing, *pour rien*. More and less than obligation conditioned by freedom from contradiction as described by Kant, the responsibility that Levinas would count to be a condition of such obligation would be a contra-Diction, the *contre-Dire* inherent in the fact that in addressing and being addressed by you I am at the same time addressing and being addressed by him and her, and other others every one of whom, *chaque fois unique*, as Derrida says, is also a you. This conflict is not a conflict of principles. It is the conflict between cases and faces. This is a situation that is tragic in a sense other than that of the tragedies that Nietzsche saw as a vehicle of the redemption of suffering. In this situation, whether or not the suffering of others be redeemable, my suffering in the face of their suffering is beyond redemption. The distance between these two senses of tragedy is a measure of the distance that, notwithstanding moments of proximity between the two philosophers, keeps Nietzsche and Levinas very far apart. Now this distance might be construed prima facie as a difference between Levinas's "spirit of seriousness" and Nietzsche's sense of fun. However, Nietzsche values redemption of suffering above substituting happiness for suffering, while according to Levinas it is for the sake of the happiness of others that I am called to substitute myself. It is arguable, therefore, that Nietzsche is the more earnestly religious of the two thinkers, and that in his suspension of the ethical he is closer to Kierkegaard in the latter's suspension of the ethical than he is to Levinas.

NOTES

1. Edmund Husserl, *Analyses Concerning Passive and Active Synthesis: Lectures on Transcendental Logic,* trans. Anthony J. Steinbock (Dordrecht: Kluwer, 2001).

2. Jacques Derrida, *De la grammatologie* (Paris: Minuit, 1967), 227; *Of Grammatology,* trans. Gayatri Chakravorty Spivak (Baltimore, Md.: Johns Hopkins University Press, 1974), 158.

3. Friedrich Nietzsche, *Human, All Too Human,* trans. Marion Faber and Stephen Lehmann (Harmondsworth, U.K.: Penguin Books, 1984), §475, 229.

12

Levinas's *Gaia Scienza*

AÏCHA LIVIANA MESSINA

THE POSSIBILITY of a rapprochement between Nietzsche and Levinas might seem either evident or quite incomprehensible. It appears evident only insofar as we remain open to the madness, even the violence that gave birth to and impels both men's thought. But it remains incomprehensible so long as we hold fast to rigid schemas and "clichés," like that which characterizes Levinas as the philosopher of goodness and fidelity to a certain god, and the one that defines Nietzsche as a cynic without ethics, destroyer of all morality and every god. For this and other reasons, I choose without hesitation to embrace the proximity between Nietzsche and Levinas. The evidence of such a relation is supported by at least three general themes. First, the irreducibility of what we might call the "matter" of philosophy to knowledge. Second, the reopening of the notion of desire contained in the word "philosophy," itself. Finally, a certain "gratuity" that crosses through both men's thought. Indeed, they express it so forcefully that, in reading them, I am invariably struck by a certain cheerfulness of expression (albeit different) in both their works.

I have enumerated three themes that go some way toward justifying the title of this essay: "Levinas's *Gaia Scienza*." If the word "*gaia*" or gaiety can denote an episode of madness, a kind of excess that tears thought up from its grounds (as also from the language in which it remains subject to reason) and sets it in the element of gratuity, then my title would translate a perfect cohabitation, free of violence, of Nietzsche and Levinas. This cohabitation would be one of friendship rather than of hospitality, a friendship in which complicity gives rise to a shared gaiety or cheerfulness, in which madness corresponds to the decision to be done with the priority of reason. Yet this association becomes difficult—or acute and more concrete—when we consider one of Nietzsche's own definitions of "cheerfulness" in *The Gay Science*. According to Nietzsche, "our cheerfulness" is "the greatest recent event—that 'God is dead', and that the belief in the Christian god has become unbelievable" (GS §343 "The Meaning of our Cheerfulness": 279). A literalist reading of this remark immediately halts the connection I am drawing between Nietzsche and Levinas. For, while he sometimes subscribes to Nietzsche's claim about the "death of God," Levinas never avoids naming God in his work. And while I would insist that only a rigid hermeneutics would characterize Levinas's thought as a fidelity to God, thus fixating it as the moralizing a priori of ethics, it nevertheless seems to me that naming God attests to the ambiguity of Levinas's thought and prevents it from being reducible to a mere thesis. We might even say that it is to the degree that "God" is always the object of an ambiguous phrase that we cannot bolt Levinas's thinking down, though we can entertain the hypothesis that the risk he takes in naming God accounts for his thought's fluidity, and perhaps also its lightness and radiance.

I will attempt in what follows to contextualize these hypotheses and show how they can be brought into relation with Nietzsche. It is in *Otherwise Than Being* (1974) that Levinas alludes to the so-called event of the "death of God." This event is named twice in the last chapter of that work, entitled "Outside" ("Au Dehors"; OB 177, 185; AE 272, 284). In the first citation, it explicitly refers to Nietzsche. The second mention occurs on the last page of the work and may be articulating what *Otherwise Than Being* claimed both as its starting point and that to which it opens; namely, what Levinas calls "the outside." In his preliminary "Note" to *Otherwise Than Being*, Levinas indicates that the work is meant *to give a hearing to* ("donner entente à") the eventuality of a "God not contaminated by Being," which is said to be a "human possibility no less important and no less precarious than to bring Being out of the oblivion into which it is said to have fallen in metaphysics and onto-theology" (OB xlii; AE 10). Levinas is here referring to Heidegger, and I will not elaborate that reference. However, it should at least be noted that, in this passage, evoking the name of God in no way implies a regression toward "onto-theology," that is, toward a foundation of the totality of beings in which the meaning and the ground of morality would also be elucidated. On the contrary, what frames this occurrence of the name of God is the declaration of a rupture more radical than what Heidegger attempted to think with the ontological difference; a rupture Levinas expresses precisely in terms of a certain disturbance or derangement [*dérèglement*]. Levinas speaks of an "ex-ception [in the sense of *ex-cipere*], disturbing the conjunction of *essence, entities,* and the 'difference'" (OB xli, trans. modified; AE 10). Hearing the name of God to which Levinas calls, and which should be distinguished from Heidegger's "hearing the call of Being," would then be intended to disturb [*dérégler*] a certain way of living or co-inhabiting this "House of the Being," where, as the "The Letter on Humanism" explains, "man abides." While I will not explore this difference between Levinas and Heidegger—which is assumed from the first pages of *Otherwise Than Being*—my attention will be directed toward the "disturbance" [*"dérèglement"*] by which Levinas demarcates his work from Heidegger's. It is precisely through his attempted differentiation that we see the proximity—and its stakes—that Levinas will establish with Nietzsche. In fact, we observe, on the one hand that, in the preliminary "Note," Levinas calls "subjectivity" what he will acknowledge as the "ex-ception" that disturbs the ontological difference. On the other hand, in part 1, subsection 4, entitled "Subjectivity," it is Nietzsche that Levinas hails and this, in terms that acknowledge precisely this exception. To quote Levinas:

> The history of philosophy, in moments of great clarity, has known this subjectivity breaking, as in extreme youth, with essence. From Plato's One without being, all the way to Husserl's pure Ego, transcendent in [its] immanence, philosophy has known the metaphysical extraction from being, even if, immediately, in the betrayal of the Said, as if it were under the effect of an oracle, the exception, restored to essence, and to destiny, returned to the rules and led only to worlds behind the world.
> (OB 8, trans. modified for fluency with the French original; AE 21)

More than anyone else, the Nietzschean human being has broken with essence. Moreover, as Levinas remarks shortly thereafter, in Nietzsche this rupture escapes the oracle that restored it to essence immediately upon its being subsumed by language, itself structured according to Being. Thus Levinas writes: "One should have to go all the way to the nihilism of Nietzsche's poetic writing, reversing irreversible time in vortices, to the laughter which refuses language" (OB 8; AE 22). Nietzschean subjectivity would then have the virtue of breaking with essence, but it is also through "a way of writing" that this break remains recalcitrant to any return to essence. Through that which Levinas calls "a way of writing, a way of giving oneself over to the world [*une façon d'écrire, de se commettre avec le monde*]" (OB 8; AE 21) that would be typically Nietzschean, the ex-ception is maintained, just as the subjectivity that stands for the exception is not betrayed in the "said" [*le dit*]. And if, as we saw in the preliminary "Note," one of the purposes of *Otherwise Than Being* is *to hear* (or give *a hearing to*) a god not contaminated by Being, then the rupture of subjectivity—which in Nietzsche is maintained or radicalized by "a way of writing"—would not fail to resonate with what Levinas means by the name "God." In this context, "God" would not name a theological or ontotheological reappropriation of that thought, but instead that which *ex-empts* (*s'excepte*) itself from any logos contaminated by Being. God would be the ex-ception; not only that which remains unsayable, ungraspable, and out of reach, but that which interrupts the possibility of taking or "seizing hold of," the possibility of keeping or even sheltering. "God" would thus be the name of the "Outside." It would denote an exposure without shelter [*sans abris*], something that links us once again to the references to the "death of God" that we noted in the final chapter "Outside" (in the section "Otherwise Said").[1]

There is no contradiction between what *Otherwise Than Being* proclaims at the outset, with the name of God, and what is stated at the book's end, with the "death of God." Not only can Levinas's "God" cohabit with Nietzsche's "death of God," it even solicits Nietzsche's event and its reflection—at least, so far as Nietzsche's affirmation goes along with "a way of writing, a way of giving oneself over to the world that sticks like the ink on our hands" (OB 8; AE 21), as Levinas writes about Nietzsche. In Levinas, "God" would remain the name of a bursting apart or a rupture [*éclat*]. Naming this god does not reascribe us to Being or to the circumstances to which the ontological difference returns us. Naming this god creates disorder, allowing the anarchical rupture *to come to pass,* as irreducible to principles *as it is to language*. As the name for the Outside, "God" comes from the "otherwise said" [*de "l'autrement dit"*]. It is there that we will situate the problem of a proximity between Levinas and Nietzsche. Now, we have already heard Levinas evoking Nietzsche with the "laughter that refuses language" (OB 8; AE 22). Can this gaiety be assimilated to or echo what Levinas calls anarchy, or a "god not contaminated by Being"? Does the rupture of anarchy not have to do, always, with the "irreducible face-to-face with the Other"? And what about the other in Nietzsche? If we suppose that Levinas would ultimately share a common end with Nietzsche—that of bursting language open [*d'éclater le langage*] and engaging thought in an "otherwise said"—why then have recourse to the name of God?

To ask ourselves how it is with the other in Nietzsche comes down to asking ourselves whether we can thematize an ethics in Nietzsche. The question is slippery because, while Levinas's work allows us to describe the adventure and the intrigue of ethics, in Nietzsche, if there is an ethics, it could well have more than one definition. Levinas's madness, as well as his violence, proceeds from the irreducibility of the relation to the Other, from which alone ontology can flow, but which also leads Levinas to interrupt his language as he attempts to state it, even if otherwise. Moreover, while what is extraordinary about his ethics resists reduction to language, it also defines the point of departure of a language that culminates—without halting for an instant—in inspiration. For this reason, it seems to me that while readers may well feel violated by this language in the sense that they are torn out of the primacy of reason, they will not fail to hear *a* language in Levinas's work. In a sense, while it is ethics in Levinas that *resists* by saying "no" to reductions—that is, reductions to neutral being or to "the neuter"—*this violence is affirmative from the outset*. It is the violence of an anarchical "yes," which keeps the work of the negative in check. Levinas's words tear the "self" from its freedom and its self-grounding. However, in being ripped out of the ground, that self is already engaged in Saying. By contrast, Nietzsche's violence begins by calling the reader into question, not by proceeding initially from the irreducibility of a relationship—that is, from the sincerity of Levinas's "yes"—but rather from the critical instability that not only disarms and defies the reader ever to find such an affirmative priority (even an anarchic one), but even, and sometimes often, humiliates him in the attempt. Nietzsche not only destabilizes; he refuses such readings. What is more, the difficulty of speaking about Nietzsche—of circumscribing his thought or setting forth its truth content—is caused precisely by the disorientation provoked by the *solitude* to which the philosopher *lays claim*. We are wounded as we confront Nietzsche's warnings to the reader; not just anyone would be his reader, whereupon he adds, with a contempt that sometimes resembles that of distress, since he never stops calling: "that everyone can learn to read will ruin in the long run not only writing, but thinking too" (TZ "Of Reading and Writing": 40). We sometimes wonder, then: were we elected to read Nietzsche? This is the impression created by these warnings that, while appearing to refute their (democratic) totality, in fact remove his writings from the totalization that such a reading would produce. Indeed, in Nietzsche's warnings there is an invitation to elect *oneself*. Hence, in "Of the Way of the Creator," (TZ 88–91), Nietzsche asks the one who *believes he must* follow the path of solitude: "show me your strength for it and your right to it" (TZ 88). This exhortation corresponds to the second metamorphosis invoked at the beginning of *Zarathustra*, the one that changes the camel into a lion (TZ 54–55). While the camel is a figure of humility and submission that says "yes" to the other because it does not have the strength to be its own beginning, to the lion it is given not only to break with ancient values but to create new ones. Solitude, then, is not a path that one follows by duty, but rather by will. We therefore do not receive Nietzsche passively, yet the critical attitude must come to grips with its own irony: Nietzsche exhorts us to solitude and to beginnings. However, the latter remain conditioned by the enigma of the "I will," in which the "new force" and "new right" come together. If therein lies the primacy of a solitude that, by exempting itself from the self-immanence of the community, elects itself and gives itself its own right, then we seem far from Levinas with Nietzsche. But it is here that a moment of Nietzsche's laughter intervenes: does it suffice to elect oneself in order to will? Should we not suppose that to will "oneself," free from alterity and in this way from all duty, holds us in the pessimistic attitude that always needs negation as a foundation for its own positivity? The question asked in "Of the Way of the Creator"—"show me your strength for it and your right to it"—is still critical. It is not there that we find the bursting open [*l'éclat*] that Levinas perceives in Nietzsche, his extreme youth, or "the laughter that refuses [even so much as] language?" The "I will" of the lion could be only a secular posture that rebuilds its world and thus its language through the simple negation of the sovereignty of the other or of God. The transformation of the "You must" into the "I will" could be circumscribed as the "self-surpassing of morality" [*"l'auto-dépassement de la morale"*] into willing.

Now the lion is only a *transitional* figure of the will, whose freedom "remains *tributary* to the object to be negated"—God. As Nietzsche writes, "But in the loneliest desert the second metamorphosis occurs: the spirit here becomes a lion; it wants to capture freedom and be lord in its own desert. It seeks here its ultimate lord: it will be an enemy to him and to its ultimate God, it will struggle for victory with the great dragon" (TZ "Of the Three Metamorphoses": 54–55).

The figure of the lion attests to the critical attitude toward the "Thou shalt," which for Nietzsche denotes an attitude that negates the "self." But the "I will" of the lion remains too stable as long as it still *knows* what it has to *negate*. It is upon this stability that the third metamorphosis is inscribed, enigmatically: the metamorphosis of the lion into a child. Nietzsche queries: "But tell me, my brothers, what can the child do that even the lion cannot? Why must the preying lion still become a child? The child is inno-cence and forgetfulness, a new beginning, a sport, a self-propelling wheel, a first motion, a sacred Yes" (TZ 55). Nietzsche's chosen readers—if at this point we may still speak of election—are not the possessors of force. It is this force that Nietzsche destabilizes by simultaneously destabilizing both its reception and its self-grounding [*son auto-fondation*]. Should we then attempt to read Nietzsche in light of what makes the negation of duty by power impossible, and in terms of what causes this opposition to fail? Would the figure of the child—which is the one that to my mind would have attracted Levinas—permit us to glimpse something like an ethics in Nietzsche?

———

I thus come back to my initial question concerning ethics, but with the following distinction: the relation to the other cannot constitute fair access to an ethics in Nietzsche. As I already indicated, for Levinas the face-to-face with the Other is irreducible; it even presents itself as an opening—onto "nothingness," solitude, and the "neuter." Levinas's gesture thus consists in tearing loose the fixity and solipsism of the "I can," thanks to the "Thou shalt" to which I am ordered by the irreducibility of this relation. Now, we have just noted that Nietzsche makes the opposite move. In the meta-morphosis of the camel into the lion, it is the transformation of the "Thou shalt" into the "I will" or the "I can" that is at stake. Yet, if the lion is a transitional figure, then this is because the "I can" contained in the lion's "I will" *is not Nietzsche's last word*. Hence, the chiasmi of "Thou shalt"–"I can" and "I can"–"Thou shalt," which might have opposed Levinas and Nietzsche, leads us on the contrary toward a point of encounter between them. This occurs precisely in the destitution of the truth of the "I can." Further, if the "I can" is not Nietzsche's last word, this is because it is rooted in the same negative essence of the will [as the camel's "I must"]. As I argued, Nietzsche's "I can" still depends on the object to be negated: God. It is thus defined as a "power of killing" or of "being able to kill" [*pouvoir tuer*]. The power of the lion is therefore dialectical. Discerning a common point between duty and willing, or between moral alienation and freedom's self-grounding, allows us to think—and this, already with Nietzsche— *a difference between the moral and the ethical*. Nietzsche attacks morality because morality—as is clear from the opening of his *Gay Science*—is defined as the devaluation of existence through its goals, which subordinate life to reasons that remain separated from existence itself. As Nietzsche there writes, for the so-called "emissaries of God," "there is something to life," simply because "there is something behind life, beneath it" (GS 74). Thus, love, life, and the will are always subordinated to the principle by which they are explained and which provides them with an end or a telos. Yet despite its self-determination, the lion never ceases accounting for itself: it is its own end. Therefore, in the figure of the lion, we again find the same schema that allowed us to think the difference between the moral and the ethical—though here it is transposed into a figure. In bringing to light the identity of these schemata, something like what I am trying to conceive as a Nietzschean ethic emerges; it would call itself, precisely, a "gay science" or "joyful wisdom." This wisdom obligates us infinitely to the present, thanks to the destitution of its ends: "My thoughts," writes Nietzsche in the same work, "must show me where I am: but they will not reveal to me where I am going" (GS §287).

Recall now how Nietzsche justified the metamorphosis of the lion into the child: "What can the child do that even the lion cannot?" asked Nietzsche. He answered, "The child is innocence and forgetfulness" (TZ 55). In the language of *The Gay Science* this is stated as, "I love [the] ignorance of the future" (GS §287). The child can forget himself because he confronts what he does not know *and cannot negate*. The lion knows what it negates, and this knowledge is the point of departure for its will. The child loses knowledge of itself. The child is innocence, but this innocence is the point of departure of an affirmation that is free from negativity, to the degree that it no longer has ends and can therefore become pure welcoming in the "ignorance of the future." In this way, the third metamorphosis can be thought of as an ethical affirmation. The "gay science" does not require power—which is always defined by negation—but innocence, where the future—which is unknown—is affirmed simply as unknown and where this ignorance is not indifference but love ("I love the ignorance of the future").

This is, in fact, the same ethical schema that we find in Levinas. In Levinas, the Other, irreducible to knowledge, is not only the unknown but, inasmuch as he is the one "over [whom] I have no power [*celui sur qui je ne peux pas pouvoir*]," as Levinas writes in *Totality and Infinity* (TI 39; TeI 28), the Other is also the one through whom time is released from its negativity. It is thus that in *Time and the Other*, for instance, the alterity of the Other is compared to the alterity of death, which is to come and over which I similarly have no power. Unlike death, which is annihilation, the Other is a "future that I can assume." The Other is not taken on according to some rule or some duty that precedes his coming but only by the infinity in which I find myself always already engaged. As infinite, the Other is indeed the one over whom I have no power. But because of this he is also the one who deprives me of that fixed ground of negativity by which the "me" [*le "moi"*] returns to the self or "to its home [*chez soi*]"—thereby opening me to the infinity of time. Indeed, in Levinas, the "Thou shalt" thus does not have a moral meaning. It denotes the modality of *departure* in a summons [*la modalité de* départ *de l'assignation*]. To be obligated to the Other, to respond to the Other, is not to have duties. It is to be torn up from oneself, to be in that situation that deprives me of my freedom as a subject but opens me to infinity. The face-to-face with the Other is not what limits my freedom as a subject. It is what, in summoning my freedom, interrupts the negativity of time, in-spiring time with infinity and pre-engaging it in this infinity. The Other thus plays the same role in Levinas's philosophy as Nietzsche's "ignorance of the future," whose "joyful wisdom" was love. The other summons me; he shows me where I am, but only insofar as, being irreducible to "grasping," to comprehension, he does not reveal to me where I am going, yet takes me there nonetheless. Different from morality, an ethics is not negation but affirmation. In Levinas, it likewise assumes the meaning of a "gay science," although Nietzsche had already opened to its unconditionality by showing that duty and power shared the same negative essence and by wagering, with the child, what the lion could not.

I have attempted to show that Nietzsche and Levinas meet at the precise midpoint of the chiasmi that might simply have reflected their opposition.

Nietzsche and Levinas converge where the fixity and the negativity of the "I can" burst open. The fact that we can *not,* that we are power-less [*qu'on ne puisse pas pouvoir*] is thus the condition of cheerfulness, innocence, and lightness. But this is a lightness that summons and orders us such that it makes subjectivity play the exceptional role of a host, taking leave of what had allowed it to determine itself. We can now weave Nietzsche's and Levinas's vocabularies together and say that the innocence of the child, wagering the infinity or the ignorance of the future, is already "responsibility." In Levinas, responsibility infinitizes humans, not in or through its force but in the breakdown of its negativity. In Nietzsche, the "self-surpassing of morality" is not an end in itself. "And life itself told me this secret: 'Behold,' it said, 'I am that *which must overcome itself again and again*'" (TZ "Of Self-Overcoming": 138). As soon as this "self-overcoming" comes to pass under the auspices of infinity, the "*Übermensch*" becomes "the traveller": "You are treading your path of greatness; now it must call up your courage that there is no longer a path behind you" (TZ "The Wanderer": 174). As in Levinas, this departure permits no turning back into the security of the self: "your foot itself has extinguished the path behind you" (TZ 174). There are no stops in the newly acquired—or rediscovered—direction of a force both ownmost and possible: "above that path stands written: 'impossibility'" (TZ 174). Thus, "innocent" in Nietzsche does not mean "uncommitted" but rather "disinterested," out of the erasure of the footprints or the self. "Responsible" in Levinas does not mean "moral" but welcoming, in the summons that brings about a departure.

In seeking something like a cheerfulness common to both Nietzsche and Levinas, we have also found a shared gravity, a seriousness that we know best in Levinas as patience and expiation. This gravity introduces a new element common to Nietzsche and Levinas: a certain pathos of writing. Indeed, something like suffering is expressed by both philosophers even as it is exhibited in their thinking itself, as its ethos. But this common element points to a difference that cannot be reduced once and for all. Of course, this difference directly engages the question of ethics and, with it, that of philosophy. One might think that the primacy accorded to the other person in Levinas interrupts Nietzsche's critical insatiability. In effect, in Levinas the face-to-face with the Other does not seem to leave any space for awaiting, whereas with Nietzsche we find ourselves awaiting an affirmation. Thus we read, in *Daybreak,* that to think is "to become silent, to become slow," which looks like a new warning to the reader. By this hypothesis, we might then infer that Levinas's pronouncing the name "God" promises that the infinite process of critique will come to an end.

Levinas's thinking would then slide into optimism, because it would in fact have proceeded from it. But could we not invert these hypotheses? Could we not say that it is indefinite awaiting that risks mystifying what was just called "the impossible"? In this respect—though it is not my intent to remain with Nietzsche on this—the messianic configuration of the impossible, which in Levinas is betrayed in the "said" [*le dit*], at least escapes the risk of mystification. The other person is indeed the one to whom I am obliged to respond, and this without delay or expectation. Now, although I do not subscribe to binaristic hypotheses here, I believe we can argue that there is, in Levinas, a revolt against the comfort that the idea of an indefinite awaiting can confer. This is one of the reasons why Levinas subscribes to the "death of God," who, as a moral god, is also the god of the promise of a coming end [*la promesse d'une fin à venir*]. But if it is the other person who interrupts this indefinite process of awaiting, then why God?

The answer to this question might not belong to a belief but to a difference of style. As I stated, Nietzsche lays claim to solitude and more than once challenges any patience accorded to the neighbor.[2] Conversely, Levinas never ceases repeating that "the Saying," that is, meaning or (the opening of) discourse, comes to me from the other person, from his approach, which is also his imminence. We thus see Levinas's style and thought turning around a series of oxymorons, which concern the relation between the neighbor and the distant one, but also that between youth and aging, lightness and gravity. Gravity, for example, resides in my exposure to the other person, which is undergoing, traumatism—but this exposure is also to be torn out of oneself; it is a departure, an opening of time and fecundity. In turn, aging is the separation or gap with regard to oneself that we encounter in effort, but in this gap of time, the infinite also *comes to pass* as a rupture or breakthrough of anarchy, a loss of time, an interruption that precedes all remembering. This allows Levinas to speak of an *underside* to interiority [*d'un* revers *de l'intériorité*], of the overturning of the economy of the Me by the for-itself [*pour soi*], of exposure at the surface of the skin, and thus of youth, sincerity, a fissioning of the secret—which we can once again call innocence. But these oxymorons proliferate out of the anarchy (i.e., the irreducibility to any beginning, origin, or presentation) that the face-to-face with the other person articulates. In effect, it is insofar as the face of the other person is not reducible to its form that he is beyond the said,

Most High. This amounts to saying that starting from the Other, time is infinitized, it is futurized: time opens itself in the very dynamic of its prolonging. Yet in this way, as we can see, the other person only receives its meaning as neighbor insofar as its meaning ("*kath auto*," as *Totality and Infinity* puts it [TI 65, 67; TeI 37, 39]) is "exteriority," unpresentable, anarchic.

There is, therefore, a double rupture. On the one hand, language is not conceived here according to the differential scheme of "signifier-signified," which abstracts language from its signification; instead, language is thought in its materiality. On the other hand, the subject is not separated from its word [*parole*], which it would use as a tool to elaborate a thought; rather, the word is given to the subject in the same way that its exceptionality is given to that subject, that is, as irreplaceable singularity and uniqueness. How to understand this double rupture?

The Other, as infinite, as the stranger, tears me out of the certainty of my identity but does so by preceding me, as it were. In this way, having no further refuge, I find I am the unique one. Uniqueness is thus conferred through exposure, but exposure is at once suffering, undergoing, and an offering. Torn out of the fixed ground of my identity, I come forth, I can say, "Here I am." If it is the other person who inspires me with the word, he inspires me not only in the trace of this departure, such that my own word is a laying bare, a suffering, and an offering—but in the trace of this departure my word is infinitized, thus laying bare my exposure and causing the infinite to reverberate in the infinity of my word. Hence, there would be nothing impossible to say—nothing unutterable—nothing that could not be said; or again, there is nothing but the unsayable to say. And thus, against what I argued earlier, I do not believe that God would be the name of the outside [*dehors*], or of exposure, but rather that God states the laying bare of every exposure. And it is not impossible to utter this name, so far as the name becomes the infinite to be said. It is simply that the irreducibility of the "face-to-face" and the primacy that the Other inaugurates represent a *step into the impossible*, into the otherwise said [*dans l'autrement dit*]. It is a venture that "does not hesitate to assert the impossibility of statement while venturing *to realize* this impossibility by the very statement of this impossibility" (OB 7; AE 20).

In fine, after what I have just argued, "God" does not have a theo-*logical* sense in Levinas. "God" does not denote the unsayable, or a Supreme Being, but instead the exception in all its exposure. Levinas's God thus announces the downfall of the theological as a discourse *on* God. But how is it that this downfall does not carry with it that of philosophy itself? And, to pose yet another question, in what sense is the "death of God," such as Nietzsche states it and Levinas takes it up, a philosophical event?

In *The Gay Science,* Nietzsche proclaims, through the "death of God," "a sequence of breakdown, destruction, ruin and cataclysm."[3] Yet if these ruins proclaim a radical change in the way we apprehend truth, then "who today could guess enough of it?" asks Nietzsche. If this event destroys our grasp of the truth, it can no longer be conceived in the present as a finite event. It follows that such an event can only open us to its awaiting, freeing the horizon from limitation. Far from submitting to a passive awaiting, this horizon "appears free to us again, even if it should not be bright" (GS §343, 280)—invites us without awaiting to "venture out again . . . to face any danger" (GS §343, 280), that is, it invites us to keep the promise of this unknown. The "death of God" is a departure, the same departure that *gives body and materiality to* [*qui donne corps*] Levinas's language; except that in Levinas it is the Other, "*Autrui*"—who is both the unknown and the signification of this departure—that is explicitly thematized as "the one-for-the-other, where the other is not assumed by the one" (OB 50; AE 85). To this, Levinas adds a specification that describes the ambiguous understanding we might have of God in *Otherwise Than Being*. First, Levinas states that signification as departure "supposes the possibility of pure non-sense invading and threatening signification" (OB 50; AE 85). This departure is really "for nothing"; it has no point. No sense is *guaranteed* at the end of this departure, which agrees with the meaning of "the death of God," understood at the end of *Otherwise Than Being* as the death of "worlds behind the scene" ("*arrière-mondes*": cf. OB 185; AE 284). There, Levinas writes, "without this madness at the outermost limits of reason, the one would take hold of itself and in the heart of its passion, recommence essence" (OB 50; AE 85, trans. modified). We can thus see that this "for nothing" is the madness on whose cord *Otherwise Than Being* balances and that inhabits its language, which shows how little this is an optimistic book. However, in another text ("Secularization and Hunger"),[4] Levinas speaks of exposure as "some other side of Nothing,"[5] which then suggests that while signification, understood as "departure," is for nothing, it remains that this disinterestedness, despite its ex-ceeding and ex-crescence, cannot itself be reduced to nothing. It exempts itself from the alternative of Being and Nothingness. Thus, Levinas's "God" does not bring about the destruction of philosophy as this God announces nothing theological or extraphilosophical and echoes like the other side of nothingness. Instead, this God is indissociable from the "death of God," indissociable from the "for nothing" by which Nietzsche thought the gaiety of such an event in the modality of a departure: "the sea, *our* sea, lies open again; perhaps there has never yet been such an open sea—" (GS 280).

————

To summarize briefly the intrigue of the proximity discerned between Nietzsche and Levinas—especially, between the "death of God" and what Levinas hears of its echo—we can say that, in *Otherwise Than Being*, "God" does not represent the impossible relationship between Saying and the said, nor even the injunction not to reduce the former to the latter. This is because God is unsayable in this logic. Instead, the name "God" denotes the overbid set on every said, by which Levinas refuses simply to give in to the impossible, as though silence should be preserved or held fast. The meaning of the "Saying" in Levinas commits him to do or to state the impossible. It is that "step beyond" [*pas au-delà*] that Levinas also calls "Goodness" [*le* "Bien"]. In this sense, if responsibility is infinite, we are always already engaged in its fulfillment, which is not its end or its realization but rather its "overbid" [*sa surenchère*]. Through the distant one [*le lointain*], Levinas shows the gratuity and anarchy—*impossible to say*—of responsibility and of its law. Through the neighbor [*le prochain*], Levinas exposes or elects us, as already committed "by the Saying to overbid," that is, precisely to say the impossible, and to exceed every aporetic law of responsibility. Where metaphysical foundations are destroyed and no measure or meaning can stand as the guarantor of existence, "the Good" or "Goodness" glimmers like the underside of "Nothingness"; "Goodness," understood as the "pre-" that our exposure to the Other always sought to say. Thus Levinas can write: "From the Good to me—assignation: a relation that survives the 'death of God'" (OB 123; AE 196, trans. modified).

But if Levinas's Other *survives* the "death of God," then is Nietzsche's God condemned to an eternal death? This question cannot have a response inasmuch as Nietzsche's word does not have a definite truth. But what we can state is that in Nietzsche, death does not lead to a self-sufficient relationship. Let us remember how Nietzsche's truth summons any pride and contempt: "Now solitude itself yields and breaks apart and can no longer contain its dead. The resurrected are to be seen everywhere" (TZ "The

Greeting": 292). Neither solitude nor death is Nietzsche's last word, precisely because Nietzsche's words happen as an indefinite rupture: "What does your truth matter, Zarathustra? State the truth that you have in yourself and be broken." Now, while this break is not embodied by a *responsive* dimension, or beating of thinking and writing, it opens to it. Nietzsche's writing indeed is not a response but an address; it does not play host to the neighbor. Nevertheless it calls to the distant one, to the friend: "It is you I am calling! Do not cover yourself in the caverns of your withdrawal and your mistrust! Be at least the reader of this book such that, thereafter, by your acts, it can be destroyed and forgotten."[6] To take one's distance, then, and to forget: therein lies the "star truth"[7]—the demise and the future—of friendship.

NOTES

1. The final section of *Otherwise Than Being* is titled "Autrement Dit"; I protect the French *adverb* in translating this as "Otherwise Said," rather than "In Other Words"—Editor. Translated by Bettina Bergo.

2. For instance in *Zarathustra*, "De l'amour du prochain."

3. See, for example, GS §343, 279.

4. Emmanuel Levinas, "Secularization and Hunger," trans. Bettina Bergo, in *Graduate Faculty Philosophy Journal* 20, no. 2, and 21, no. 1 (1998): 3–12.

5. Levinas, "Secularization," 10: "It is an incessant recommencement of hunger struggling against the same stony surface . . . yet in this way as if calling to some other side of Nothing [*l'envers du Rien*]. A call without prayer"—Trans.

6. Friedrich Nietzsche, *On the Future of Our Educational Institutions*, trans. Michael W. Grenke (South Bend, Ind.: Saint Augustine's Press, 2004): five lectures presented in 1872 at the University of Basel.

7. See GS §279.

13

Levinas: Another Ascetic Priest?

SILVIA BENSO

In fond memory of my father.

Nietzsche's Critique of Morality

On the Genealogy of Morals offers Nietzsche's most systematic, pervasive, and devastating criticism of all moralities based on the notion of a transcendent good inhibiting life, the enjoyment of life, and the will to power. Nietzsche does not simply question a certain morality; rather, he challenges "the *value* of morality," and especially of that "morality of pity" (GM Preface: 5) in which "'moral,' 'unegoistic,' '*désintéressé*' [are taken] as concepts of equivalent value" (GM 1:2). Nietzsche's well-known criticism can be reformulated as focusing on three issues: altruistic morality stems from *ressentiment,* fosters asceticism, and displaces the value of life onto an ascetic ideal. All three notions, *ressentiment,* asceticism, and ascetic ideals, are characterized by the same structural or formal movement—the movement of negation: of the other, of oneself, and of life. One could thus legitimately conclude that the morality of *ressentiment* is a morality of negation, the minister of which is the figure of the ascetic priest. In criticizing morality,

I argue, Nietzsche is condemning this notion of *negation* that functions as its foundation.

Two types of negation can be retraced in Nietzsche, which can be named affirmative negation and negative negation. Affirmative negation is the movement of denial enacted by the noble (GM 1:10). This negation stems from a first affirmation within the self; therefore, it is autonomous. Negative negation belongs to the rabble, who can assert themselves only by means of what Deleuze calls a "paralogism."[1] This group proceeds to affirmation only through a previous negation of what is other than itself. Negative negation starts in heteronomy, outside the self, from the other to which it says "No" (GM 1:10). Whereas affirmative negation is favored by Nietzsche, who pursues it in many of his works (from the early *Birth of Tragedy* to the later *Thus Spoke Zarathustra*) as a form of activity and affirmation of differences, negative negation is sharply rejected by him because of its reactive character.

Nietzsche's hermeneutic strategy for evaluating the dangerousness of a given morality is that of reading moral values as symptoms of the health conditions of the will that underlies them. If the proposed values reveal an affirmative structure, the will behind them is salubrious, nonreactive, and concerned with an affirmation and enhancement of life. Such values can be embraced with confidence. However, if the proposed values prove to come out of a dialectical structure of negation and *ressentiment,* the morality founded on them should be rejected since it fosters self-infliction of pain, debasement, *décadence,* and nihilism, and the will that proposes them is itself reactive, sick, and degenerated. Altruistic morality is the danger of dangers when it comes to the assertion of the value of life because, by operating through negation, such a morality denies life.

The minister of altruistic morality (that is, the ascetic priest) as a type "appears in almost every age; he belongs to no one race; he prospers everywhere; he emerges from every class of society" (GM 3:11). Nietzsche's age, as well as ours, is not immune to such a presence. Moreover, not only is the priest's activity endemic to different epochs; it is also contagious. The ascetic priest thrives on the existence of some herd whose weakness he can parasitically exploit. Therefore, his own well-being is conditional upon the diffusion of a nihilistic (that is, altruistic) morality. The priest must encourage negation. As long as there exist priest-type individuals, morality represents the danger of a deadly contagion, which the physician of culture (the Nietzschean philosopher) needs to combat.

On the Necessity of the Confrontation
Between Levinas and Nietzsche

The latest appeal to ethics in continental philosophy comes from Levinas. Two main claims give his philosophy its ethical connotation. The first is the radical assertion that ethics is first philosophy, *philosophia prima* (TI 304). The second is that ethics is essentially heteronomy, a response to an appeal that comes from the other and never returns to the structures of identification of the same.

Any ethics that wishes to claim some credibility after Nietzsche cannot exempt itself from a confrontation with Nietzsche, I argue. To move against Nietzsche is in fact not yet to disprove Nietzsche. Despite the awareness of its anti-Nietzschean motif (OB 177), Levinas's philosophy must show that it does not result in an ironic, or even dialectical, confirmation of the powerfulness of Nietzsche's critique. More specifically, Levinas's ethics must be capable of withstanding two conditions. First, it must not display the reactive structure characterizing *ressentiment;* that is, it must prove not to be another case of slave morality. Second, and consequently, Levinas must prove that he is not the latest incarnation of the ascetic priest; that is, he must demonstrate that he is not advancing another example of asceticism and the ascetic ideal. Were Levinas's philosophy incapable of satisfying these two demands, then the force of his ethical project would be neutralized by the power of Nietzsche's critique. Conversely, were Levinas's answer to the two demands satisfactory, then his philosophy would not only prove that it is capable of saying something meaningful about ethics after Nietzsche's criticism; it would also undermine such a criticism and therefore also the devastation provoked by Nietzsche when it comes to the possibility of ethical thought. In either case, the confrontation between Nietzsche and Levinas is crucial.

Levinas's Appeal to Ethics: A Nietzschean Reading

Let me start with a characterization of Levinas's ethics from the perspective of a Nietzschean reader concerned with emphasizing the reactive aspects that assimilate Levinas's project to the morality of *ressentiment* and thereby turn Levinas into an ascetic priest.[2] On such a reading, in Levinas's philosophy the place of the Nietzschean noble would be taken by the "I." In *On the Genealogy of Morals* the nobles are spontaneous, active, and self-sufficient (GM 1:10). Similarly, in *Existence and Existents* Levinas describes the I as virility, solitude, and mastery of existence (EE 65–69). The atheistic separation and self-sufficiency of the I is reaffirmed in *Totality and Infinity*. The egoism of the I, its being satisfied by and within itself, is there described as contraction upon itself, enjoyment, and happiness (TI 107–83). The I is for itself, alone, immanent to its world, which appears as its home, its dwelling, the space where it feels at ease, even in fear (TI 152–74). The I's feeling of happiness and egoism receives a substantial contribution through possession and work (TI 158–68). The world becomes an economy, the law of which is established by the I through representational knowledge, which is spontaneity, creation, and legislation. Through it, the I constitutes itself as stable and enduring. At the origin, for Levinas, there is a citizen of paradise (TI 144) who is not dialectically constituted as an antithesis to the other or to the infinite. Like Nietzsche's noble, Levinas's I is lord and master of its own existence.

Yet, Levinas claims, the mastery of the I gets interrupted by the appearance of the face (TI 187–219), which signifies otherness and whose first expression immediately presents the I with a prohibition in the form of the commandment "You shall *not* commit murder" (TI 199, emphasis added). "No" is the other's first word (CPP 55). The other's first signification questions the power and mastery of the I, forces the I to justify its activity and spontaneity, and (ideally) compels the I to end its conditions of blessed egoism and solipsism. The other asks the I for a suspension of the I's will to power. It commands a negation of the I's enjoyment of life and an *epoché* of its domination and mastery. The Nietzschean interpreter would have no difficulties recognizing that a familiar type is disguised behind these requests: the other is a figure of *ressentiment*, the activity of which is marked by the negative attempt to stop the expansive forces of life and egoism, as if it were possible "to demand of strength that it should *not* express itself in strength" (GM 1:13).

Otherwise Than Being—the book where Levinas describes the figures of passivity by which the ethical self responds to the visitation by the face of the other—would be for the Nietzschean reader the clearest elaboration of such an ethics of *ressentiment*. In such a work, the other is said to command the I to become powerless, to take care of the other, to open the doors of the I's own warehouse and sate and slake the other even when the other leaves constitutively undetermined the content of her or his command—hence (and here is where the Nietzschean interpreter would put forward her criticism) the I's infinite guilt, its inadequacy and inability to be good enough to respond responsibly to the other's demands; hence the I's becoming the other's hostage, that is, the hostage of an unfulfilled and unfulfillable obligation toward the other. Because the other, described by Levinas through the images of the poor, the orphan, the widow, and the stranger, is unable to implement self-(im)position as a sovereign, the other demands proximity, the Nietzschean reader would argue. In this demand, the deceitful trick (the idealistic deception, the Nietzschean interpreter would relentlessly contest) that the other plays upon the I lies in the constant displacement of the possibility of achieving real and effective nearness. The other is always a step beyond, always further than the I can reach (the ascetic ideal! the Nietzschean would retort), always at a distance, a trace, and an immemorial past.

Despite the other's infinite inaccessibility, the I should still be directed by the other rather than by itself, Levinas claims; this should be so to the extent of becoming passive, more passive than passivity (asceticism! the Nietzschean would exclaim), substituting itself to and for the other and rejoicing and suffering not for itself but for the other, in place of the other (OB 90). The I should renounce being the creator of meaning, even of the meaning of *its* life, and receive such a meaning from the encounter with the other. On a Nietzschean reading, this would certainly correspond to an inhibition of the I's creative activity of interpretation, which is replaced by the unidirectionality of the relation oriented by the other and the other's appeal and demands. From this perspective, the other becomes the giver of all meaning, the donation of which happens through that first "No" with which the encounter begins.

That this is an inversion of the noble morality and not a substitution of a previous mastery (the I's) with a new one (the other's) is confirmed to the Nietzschean interpreter by that first negation that characterizes the appearing of the other. The alleged "mastery," to employ a Nietzschean vocabulary, that the other imposes on the I bears the features of what the Nietzschean interpreter would consider a reduction to the rabble: the other is the poor, the weak, the destitute, Levinas argues; therefore, it is to a proximity to this condition that the other calls the I. Whereas the other may be described as a master, nevertheless the other is only the master of her or his own destitution, since the other's is a mastery without possessions, Levinas claims. That is, the other is a master of nothingness, the Nietzschean would retort. Therefore, the Nietzschean reader would continue, the other cleverly inverts such evident lack of strength by transforming it into what Levinas calls ethical authority. According to this, powerlessness and passivity become the victorious keys of affirmation. The aim is somehow to force the I to be ashamed of its own power, to feel guilty, to renounce its egoism, to become subjected to the other and to transform itself into an "*Autrui*-ist," that is, to be directed by *Autrui* and become good. In its negativity, the first imperative with which Levinas's other greets the I would be considered by the Nietzschean reader as an expression of the other's *ressentiment* and of the other's inability to cope with its own lack of physical (or psychological for that matter) power of self-affirmation. Rather than fighting, the other surrenders by placing an infinite demand that amounts to a surreptitious victory. This is what Levinas calls ethical resistance (CPP 55), but what for the Nietzschean reader is a mere product of *ressentiment*.

Viewed from such a Nietzschean perspective, the move that represses the I's instinct for domination amounts to the affirmation of an ascetic ideal. For Levinas, the other is always beyond, *à-Dieu*. The other comes from an immemorial past of which there is neither grasp nor control, and the other's appeal to the I to become good still concerns the beyond. The reward for the I's renunciation of its egoism of life and being, or what Levinas calls the ontological I, is the transmutation of the I into an ethical self. Yet, the Nietzschean interpreter would object, the good toward which Levinas's ethical self should strive is always beyond being; it is the desire for the infinite that never gets fulfilled because the infinite does not expose itself to possession (TI 33–35). That all this amounts to an ascetic ideal is further confirmed for the Nietzschean analyst by the marginalized role history plays within Levinas's philosophy: the forces of life do not serve the immanence of action but the transcendence of eschatology.

When interpreted from this (perhaps overly) Nietzschean perspective focused on power, affirmation, and activity, Levinas's ethics would maintain all the features of the morality Nietzsche so sharply condemns. When the ascetic priest begins to philosophize, Nietzsche warns, the result is metaphysics. It is therefore very appropriate that Levinas reserves the term "metaphysics" to his thought. And on a Nietzschean account it is again very appropriate that for Levinas metaphysics indicates the philosophy of the beyond, of the infinite, of the transcendent—what the Nietzschean has no difficulty identifying as the ascetic ideal. The Nietzschean interpreter would conclude that Levinas's philosophy offers powerful theoretical tools for a successful infection and spreading of that debasing disease that is ethics and that Levinas's success as an ascetic priest—and the consequent fatal contagion—increases every time a new reader joins Levinas's audience and lets her- or himself be convinced by his thinking.

Levinas's Appeal to Ethics: A Retrieval

The assimilation of Levinas's philosophy with slave morality is what may immediately occur to the shrewd and unsympathetic Nietzsche scholar (but perhaps an excessively naive Levinas reader, I argue). However, a more attentive reading of Levinas's philosophy, that is, a reading that is faithful to the internal structure of his thinking, will reject the assimilation and absolve Levinas from the charges of being an ascetic priest. Such a reading, on which I will now embark, will liberate Levinas's project from Nietzsche's condemnation while simultaneously regaining for philosophy the possibility of a meaningful ethical discourse after Nietzsche.

The task of rehabilitating Levinas is not unproblematic. Levinas seems to take a special pleasure in employing terms and concepts that invite the very criticism and condemnation that Nietzsche advocates. Nevertheless, retrieving Levinas's philosophy from the grips of Nietzsche's criticism remains inevitable if one wants to assert the continuing relevance of ethics and all ethical projects. More fundamentally, such retrieval becomes crucial if one wishes to assert different modalities of relations between the self and the other than those contemplated by Nietzsche. The goal of reasserting the valence of ethics after Nietzsche cannot be successfully pursued simply by claiming that Levinas's notions are situated on a level (that is, the ethical level) different from the analogous concepts criticized by Nietzsche (which would still move on an ontological plane). The invocation of a difference of levels is precisely the displacement that the ascetic ideal performs and Nietzsche deconstructs. Nor is it enough to claim that Levinas does not recur to traditional ethical concepts such as virtue and duty, as if this lack were sufficient to construe a different model of ethics and hence could provide a satisfactory exemption from a Nietzschean criticism. A more structural analysis is required.

What characterizes ascetic morality, the ascetic ideal informing such a morality, as well as the ascetic priest, is the structure of negation—of the other, of oneself, and of life. The very engine of such a morality, *ressentiment,* is negation; it gives birth to phenomena of repression and denial, as Nietzsche portrays it in his description of the origin of (bad) conscience, responsibility, and guilt. The strategy I will employ to retrieve Levinas from a Nietzschean criticism will be to show the following: not simply *ressentiment* (a psychological feeling) but rather negation (a structural movement) is alien to Levinas's philosophy. The rest of my analysis will focus on three moments constructed around a common structure of negation: the lack of external negation, the lack of internal negation, and the lack of the ascetic ideal in Levinas.

The Lack of External Negation

Despite the scarcity of his references to Nietzsche, it seems legitimate to infer that Levinas shares with Nietzsche a philosophically deep aversion to negation. More radically than Nietzsche, however, Levinas extends his contempt to include not only what has been identified earlier as negative negation but also affirmative negation. The reason for Levinas's double rejection lies, I argue, in the formal character of negation, rather than in its genealogy. From a formal point of view, negation is the main feature characterizing dialectics, since negation is inherently bound to the object of its denial. Every dialectical project aims at keeping together the I and the non-I (the other) precisely through negation, in a connection that can be more or less stringent, more or less open. When dialectics operates, there arises a link or dependency between the two terms or beings that no revolt can ever dissolve.[3]

It is immediately evident how negative negation, that is, the negation carried out by slave morality, depends on the existence of the non-I, which the self needs to deny for its own self-assertion. Nietzsche identifies the reactive character of negative negation in this dependency, which binds the I and the non-I together as an a priori *condition* for the affirmation of the I. That affirmative negation also is, despite Nietzsche's effort to say the opposite, somehow dependent on the existence of the non-I is more difficult to assert, since the non-I enters the scene at a later stage, when the I has already affirmed itself independently from the non-I. In his philosophy, Levinas challenges precisely the independence of the I enacting affirmative negation. Such an I, according to Nietzsche, is autonomous. What Levinas's entire philosophy questions is the nature of this autonomy.

Although the reference to Nietzsche is never explicit, for Levinas Western subjectivity since Parmenides has been shaped (with very few exceptions) by an autonomy and an egoism (CPP 48) analogous to those Nietzsche favors. However, as Levinas claims, the identity of the subject is never a status but rather a process of identification (TI 36). To reestablish continuously the autonomy of its identity, the I needs to reduce to itself "all that is opposed to it as *other*" (CPP 48). Since the I's inception, the I's need for integration (that is, for a necessarily totalitarian, continuous self-assertion) contemplates the other not as an absolute other but rather, always and already, as another from the self, that is, as a *relative* otherness (and hence Levinas's complaint about the artificial alterity of this other). Thus, exactly like Nietzsche's noble, the I engages in an activity of reduction to itself, its own non-I (representational objects, nature, bodies, and so on), with the goal of being able to enjoy its own power and strength more satisfactorily. If the dependence of the autonomous I on the non-I is not *a priori* (that is, if it is not a *condition* for self-affirmation, as is the case for Nietzsche's slave), nevertheless such a dependence comes *a posteriori,* as a *necessary consequence* of the process of self-identification. In the case of Nietzsche's affirmative negation, this movement means that the masters could not appreciate the extent of their mastery unless there *are* slaves to be mastered. Even the beast of prey depends on its victim to be the ferocious predator that it is. Otherwise, it is only a hungry animal. The presence and negation of some non-I, at whose expense the process of self-identification is carried out, becomes essential. The deceiving alterity of the other within any dialectical system mirrors the deceptiveness of the autonomy of any I (even the I of positive affirmation) within such a dialectical movement of thought.

Stated more clearly, albeit perhaps also more abruptly: in (either negative or affirmative) negation, the negator and the negated always stand in a relation binding and committing the one to the other. The I of negative negation (in Nietzsche's description, the slave) posits *itself* as a negation of *its other*. The I of affirmative negation (in Nietzsche's analysis, the master) considers *its other* as an impediment and a negation of *itself*. No matter where the negation is generated, the I and the non-I (*its* non-I) remain within the horizon of one and the same system, since, as Hegel would claim, negation is always determined, that is, it is always *reciprocally* determined. Therefore, when Nietzsche claims that the noble is autonomous, he is mistaken. There cannot be real autonomy—or real heteronomy, and this is Levinas's point—when some form of negation is present. Formally, although this may not be true genealogically, the nobles are not much different from the slaves as to their participation in dialectical dependency. Certainly there is a dialectics of the noble and a dialectics of the slaves, and the differences between them are not irrelevant. But negation as a formal feature assimilates both.

Levinas's criticism of Western philosophy turns Nietzsche's criticism against itself to include Nietzsche as part of Nietzsche's own targets. Conversely, the complete absence of negation, that is, the possibility of an absolute separation as delineated by Levinas, eliminates the structural motif from which *ressentiment* arises. It is to this absence in Levinas that I now turn.

Levinas's project aims at withstanding dialectics by withstanding the negation that lies at its core. For him, the relation between the ego and the other cannot be dialectically, that is, oppositionally, constituted. Between the I and the other there is distance, which allows for the separatedness and absoluteness of each of them. That is, in Levinas both the I and the other stand as autonomous and independent from each other when it comes to their existence. Neither is constituted in relation to the other because between them there is no reciprocity. Exteriority rules their existence. Although this may create difficulties of a different order, the relation between the I and the other is said to be a "relation without relation" (TI 80). This is what Levinas characterizes as ethics.

First, let me illustrate the I's "autonomy"—which Levinas identifies as separatedness, to distinguish it from ontological autonomy. As already mentioned, the I enjoys the world (and the presence of a Nietzschean motif in this could be explored), possesses the world, and shapes it through its activity of labor. In such accomplishments, the I is solitude, distance from its creator, atheism, joy, and plenitude of life. As if truly inspired by Nietzschean themes, Levinas's I is master because it does not lack anything. It is the artistic creator of its own world and representations. It is a "here I am" of Pascalian memory that imposes itself upon the world—its world. The fact that the ontological "here I am" can transform itself into the availability of infinite ethical responsibility (the *hineni* of Abrahamic memory) is subsequent to the encounter with the other, who does not found the I (even when the other precedes the I), since the I is already there. Here lies the nondialectical paradox of Levinas's philosophy: ontologically the I is already there, without the other, with no need for the other in order for itself to exist, and yet ethically the I is already haunted by the other who comes before, precedes the I at all times in the other's own separation and absoluteness.

The other's separatedness or "autonomy" is, for Levinas, as originary as the I's separation. Retrieving the ontological argument, Levinas gives his own version of it in terms of the other: "the exteriority of a being is inscribed in its essence" (TI 196). This means that the otherness of the other is absolute, that is, absolved from the identity of the same: it "is not formal, is not the simple reverse of identity, and it is not formed out of resistance to the same, for in limiting the same the other would not be rigorously other" (TI 38–39). As Levinas phrases it, the other is *Autrui*, the absolutely or wholly other who remains irreducible to any content of the I's consciousness. Between the I and the other there is no common theoretical ground.

The relation that the I and the other are called to establish (ethics) but in which they are already is this "relation without relation," in which each is maintained in her or his own separatedness. The relation is a face-to-face—on both sides. There is no foundationalism of the I through the other, or vice versa. The temporality of the I and the other, and of their relationship, is not synchrony, in which the before and the after of foundationalism find their place in a chronological order. Rather, it is diachrony, that is, two different, incommensurable temporalities in a time that is that of inspiration and prophecy.

What appeared as a first negation, the initial "You shall not kill" with which the other greets the I, must be thus reinterpreted not as a denial of the I and its power of affirmation but as an affirmation of the other's existence in its own separatedness. It becomes an appeal, an injunction, and an order only because in their separatedness the I and the other are already in the ethical relationship, in a face-to-face prior to any representation. That is, the ethical relationship precedes the separatedness of the I and the other, but it does not sublate it, or them. In this sense we can say that in Levinas's ethics the I and the other are independent in a more fundamental way than is the Nietzschean master. It is not negation that acts in ethics. If anything, it is a philosophy of separation and proximity in which there is no reduction of the one term to the other.

Because of the lack of negation (whether affirmative or negative), Levinas's position certainly cannot be qualified as that of a Nietzschean master. But neither can Levinas's thought be qualified in terms of *ressentiment*.

Levinas stands with Nietzsche in performing a strenuous critique of nega-tion, but moves further than Nietzsche in assimilating both kinds of nega-tion (affirmative *and* negative) as a single mode of denial. While liberat-ing him from the charge of being moved by *ressentiment,* this move affords Levinas a new meaning for heteronomy and ethics.

The Lack of Internal Negation

At this point, the Nietzschean reader might argue that Levinas's ethics still operates a negation in terms of the imposed self-denial of the I, which, despite its separatedness, is directed by the other's demands. Asceticism implies self-abnegation. Levinas's notion of heteronomy is precisely this movement, the Nietzschean interpreter could claim. It therefore becomes necessary to show that despite or even because of its specific heteronomy, Levinas's ethics does not reintroduce negation at the stage of the individual, causing its exhaustion rather than its empowerment. It must be shown that besides not being structured by external negation, Levinas's ethics does not produce asceticism.

Two considerations must be developed at this juncture. The first concerns the origin of the ethical relation. According to Levinas, the I is involved in an ethical relation with the other *before* any theoretical acknowledge-ment or recognition of norms—that is, before moral choices (TI 25, 113). Heteronomy, or orientation by the other, is inscribed in the I's separated-ness. Ethical responsibility is neither "the recall of some prior generous dis-position toward the other," nor "a decision resulting from a deliberation" (TO 113). In other words, ethics is not chosen, is not the product of voli-tion, of an intentional act of the will (to power or to *décadence*). On the contrary, ethics is an-archic. It does not start because it always is.

The second consideration concerns the meaning and implications con-tained in the notions of power/empowering (and hence debasement) for Nietzsche and Levinas. Because of the lack of external negation, in Levinas mastery as well as power cannot be understood as a violent, tyrannical, or dominating physical force of imposition. What could be considered as, in Nietzschean terminology, the Levinasian master, that is, as the I in its sepa-ration, is not "a beast of prey" (GM 1:11) but rather a separated existent. On the other hand, the other does not oppose the power of the I with any physical resistance. Rather, the other exerts resistance by subtracting itself from the I. The halting of the killing is by withdrawal, not by oppression or repression (TI 198, CPP 55). This institutes a distance between the I and the other that places the other in a dimension of unreachable height. The other is my master and my lord not because the other dominates me but because the other commands to me from a distance, which is the distance of destitution rather than force and violence (CPP 58). Asymmetry rules the ethical relationship for Levinas. Not the community of association (GM 3:18) but proximity, that is, once again, nearness in separation, becomes the way by which the I encounters the other. À la Nietzsche, Levinas's perspective is not immediately egalitarian. Justice is the preservation (and proximity) of differences (although not in the aristocratic sense Nietzsche advocates), and only thus an appeal to democracy.

In Nietzsche, on the other hand, the notions of mastery and power subtend the notion of the will to power. As Heidegger remarks, the will to power implies a metaphysics of the will, or at least a voluntarism,[4] that unfolds as one more instance of subjectivism and the bad infinite (in the Hegelian sense). Conversely, Levinas's notion of power avoids subjectivism and voluntarism because it does not originate from the subject. The powerful I is for Levinas the one who, thanks to the other, has been liberated from the limits and constraints imposed by self-concern and self-interestedness. Through this liberation, the I gains freedom from and for itself and thereby can afford the generosity of giving even its own being. The result is not a weakening of the I but its empowerment as gift giver. This implies a novel form of subjectivity. Similar perhaps to the Nietzschean *Übermensch,* whose generosity, like the sun's, stems from excess rather than from a voluntaristic, guilt-led attempt at being altruistic, Levinas's I is so full, rich, and wealthy that it can afford emptying itself out, exposing itself, and even giving itself to the other. This is its ethical power.

It is not toward a negation of all subjectivity, toward its ascetic abnegation, that the appeal from the other is directed, but toward its declension: for Levinas, the I becomes an accusative, a Me. And the Me is always appealed to as a first person, in its uniqueness and irreplaceability. In a move that Nietzsche would appreciate, no conformity with the herd or universalization of the I is possible for Levinas. That the Me be defined in terms of passivity, absolute passivity, passivity more passive than any passivity (rather than being defined by activity), is not relevant at this point because the structure of (self-)negation, even in passivity, has been relinquished. The movement is from a closed subjectivity trying to impose its own closure on the external world to an open subjectivity responding in terms of generosity and gift giving. The other does not deny the I, does not alienate it; the other keeps the I awake as a one-for-the-other, as an exposure, as a Me capable of the excesses of generosity. This is not a submission to what is other-than-the-I, to a non-ego (OB 54, 112). It is, rather, the mobility, fluidity, porosity, and displacement that the I, as a Me, reaches through the other. To retrieve this dimension is for the I to place itself at the origin of its genealogy, since ethical responsibility—the Me—is "prior to the will's initiative (prior to the origin)" (OB 118). In other words, in suffering, substitution, being a hostage, in the ethical categories by which Levinas describes the relation with the other, the self gets reinforced, although through a different modality of subjectivity. Not only does Levinas reinstate the possibility of ethics, he also describes a different subjectivity for it. In being heteronomous, the I does not renounce its separatedness; that is, the self is never denied. What the self gives up is what renders it a resentful, and hence violent subject: the structure of (self-)negation.

A major accusation Nietzsche advances against asceticism is that it represses sensuality, corporeality, and the body. Levinas's notion of passivity, however, is based precisely on sensibility, which is understood as the possibility of being affected, or affectivity. The declension of the I as Me, as an accusative passive to the demands of the other, is for Levinas a celebration of the body. Nietzsche would agree that it is not the presence of suffering per se, but rather the modality of suffering that makes a life ascetic. Therefore, it is not the presence of suffering that may constitute a charge against Levinas. Levinas finds an ethical justification for suffering in the form of responsibility for the other. Nevertheless, unlike ascetic morality—which also provides a justification for the suffering endemic to human existence (GM 3:28)—Levinas's justification does not posit self-denial as the supreme goal of life. Negation does not appear, not even as self-negation. Therefore, the analogy between the categories of suffering, subjection, and substitution that Levinas employs, and the same categories that Nietzsche criticizes is only superficial, nominal and not semantic. Any such critique neglects the structural novelty of Levinas's project. It is not hetero-directedness that should be criticized, but rather the ab-negation—of life and self—that is usually associated with such a heteronomy. In subtracting himself from negation, Levinas escapes also its criticism, since, having dissociated heteronomy from (self-)negation, he is able to retain the former while relinquishing the latter.

In other words, Nietzsche and Levinas have a common enemy: negation. Nietzsche fights it by condemning what he sees as the most powerful instances of negation—morality, asceticism, Christianity. Levinas, on
the contrary, having severed ethics from negation, can still fight the latter
without having to dismiss the former. In still different words, Levinas fights
not against the symptoms of the morality that Nietzsche rejects—this is
the peculiarity of the anaesthetizing rather than therapeutic method of the
ascetic priest (GM 3:17); rather, he fights against the causes at work in such
a morality—mainly, negation, the consequence of which is the ontological
ego. The result is an enhancement of life and sensibility. But since sensibility is defined in terms of affectivity, the reevaluation of life becomes a
reevaluation of passivity—although a passivity that precedes all distinctions
between active and passive, that is, between master and slave and between
master and slave expressions (morality/dialectics/ontology [or anything
else]).

The Lack of an Ascetic Ideal

One more issue remains to be examined: whether Levinas's notions of the
other and the goodness toward which the other directs the self work as
ascetic ideals for the ethical self. For Nietzsche, the ascetic ideal displaces
the value of life into another world, connoting the mundane existence of
negative attributes of lack and imperfection. This dislocation does not apply to Levinas, despite the fact that for him the desire for infinite goodness
is admittedly insatiable and goodness itself is transcendent, beyond being—
and, analogously, that the other always speaks from the inaccessibility of
the beyond, from a temporality that is never that of synchronicity but of
diachrony, ungraspable and unreachable. Levinas's phenomenology of desire clearly manifests how for Levinas desire does not originate from lack
but from plenitude. That is, there is nothing in mundane existence that is
in need of fulfillment or replacement by redemption. Again, goodness does
not repress the I through its limitations. It rather enhances the I by opening
it up to its possibilities, not for power but for becoming good.

Need originates from a lack in the soul; it stems from and is oriented toward the subject. It is nostalgia in need of a fulfillment that, while fulfilling,
also erases the subject by restoring it to a primordial unity with the object

of need. On the contrary, for Levinas desire is animated by what is desired, it moves from the other. Rather than fulfilling the desirer, desire "hollows it out, at the same time in a strange manner nourishing it or me ever again with new hungers" (ED 193). In its being beyond satiation, desire escapes the economy of closure that need attempts to establish. The I is opened up by this emptiness that nourishes without satiating it. Heteronomy, but not negation of the desirer, is at the core of the desire for goodness. Levinas writes that "truth is sought in the other, but by [her/]him who lacks nothing. . . . The separated being is satisfied, autonomous, and nonetheless searches after the other with a search that is not incited by the lack proper to need nor by the memory of a lost good" (TI 62). That is, the desired is not meant to complement (Plato), supplement (Hobbes or Hegel), or even substitute and replace the desirer (Christianity). In Levinas the desirer, because of its separatedness, is not "a being indigent and incomplete or fallen from its past grandeur" (TI 33), which the ascetic ideal should sublimate by an annihilation amounting to redemption. For Levinas, the infinite, the good—in short, everything that Nietzsche characterizes as the ascetic ideal—certainly calls into question the I's spontaneous freedom (TI 51). But transcendence for Levinas is not negativity any more than the other is negation of the I.

Levinas makes this point explicit in a passage that, in certain respects, reminds its reader of Nietzsche's criticism of the ascetic ideal. "The movement of transcendence is to be distinguished from the negativity by which discontent [human beings] refuse the condition in which [they are] established. . . . The 'otherwise' and the 'elsewhere' they wish for still belong to the here they refuse" (TI 41). Conversely, from its absolute alterity, the infinite to which Levinas subscribes does not deny imperfection. It rather designates a distance, "a passage to the other absolutely other" (TI 41), which does not remain on "the common plane of the *yes* or *no* at which negativity operates" (TI 41). In being designated as height, nobility, and mastery, the transcendent cannot be a mere negation of the imperfect, of the mundane. In "God and Philosophy" Levinas acknowledges that the "in-" of "infinite" must be read not only as a separation of the infinite but also as meaning that the infinite is found within the finite.[5] And in *Totality and Infinity* Levinas says: "This 'beyond' the totality and objective experience is . . . not to be described in a purely negative fashion. It is reflected *within* the totality and history, *within* experience" (TI 23).

Levinas's affinity with Nietzsche in rejecting any explanation that denies our world and existence in favor of another world is explicitly acknowledged in the opening pages of *Otherwise Than Being*. The God that dwelled above the earth is dead. Any recourse to a *Hinterwelt* is now forbidden (OB 8). Levinas's rejection is restated when he situates his work in continuity with Nietzsche's project of demythologization: "in this work which does not seek the restoration of any ruined concept . . . after the death of a certain god inhabiting the world behind the scenes" (OB 185). The transcendence Levinas advocates is not a being otherwise but an otherwise than being (OB 3). Not a negation, transcendence is rather a positivity that does not annihilate (TI 41–42). The relation to it is what Levinas calls "metaphysics." The infinite does not direct the ethical self beyond the world but to *this* world, toward an enjoyment of the fruits of the world.

It is true that, for Levinas, the fruits of the world acquire their meaning not by themselves but by becoming *gifts* for the other, that is, through the ethical dimension. Nevertheless, the ethical relation that is thus enacted retains all the features of an immanent ethics, an ethics where the call from the other and the response to it occur and unfold in *this* world. In this worldly gift giving, there is no negation of the other or of the I. The gifts from the I are met by the other with ingratitude. This move of nonreturn prevents a negation of the other by the I's return to itself. The gifts are pure generosity without remuneration. Their being pure gifts means also that to exist the I does not need the other's recognition. The I is sacrifice, but sacrifice, when it stems from plenitude, is gift giving, expenditure, and excess—heteronomy that does not deny autonomy; it only redefines it.

To conclude, Levinas accepts old Jewish categories, but he twists them in a direction that is immune to Nietzsche's charges. Bearing with Nietzsche in criticizing negation, Levinas goes further than Nietzsche in retrieving an ethics and a subjectivity that, simultaneously, condemn Nietzsche's ontological imperialism, absolve themselves from Nietzsche's criticism, and even espouse some clearly Nietzschean themes such a lack of negation, separation, sensibility, immanence, and faithfulness to the earth. Levinas is not an ascetic priest, nor is his metaphysical project a reproposal in new terms of the old ascetic ideal. Metaphysics must be understood as a rupture of participation in the totality that the dialectics of negation constitutes. Unlike the ascetic priest, Levinas does not infect the reader with a dangerous and fatal disease. Conversely, he signifies the death of the ascetic priest, since after Levinas there can be ethics without *ressentiment*, asceticism, and the ascetic ideal. It is an ethics of exposure, expenditure, and nonreturn. As Nietzsche would appreciate, it is an excessive ethics.

NOTES

An earlier version of this essay appeared in *The Journal of the British Society for Phenomenology* 2 (1996): 137–56. The essay has not been significantly changed in content, although it has been shortened for editorial reasons. The form has also been considerably edited for clarity and readability.

1. See Gilles Deleuze, *Nietzsche and Philosophy*, trans. H. Tomlinson (New York: Columbia University Press, 1983), 122.

2. I thank Daniel Conway for pointing out to me the dangers of asceticism inherent in Levinas's ethical project.

3. Therefore, the inanity of Kierkegaard's protest against Hegel's system.

4. Martin Heidegger, "The Word of Nietzsche: God Is Dead," in *The Question Concerning Technology*, trans. W. Lovitt (New York: Harper and Row, 1977), 95 ff.

5. Emmanuel Levinas, "God and Philosophy," trans. R. Cohen, *Philosophy Today* 22 (1978): 133.

14

Apocalypse, Eschatology, and the Death of God

BRIAN SCHROEDER

Who would still dare to undertake projects that would require thousands of years for their completion? For what is dying out is the fundamental faith that would enable us to calculate, to promise, to anticipate the future to them . . .
—Nietzsche, *The Gay Science*

Of peace there can only be an eschatology.
—Levinas, *Totality and Infinity*

The Death of God

Nothing separates the thinking of Nietzsche and Levinas more than the question of the "death of God," its extent and significance, and yet despite this distance they are drawn together in this very questioning, even if this signals an impossible resolution. In the case of Nietzsche, philosophical and theological arguments concerning the death of God abound, ranging from the simple assertion of God's nonexistence, to the paralysis of nihilism attending such an event, to the absolute release into a total freedom. For Levinas, the matter is more obscure, but it is perhaps best construed as the demise of a certain conception or set of interpretations about God (OB 185). Nietzsche incisively realizes that the death of God is foremost an ethical issue: the primary questions for the "philosophers of the future" (GS §§289, 343, 372) are those of the meaning and value of existence, not of epistemic certainty or metaphysical being. It is precisely here that these two very different nomads wend their paths over similar ground. More than indicating simply the loss, end, or completion of certain ideal grounds of truth, value, and meaning, the death of God is—and here is arguably the most important point of convergence between the generally disparate positions of Nietzsche and Levinas—the seeming withdrawal of any determinate sense of ground (*Grund*). If the only ground left after the death of God is a certain (in the sense of both surety and particularity) groundlessness, then what remains is a perpetual nomadic exile, an endless tarrying that leaves us vulnerable and exposed, but also for this reason wholly responsible not only for ourselves but for the Earth and its inhabitants or, as Levinas would have it, for the other. Nietzsche avers this only by affirming the death of God, but this is an affirmation closed to Levinas, who nevertheless acknowledges, accepts, and avows the same sense of destitution and responsibility.

There is an ironic seriousness in thinking the relationship between Nietzsche and Levinas on the grounds of their respective interpretations of the meaning of the death of God, a matter about which Levinas is taciturn but which is nevertheless pivotal in his critique and subsequent rejection of onto-theological metaphysics on the grounds of its violent totalizing tendencies, as well as its nihilistic impulses. This "greatest event" for Nietzsche, the watershed of so-called European nihilism, is for Levinas the culmination of Western ontology insofar as it represents the rejection or abandonment of absolute alterity and the subsequent theoretical totalization of being and the other. For both, however, the death of God also represents the great challenge for any fully active and affirmative thinking of the future, and herein lies the irony: even if the "violence" of Nietzsche's "non-saying of dance and laughter" may well be the very affirmation needed to overcome the egological self and the nihilism of history, as Levinas admits, one still "must return to language to convey, even if in betraying them, the pure and the unutterable" (CPP 147–48). With the death of God follows the death of the subject, and yet the subject is the one who is not only constituted by language, be it the logos, historical consciousness, or the voice of the other, but also the one who commands language and thereby shapes and gives meaning to the world. Language is thus both the liberator and the prisoner.

Who is this subject that has died along with God and yet still endures? She is the fecund moment of future possibility, whether construed in relation to the "innocence of becoming" (Nietzsche) or as "persecuted" and "hostage" (Levinas). Zarathustra's metamorphosed child (TZ "The Three Metamorphoses") bears a striking resemblance to the "youth" that Levinas affirms, albeit with an important caveat: "But youth here does not mean simply the incompleteness of a destiny newly entered upon, possibly calling for the essence. Youth, which the philosopher loves, is the 'before being,' the 'otherwise than being'" (CPP 147). Here is precisely the tension, perhaps irresolvable, of the matter at hand—namely, how the death of God gives rise, in Nietzsche's words, to "we who are homeless . . . we children of the future" (GS §377), and yet who are also, for Levinas, the "trace" of the infinitely other. Put another way, if the death of God signifies an irreversible forward movement of history and thought, then is it possible to respond to the trace apart from an ultimately backward movement, a movement to the absolutely primordial or "pre-original" (OB 5–6 ff; cf. EI 88; LR 183), as Levinas would have it?

While defined in relation to the yet to come, such a youthful subject has found, writes Levinas, several "marvelous moments" of previous historical expression (CPP 147). While acknowledging that the "Nietzschean man above all was such a moment," he nevertheless sees Nietzsche's work and vision as being ultimately nihilistic "poetic writing . . . laughter which refuses language" (OB 8). "The philosopher," moreover, "finds language again in the abuses of language of the history of philosophy, in which the unsayable and what is beyond being are conveyed before us. But negativity, still correlative with being, will not be enough to signify the *other than being*" (OB 9). Perhaps what attracts Levinas to Nietzsche is that which paradoxically also distresses him: such laughter may all too easily forget what is required for its very sustenance and continuance, namely, responsibility.

The heart of the difference between Nietzsche and Levinas—the status of the "beyond"—leads each to seek a path whereby an absolute affirmation is possible on the part of the subject, without an invariable lapse or fall back onto the negativity of either a dialectical negation or a simple refusal or denial. Nietzsche names the moment of this future affirmation the *Übermensch;* for Levinas, however, such a naming is impossible. The difference between the actuality and the impossibility of this sovereign act of naming is qualified for our purposes here as the distinction between the terms "apocalypse" and "eschatology." The question that haunts any possible relationship between Nietzsche and Levinas hinges on whether this difference/distinction necessarily entails an absolute disjunction of terms. In other words, is the "logic" that governs the relation between this actuality and impossibility a logic of exclusion, of either/or, or does it admit the possibility of a radical conjoining that refuses the totalizing impetus of a dialectical framework?

At once the culmination of the modern consciousness in all its self-alienation and also the marker of the advent of postmodernism, which understands itself philosophically as postmetaphysical or postsubjective, the death of God not only denotes the so-called end of history but also invokes the question of origin. From an apocalyptic perspective, as represented philosophically in Hegel and Nietzsche, the genesis and the death of God are inseparable moments of the same forward process, made possible as such by the *kenosis* of Godhead itself, effectively abolishing all pure transcendence and securing immanence as the fullness of actuality.[1]

For Nietzsche, the apocalyptic death of God is final and irreversible. Here Nietzsche breaks from Hegel, in that the negativity of this event is absolute and culminates in the complete negation and dissolution of the conscious subject via the affirmation of the eternal recurrence by and as the will to power in the person of the *Übermensch*. For Levinas, however, the death of God marks the very ending of everything that the West has known previously as "God," and this poses perhaps the ultimate challenge to his Judaism. Viewed positively for Levinas, the modern death of a certain God helps clear the way for the "metaphysical" desire for the Other, for the eschatological dimension of messianic peace embodied in the "youth" of the future.

Apocalypse and Eschatology

It is difficult, if not impossible, to consider any possible engagement between Nietzsche and Levinas without reference to the religious and theological grounds out of which their thinking emerges. Indeed, it is the very problem of ground that both unites and separates their thinking. If there is one consequence of the modern realization of the death of God that stands out, it is the disappearance or dissolution of the concept of ground, and most of all an ethical ground. This is the advent of nihilism, yet perhaps it is only in this context that a transvaluation of the concept of ground can occur. Nietzsche and Levinas are in agreement that all previous ethics are groundless and ultimately illusory, either because they refer back to a metaphysical nothingness (Nietzsche) or because they manifest a totalizing, violent ontology (Levinas).

The common problem that confronts Nietzsche and Levinas is how to think from a new standpoint that is removed from all traditional conceptions of ground and yet is still open to a thinking of the future from the stand-point of the "subject." If the ground of subjectivity is groundless, then the conventional ways of conceiving origin and end, *arché* and telos, must also be radically rethought. Here is where the history of Western philosophy comes up short for both Nietzsche and Levinas and why it is necessary to consider their relationship to the theological and religious traditions.

The terms "apocalypse" and "eschatology" are often conflated in mean-ing even though in actuality they are significantly different. Both terms convey, however, a sense of *terminus*. What distinguishes their respective meanings though is the dimension of knowledge—specifically, knowledge of the end of history. That is to say, even though both concepts connote a teleological dimension, only apocalypse truly conveys this meaning insofar as it posits a telos able to be comprehended as such. Eschatology, on the other hand, makes no determinative proposition regarding the nature of the end or completion of time or history, or even whether it will of neces-sity occur. This difference is fundamental and crucial; however, it is still not decisive for determining the relationship between Nietzsche and Levinas with respect to the meaning of God's death.

Apart from its etymology, the definition of eschatology is also signifi-cantly shaped by Greek thought, which first apprehends philosophically, Levinas notes, the concept of radical transcendence, as expressed initially in Plato's idea of the Good "beyond being" (TI 103). Yet ever since Aristotle, much philosophy and theology has tried to either distance itself from or defend itself against such transcendence, declaring it outside the bounds of rational thought and therefore but a figment of phantasmal imagination. Hegel stands out as the culmination of this effort and is also the first purely apocalyptic philosopher, declaring that all truth is disclosed and known via its linguistic articulation. Divine reason, *Geist* as history itself, is thus the voice of the apocalypse, but a voice ultimately silencing all dissonant voices within the totality. Philosophically, apocalypse thus signifies the uncovering or disclosure of the world and history as fundamentally rational in their to-tality, exposing along with myth and mystery all transcendent conceptions of reality, all metaphysical dualisms, as groundless insofar as they are essen-tially unknowable.

A simpler tactic would be to cast the distinction between apocalypse and eschatology principally in terms of the relation between Christianity and Judaism in order to consider the relationship between Nietzsche and Levi-nas. Their thinking is too complex, however, to be reduced solely to such a move, even if it cannot be understood adequately without reference to that relation. For, despite his trenchant critique of Platonist and Christian metaphysics, the proclamation of the death of God is for Nietzsche a theological assertion and in full continuity with the Christian theological tradition, even if it is a full reversal of it and thereby apocalyptic in its bringing to a close all previous conceptions of the absolute in naming the death of God as the will to power and eternal recurrence. And Levinas's recourse to the phenomenon of prophetic eschatology to counter what he will call "ontology," or apocalyptic philosophy, is grounded in the tradition of post-exilic Israel that gave rise to Judaism, which in its turn is a response to Christianity. While this is a refusal on Levinas's part to engage in theology (cf. OB 196n19, 197n25; OG 56), that is, to name God, and especially the death of God, it is nonetheless a breaking of a certain silence in that it finds a voice not only in the scriptures but also in the philosophical tradition. "The totality that includes all eschatology and every interruption," he writes, "could have been closed if it were silence, if silent discourse were possible, if a writing could remain for ever, if it could, without losing its meaning, renounce all the tradition that bears it and interprets it" (OB 171). Levinas employs terms such as "prophetic" and "messianic" in relation to "eschatological" not to provide reactive tropes with which to counter philosophy but to express the uneasy but intertwined relationship between Jerusalem and Athens. Clearly, the messianic is a Jewish notion, one never entertained by Greek thinking and never fully realized by Christianity, but the eschatological dimension of an exteriority beyond the totality is decidedly Greek, even if it is also present in the prophetic revolution of Israel.

The early apocalypticism of Christianity broke with all previous conceptions of time and history, becoming quickly estranged even from its original historical ground in Judaism, especially after the Diaspora. Christian orthodoxy negated the initial apocalyptic orientation of the early faith and replaced it with only a different variant of primordial thinking (that is, a thinking predicated on the return to the origin), so that in time apocalypse became an almost foreign and dangerously heterodox concept. The pervasiveness of the traditional or "orthodox" perspective is now such that its effect has clearly extended beyond theology, affecting even the secular world of postmodernity, as denoted by this world's apparent incapacity to project and advance a genuinely new sense of beginning. This issue is whether any primordial ground—and this includes the thinking of Levinas—is actually open to the future. From an apocalyptic standpoint, only the death of God absolutely reverses all backward looking primordial thinking and reveals the ground of such thinking as abstract, illusory and perhaps even delusional. The postmodern world is characterized in part by its inability to recognize the actual dissolution of previous forms of consciousness and hence prior conceptions of history. Yet this is a contradiction within postmodernity itself, for no other age so completely embodies apocalypse and forms a totally new horizon, even if that horizon is nihilistic, and so much so that the ethical ground in apocalyptic thinking is conspicuously concealed. The challenge, then, is the determination of a new "ground," a veritable groundless ground, one that is not a *Grund* but an *Abgrund* for meaning, truth, and value. But this is not tantamount to naming such a ground "nothingness" and simply falling back into the traditional metaphysical thinking of ground. Rather, it is to understand ground in a wholly new way—as the activity of ungrounding (*Ungrunden*) that reveals the fundamental way of being in the world as nomadism.

Nietzsche and Apocalypse

A fundamental aspect of apocalyptic thinking is its serious engagement with the question of nihilism, an engagement that seeks not only to overcome nihilism but also to affirm its necessity as the groundless ground of freedom. Nihilism is moreover precisely apocalypse itself, and far from designating an ultimate collapse, it actually demarcates the fullness of historical continuity, drawing us necessarily into the domain of the ethical, or of our fundamental dwelling with others in the world.[2] This is in fact the very nihilistic point of apocalyptic thinking: the absence of an absolute ground that makes possible the proliferation of multiple grounds, the manifestation of creative imagination and willing itself, thus enabling the negation and overcoming of nihilism as a purely negative ground.

Does apocalyptic thinking bar the path or portal to the possibility of an unforeseen possibility, a future possibility that is not coincidental with death—an impossible possibility? In other words, are apocalypse and eschatology, inasmuch as these concepts apply to the thinking of Nietzsche and Levinas, mutually exclusive? Or is it possible to think both concepts together in a way that brings together not only the past and present in terms of an openness to the future but also, and perhaps more important, in such a way that the past and future coalesce in the here and now, in a present always already past and always yet to come? What would be the name of this moment, this *Augenblick?* Is it "infinity"?

If Nietzsche is that thinker who has impressed most upon modernity the need to reconceive infinity (cf. GS §§124, 125, 374), then it is Levinas who has most ardently taken up that task. Despite their profound differences, they are united in their mutual eschatological orientations. Both retain the element of surprise, of radical transformative potential, as essential to the realization of the future. But the ground of that orientation is decidedly different.

Marking the highest affirmation of this existence, even if it is the nihilistic event par excellence, the death of God is for Nietzsche also the reversal of nihilism. Only thus is its negativity overcome by its transfiguration into an absolute Yes-saying that can only occur simultaneously alongside an equally powerful No-saying. While this is a dialectical movement, unlike the death of God in Hegelian idealism, Nietzsche's construal of this death refuses the teleological dimension of Spirit that remains bound to a version of the archaic myth of the eternal return, and therefore to a conception of temporality that is not fully open to the future, in the sense of being unbound to a determining logic or logos. In the eternal return, time moves both forward and backward, endlessly creating, destroying, and re-creating itself, but all the while remaining bound in its infinite reversibility to an absolute primordial beginning. The death of God signifies a dual movement of diremption and conjoining: a break with the past but also a new nonmetaphysical unity, a bonding of transcendence and immanence, of infinity and finitude, of eternity and space-time. This is evinced most prominently in Nietzsche's notion of the "eternal recurrence," wherein time is reconceived and experienced as irreversible and forward moving, thereby realizing what is impossible for a purely primordial thinking, namely, the radical dimension of futurity. At the heart of this teaching is the relation between the apocalyptic and the eschatological.

Hegel is the first to announce philosophically the death of God, and while this does have a direct impact on Nietzsche's thinking, there is a significant difference between the two accounts. Hegel only comprehends the death of God on the purely conceptual level, ultimately returning the concept (*Begriff*) to itself, and so he does not fully break with the orthodox theological conceptions of the transcendent Godhead. According to Hegel, the death of God is continually enacted in the dialectical unfolding of Spirit, whereas for Nietzsche, the death of God is final and irreversible. God is "the will to nothingness pronounced holy" (AC §18), Nietzsche declares, enunciating a nothingness fully and actually present, here and now. Nietzsche differs from Hegel insofar as the negativity of the death of God is absolute and culminates in the complete negation of the knowing subject, decentering self-consciousness and releasing all into the infinity of absolute nothingness. Philosophically, this apocalyptic event announces itself as the end of metaphysics, the end of history, and culturally, as the nihilism that is simultaneously the fulfillment of absolute freedom.

Nietzsche's apocalyptic reversal of the primordial alterity of God also reverses if not shatters the philosophically knowable ground of God's kenotic death. Now the ground becomes groundless as absolute becoming, an infinite, irreversible, temporally forward process of ungrounding. Unlike the Hegelian realization of the death of God, in which the primordial otherness of divinity is nullified and transformed into the fullness of historical actuality, in Nietzsche this alterity is once again recovered, although now not in the sense of an eternal return to a primordial plenum or transcendence, but instead as the openness to historical futurity, as eternal recurrence. Here one finds a new or different sense of origin that is not determinate or knowable. Yet, despite this irrevocable break with and dissolution of metaphysics, one signaling the advent of a new infinite horizon, it is textually difficult to locate in Nietzsche a once-and-for-all origin that is synonymous with apocalypse. He arguably rejects a notion of God as providential origin when he hypothesizes that if existence does have a final purpose, it would have long ago realized it since the universe is infinite. Nietzsche's "new 'infinite'" (GS §374) is but the destruction of a particular horizon, although one that truly makes possible an endless multiplicity of horizons, or interpretations which in turn are equally destroyed.

The death of God is for Nietzsche absolute and fully historical. In rendering possible a new conception of the future as eternal recurrence, transcendence is radically inverted as immanence, undermining any and all previous metaphysical grounds for ethics and unmasking the will to power as the simultaneous ungrounding and transfiguring of all valuation. Refusing the formation of any *Grund* to substantiate, validate, or render meaning, Nietzsche doubts "whether a philosopher could *possibly* have 'ultimate and real' opinions, whether behind every one of his caves there is not, must not be, another deeper cave—a more comprehensive, stranger, richer world beyond the surface, an abysmally deep ground [*ein Abgrund hinter jedem Grunde*], under every attempt to furnish 'grounds' [*Begründung*]" (BG §289). The death of God exposes the paradoxical groundless ground of chaos as the flux of shifting veiled appearances, devoid of substantive identity and truth-fulness. In confronting this nihilism, the emphasis falls now on the will to power as the nonmetaphysical locus of valuative meaning. Apocalypse is the realization that history is the actualization of the collapse of eternity into time, the total dissolution of primordial transcendence, and the shattering of everything that human consciousness has previously known as the "I," self, ego, or subject. Thus construed, apocalypse is the literal and histori-cally actual death of God. This, in turn, permits a new sense of "self," one that is neither subjectivity nor consciousness in the traditional meaning of those terms but rather, to use a contemporary coinage employed by neither Nietzsche nor Levinas, a singularity.

Levinas and Eschatology

For Levinas, the death of God is posed not so much as an event but as a question; it is principally a matter of which version of God is no longer tenable:

> This loss of unity has been proclaimed—and consecrated against the grain—by the famous paradox, become commonplace, of the death of God. The crisis of sense is thus experienced by our contemporaries as a crisis of monotheism. . . . The status of his [that is, God's] tran-scendence, despite the immanence of his revelation—a transcendence new with respect to the unbridgeable transcendence of the Aristotelian god—the status of this transcendence of the supernatural was never es-tablished.   (BPW 47)

Levinas's insistence on the preoriginal alterity of the wholly other—or God—opens the dimension of the future as fecundity in a radically dif-ferent way, one that leaves the domain of being and history in favor of a relationship with that which is "otherwise than being," with "illeity" (cf. BPW 61–64; OG 69). Transcendence thus signifies for Levinas, to use the language offered in *Totality and Infinity*, "metaphysics" or "religion," which he defines as the ethical relationship between the self and the Other, predicated on the face of the Other as the trace of the absolutely other.

Even if metaphysical transcendence is emphasized in terms of the ethi-cal relationship and not with regard to divinity, this profoundly affects

Levinas's interpretation of eschatology. Its meaning undergoes a radical transformation in his thought, in part because his Judaism is so strongly affected by his incorporation of Greek philosophy, which in turn affects his understanding of messianism, prophecy, and eschatology. It is altogether significant that Levinas opens his preface to *Totality and Infinity* by invoking these concepts (which while not taken up explicitly in the remainder of this work nevertheless condition its entire reading), as they serve in part to elucidate his critical distinctions between ethics and politics, metaphysics and ontology, infinity and totality, and other and self/same. Prophetic eschatology, which "institutes a relation with being *beyond the totality* or beyond history, and not with being beyond the past and the present" (TI 22), disrupts the totalizing, violent maneuvers of a sovereign theoretical reason, characteristic of philosophy in general. The central issue here for Levinas is the status of the immemorial past, or "an-archy" (CPP 127–39; cf. OB 101), which ruptures the absolute totality announced in apocalyptic thinking. The status of the "beyond," and thus also of "transcendence," is one of the most problematic aspects of Levinas's thought, and its connection to the notion of eschatology tends to lead many to construe his philosophy as but another variant of onto-theology. Well aware of this proximity to a metaphysical, or ontological, tradition that he refuses, Levinas writes in a critical passage:

This "beyond" the totality and objective experience is, however, not to be described in a purely negative fashion. It is reflected *within* the totality and history, *within* experience. The eschatological, as the "beyond" of history, draws beings out of the jurisdiction of history and the future; it arouses them in and calls them forth to their full responsibility. . . . The eschatological notion of judgment (contrary to the judgment of history in which Hegel wrongly saw its rationalization) implies that beings have an identity "before" [*avant*] eternity, before the accomplishment of history, before the fullness of time, while there is still time; implies that beings exist in relationship, to be sure, but on the basis of themselves and not on the basis of the totality. . . . The first "vision" of eschatology (hereby distinguished from the revealed opinions of positive religions) reveals the very possibility of eschatology, that is, the breach of the totality, the possibility of a *signification without a context*.   (TI 23)

The messianic dimension of eschatology reveals itself as a "'vision' without image," as the ethical expressed in the face of the Other, as ethics qua "optics" (cf. TI 23, 78, 174),[3] thus opening a new way of understanding subjectivity as arising from the eschatological vision. Here, "messianic" refers neither to a soteriology nor to the realization of the providential fulfillment of a collective desire but rather to the universal embrace of a philosophy of peace, predicated on the promotion and maintenance of alterity, plurality, and difference. And while Levinas does invoke the notion of prophetic eschatology, this is likewise used in a heterodox sense, scarcely resembling anything that the prophetic tradition of Israel understood as eschatological. In Levinas's use of the term, eschatology is arguably shaped more by the Greek world than it is by the Jewish world, although his sense of time is clearly informed by his Judaism. Eschatology is a concept that developed primarily as such during the Christian period from Paul to Augustine, and any prior conceptions of eschatology remain, for the most part, somewhat vague and debatable. Indeed, what common aspects of eschatology one finds in the Jewish prophetic tradition are generally linked to a nationalistic, not individualistic, conception of messianism. This fundamentally historical conception of eschatology is therefore properly understood as apocalyptic and is precisely what was recognized by early Christianity and reversed soon after by ecclesiastical orthodoxy.

The apocalyptic dimension of eschatology is refused by Levinas, though he does retain the crucial aspect of the messianic. But is Levinas truly opposed to any and all conceptions of historical eschatology? Or does he instead transform the notion of eschatology so as to permit a retention of a primordial memory of ethical meaning, without regressing into the older pre-prophetic myth of the eternal return that captivated the ancient Hebrews along with the other Mesopotamian peoples of the time, a myth subsequently revived and given new impetus and expression by Christianity? This raises the question of whether and, if so, to what extent Levinas has been influenced by such orthodoxy. For example, while recognizing numerous differences, there are striking parallels between the philosophy of Levinas and that of Plotinus,[4] who so heavily influenced orthodoxy, not to mention the more obvious and often addressed connection with Plato. And certainly both Plato and Plotinus and the ensuing traditions of Platonism and Neoplatonism are bound to certain conceptions of eternal return, re-inscribing the archaic myth as a new philosophical myth focused on the reunification of the soul with the One. Even if this is clearly not Levinas's agenda, his notion of metaphysical desire (TI 33–5), as a movement toward the beyond, or the Invisible, betrays a certain inclination to return, despite his strong opposition of the archetypes of Abraham and Ulysses. In this sense, also, Levinas's understanding of eschatology is perhaps more Greek than it is Jewish.

Eschatology Beyond Apocalypse

Nietzsche's thinking marks the advent of a possible absolute affirmation of existence here and now, an affirmation that is simultaneously fully actual and yet to be realized. Here is precisely where apocalypse (the revealed actualization) and eschatology (the hidden yet to come) coincide. The apocalyptic ground revealed or unveiled by the death of God is at the same time the absence of any substantial ground. If this is so, then with the death of God the trace of the infinite other, the beyond or otherwise than being for Levinas, is also absolutely reversed. In other words, all trace of an absolutely immemorial past is destroyed but also transfigured in meaning as the future beyond, as a new differential unity or *coincidentia oppositorum* that is simultaneously apocalyptic and eschatological. Only thus is the death of God conceivable as the *event* that makes possible a unity between the messianic and the *übermenschliche,* a unity that allows for the infinite to be "*within* history or the totality" in a truly meaningful way. Otherwise, the eschatological ethics proposed by Levinas remains perpetually bound, at least from a philosophical point of view, to a certain nonactuality. The death of God is the necessary condition for the "atonement"[5] of the apocalyptic and the eschatological, the philosophical and the prophetic, the knowable and possible.

Is eschatology a possible name, then, for the very openness to the realization or embodiment of the great Yes-saying to life, made possible by the apocalyptic death of God? Such an event breaks with the archaic myth of the eternal return, which understands infinity only as the perpetual movement backward toward an elusive past and permits no actual sense of future eschatological possibility. The death of God is, at the very least, the death of a certain conception of God, one already dead in the sense of never having been; namely, the rational god of the philosophers as well as the archaic divinity. Understood apocalyptically, however, the death of God provides an opening for the receptivity of the fully immanent presence of divinity, of infinity *within* the totality, but also for the eschatology of infinity as the absolute openness to the horizon of future possibility. With the death of God, the tyranny of any and all oppressive and coercive transcendence is vanquished, leaving in its wake an inevitable nihilism, but a nihilism that liberates in a joyous affirmation of life here and now.

As Levinas argues, transcendence and ethics are so inseparably conjoined as to constitute one and the same thing. But what is this "transcendence" if not a full disavowal of everything previously known as transcendence? The question of transcendence and its meaning is indeed the Archimedean point on which rests the status of the relationship between apocalypse and eschatology, in all the fullness of meaning that these terms convey. Integral to an eschatological conception of ethics is the conviction that an absolute alterity cannot be adequately thought. This is perhaps the principal difference between the apocalyptic, which maintains that absolute alterity can be thought, and eschatological modes of thinking, and so it would seem the ultimate obstacle toward reconciling these two approaches. This is precisely the hurdle that must be overcome if one is to think the ethical meaning of the death of God, one that Levinas attempts to clear in saying and unsaying absolute alterity-in-the-same.[6] This is a—if not the—principal task for the thinking of the future if it is to hold apocalypticism and eschatology in some balance.

While Nietzsche is an apocalyptic thinker, he is also an eschatological thinker, and it is here that he is drawn into a certain proximity with Levinas, despite their vastly different positions regarding the death of God and the fact that Levinas refuses to conjoin completely the apocalyptic and the eschatological, for reasons already indicated but also because of his fidelity to his Jewish tradition. But they are also brought closer together insofar as they each negate in their own way the Hegelian thesis of the primacy of reason. If Hegel is rightly interpreted as the first fully apocalyptic philosophical thinker, then Nietzsche goes beyond or transcends him inasmuch as he overcomes or transcends the absolute finality of the dialectic, not through some deeper or more obscure "cunning of reason" but rather through the hyperrationality of the will to power. Certainly, nihilism follows his every step and foreshadows the indeterminacy of the future, but unlike Hegel, who only sidesteps nihilism as an abstract moment in the dialectic, Nietzsche's affirmation of the necessary inevitability of nihilism, as a continually recurring event, is the first truly modern affirmation of eschatology.

Is it possible to think of eschatology as the transcendence, or overcoming, of transcendence? Would such a transcendence also be simultaneously a transcendence of immanence, or at least of any prior conceptions thereof? In its most radical interpretation, the death of God is the complete deconstruction of all operative or previously known conceptions of totality, whether conceived in terms of a pure transcendence, a pure immanence, or some intertwining of transcendence and immanence. Is eschatology then a transcendence of every possible totality and the simultaneous death of God and death of the subject? Could this simultaneous death make possible an infinite responsibility to totality, such as one encounters in Nietzsche, that does not render either the Other abstract or the self sovereign? But if the death of God is finally also the transcendence, and thus destruction, of totality, including and perhaps especially, in light of the critiques of Nietzsche and Levinas, every Hegelian *Aufhebung* (that is, every negation that preserves what it negates), then is infinite responsibility itself a negation of totality that destroys every possible totality, or at least dissolves the hold of totality in each and every moment that infinite responsibility is recognized? Nietzsche's understanding of responsibility, which ushers in a new conception of infinity alongside a "new *justice*" (GS §289), is just such an affirmation of totality, one that is also, and by virtue of it, an affirmation of nihilism, or the dissolution of totality. Such a sense of responsibility is grounded, or rather ungrounded, on the affirmation of the apocalyptic death of God, the death of transcendence itself—"*a divine way of thinking*" (WP §15). Now the mantle of responsibility lies solely and fully on the shoulders of humanity, and it is of a purple that will fade with time, but for that reason must be continually dyed and mended.

Responsibility is inseparable from nihilism, and Nietzsche's affirmation of the inevitable necessity of nihilism the first truly modern affirmation of the *eschaton*. Given that this is a concept of responsibility that necessitates that any ethical thinking is a nihilistic thinking in that it demands a negation of totality, it denotes a decisively distant move from the position of Levinas, which is predicated not only the existence of the Infinite, or God, but also on the trace of that absolutely other within the totality in and as the face of the Other. But such a God, in Nietzsche's view, is nihilistic and negates the totality in its very being. Thus the death of God, while nihilistic in its affirmation of nothingness, is also the self-overcoming of nihilism, which results in an "ecstatic nihilism" (WP §1055). This is not a final overcoming of nihilism, however, in the sense of returning to a positive ground that vanquishes nihilism absolutely. Rather, the death of God, the nihilistic event par excellence, liberates us from the absolute nihilism of transcendence (the old god), and therefore impresses on us the necessity to assume responsibility for totality, for immanence grasped as the open horizon of eschatological possibility. Now nothingness is no longer simply nihilism, nor is Godhead, for that matter, since the kenotic death of God, as interpreted here, is but another name for the absolute nontotalizable unity of transcendence and immanence, a new unity that is fully open to the future in all its potential.

In Nietzsche's thinking what is negated is not only all previous conceptions of ethical and political being, but also every thinking in which there is any ethical and political subject or subjectivity, or at least any that has been previously thought. Here, perhaps, there is a realization of the prophetic dimensions of both Nietzsche's and Levinas's thinking that can call forth and affirm, in their respective ways, the eschatological youthful saying of the children of the future. Levinas's interpretation of eschatology is predicated on the possibility of a subjectivity that does not lose its identity in the face of its relation to alterity, and it is here that he reveals his primary relation to a religious (metaphysical) rather than a philosophical (ontological) tradition. But if Nietzsche, and not Levinas, is our first truly modern philosophical thinker of eschatology, then his is a standpoint that makes Levinas's eschatological ethics impossible, or at least incomplete. Eschatology concerns the end, but there is no thinking of the end without a thinking of the beginning, and it is here that the nonapocalyptic eschatology of Levinas speaks most forcefully: "The first saying is to be sure a word. But the word is God" (CPP 126). Nietzsche's apocalyptic eschatological thinking, on the other hand, would end not only modernity itself but also any archaic sense of beginning, inaugurating a new sense of beginning, though doing so by destroying, or at least decentering, the subject of thinking by apocalyptically vanquishing all vestiges of the *Grund* of that thinking—God.

NOTES

1. No one has argued this point more than Thomas Altizer, who is also to be credited with identifying Hegel and Nietzsche as apocalyptic thinkers.
2. I develop this line of thinking in "Can Fig Trees Grow on Mountains? Reversing the Question of Great Politics," in *Difficult Justice: Commentaries on*

Levinas and Politics, ed. Asher Horowitz and Gad Horowitz (Toronto: University of Toronto Press, 2006), 148–71.

3. See my "The Listening Eye: Nietzsche and Levinas," *Research in Phenomenology* 31 (2001): 188–202.

4. See my "A Trace of the Eternal Return? Levinas and Neoplatonism," in *Levinas and the Ancients,* ed. Brian Schroeder and Silvia Benso (Bloomington: Indiana University Press, 2008), 210–29.

5. See my "Absolute Atonement," in *Thinking Through the Death of God: A Critical Companion to Thomas J. J. Altizer,* ed. Lissa McCullough and Brian Schroeder (Albany: SUNY Press, 2004), 65–87.

6. I am indebted to Bettina Bergo for reminding me of this important aspect of Levinas's philosophy and for her numerous helpful comments and suggestions.

Bibliography

Works by Emmanuel Levinas

Altérité et transcendance. Montpellier: Fata Morgana, 1995.

Alterity and Transcendence. Trans. Michael B. Smith. New York: Columbia University Press, 1999.

L'au-delà du verset: Lectures et discours talmudiques. Paris: Minuit, 1982.

Autrement qu'être ou au-delà de l'essence. Dordrecht and Boston: Kluwer Academic Publishers, 1974, and Paris: Livre de Poche, 2004.

"Bad Conscience and the Inexorable." In *Face to Face with Levinas,* ed. Richard A. Cohen, 35–40. Albany: State University of New York Press, 1986.

Beyond the Verse: Talmudic Readings and Lectures. Trans. Gary D. Mole. Bloomington, IN: Indiana University Press, 1994.

Collected Philosophical Papers. Trans. Alphonso Lingis. The Hague and Boston, MA: Martinus Nijhoff, 1987.

De Dieu qui vient à l'idée. Paris: Vrin, 2000.

De l'évasion. Montpellier: Fata Morgana, 1996.

De l'existence à l'existant. Paris: Vrin, 2002.

Difficile liberté: Essais sur le Judaïsme. Paris: Albin Michel, 2000.

Difficult Freedom: Essays on Judaism. Trans. Seán Hand. Baltimore, Md.: Johns Hopkins University Press, 1997.

Discovering Existence with Husserl. Trans. Richard A. Cohen and Michael B. Smith. Evanston, Ill.: Northwestern University Press, 1998.

Du sacré au saint: Cinq nouvelles lectures talmudiques. Paris: Minuit, 1977.

Emmanuel Levinas: Basic Philosophical Writings. Ed. Simon Critchley, Adriaan Peperzak, and Robert Bernasconi. Bloomington: Indiana University Press, 1996.

En découvrant l'existence avec Husserl et Heidegger. Paris: Vrin, 1949; 1982.

Entre Nous: Essais sur le penser à l'autre. Paris: Grasset, 1991.

Entre Nous: On Thinking-of-the-Other. Trans. Barbara Hashav and Michael B. Smith. New York: Columbia University Press, 1998.

Ethics and Infinity: Conversations with Philippe Nemo. Trans. Richard A. Cohen. Pittsburgh, Penn.: Duquesne University Press, 1985.

Existence and Existents. Trans. Alphonso Lingis. The Hague and Boston: Martinus Nijhoff, 1978.

God, Death, and Time. Trans. Bettina G. Bergo. Stanford, Calif.: Stanford University Press, 2000.

A l'heure des nations. Paris: Minuit, 1988.

Hors sujet. Montpellier: Fata Morgana, 1987, and Paris: Livre de Poche, 1997.

L'humanisme de l'autre. Montpellier: Fata Morgana, 1972.

Humanism of the Other. Trans. Nidra Poller. Urbana: Illinois University Press, 2003.

Les imprévus de l'histoire. Montpellier: Fata Morgana, 1994, and Paris: LGF, 1999.

In the Time of the Nations. Trans. Michael B. Smith. Bloomington: Indiana University Press, 1994.

Is It Righteous to Be? Interviews with Emmanuel Levinas. Ed. Jill Robbins. Stanford, Calif.: Stanford University Press, 2001.

The Levinas Reader: Emmanuel Levinas. Ed. Seán Hand. Oxford: Blackwell Publishers, 1989.

New Talmudic Readings. Trans. Richard A. Cohen. Pittsburgh, Penn.: Duquesne University Press, 1999.

Nine Talmudic Readings. Trans. Annette Aronowicz. Bloomington: Indiana University Press, *1990.*

Noms propres. Montpellier: Fata Morgana, 1975.

Nouvelles lectures talmudiques. Paris: Minuit, 1995.

Of God Who Comes to Mind. Trans. Bettina G. Bergo. Stanford, Calif.: Stanford University Press, 1998.

On Escape. Trans. Bettina G. Bergo. Stanford, Calif.: Stanford University Press, 2003.

Otherwise Than Being; Or, Beyond Essence. Trans. Alphonso Lingis. Dordrecht and Boston: Kluwer Academic Publishers, 1978, and Pittsburgh, Penn.: Duquesne University Press, 1998.

Outside the Subject. Trans. Michael B. Smith. Stanford, Calif.: Stanford University Press, Meridian, 1993.

Proper Names. Trans. Michael B. Smith. Stanford, Calif.: Stanford University Press, 1997.

Quatre lectures talmudiques. Paris: Minuit, 1968; 2005.

Le temps et l'autre. St. Clément: Fata Morgana, 1979, and Paris: Presses Universitaires de France, 2004.

La théorie de l'intuition dans la phénoménologie de Husserl. Paris : Vrin, 2000.

The Theory of Intuition in Husserl's Phenomenology. Trans. Andre Orianne. Evanston, Ill.: Northwestern University Press, 1973, 1995.

Time and the Other. Trans. Richard A. Cohen. Pittsburgh, Penn.: Duquesne University Press, 1995

Totalité et Infini. Essai sur l'extériorité. The Hague and Boston: Martinus Nijhoff, 1961, and Paris: Livre de Poche, 1990.

Totality and Infinity: An Essay on Exteriority. Trans. Alphonso Lingis. Pittsburgh, Penn.: Duquesne University Press, 1969.

Unforeseen History. Trans. Nidra Poller. Urbana: Illinois University Press, 2003.

Levinas and Philippe Nemo. *Éthique et infini.* Paris: Fayard, 1982.

Levinas and Jacques Rolland. *Dieu, la mort et le temps.* Paris: Grasset, 1993.

Articles by Emmanuel Levinas

"God and Philosophy." Trans. Richard Cohen. *Philosophy Today* 22 (1978): 127–45.

"Martin Buber and the Theory of Knowledge." In *The Philosophy of Martin Buber,* ed. Paul Arthur Schilpp and Maurice Friedman, 133–50. La Salle, Ill.: Open Court, 1967.

"Secularization and Hunger." Trans. Bettina G. Bergo. *Graduate Faculty Philosophy Journal* 20, no. 2, and 21, no. 1 (1998): 3–12.

"Some Reflections on the Philosophy of Hitlerism." Trans. Seán Hand. *Critical Inquiry* 17, no. 1 (1990): 63–71.

"Useless Suffering." Trans. Richard A. Cohen, in *The Provocation of Levinas: Rethinking the Other,* ed. David Wood and Robert Bernasconi, 156–167. London: Routledge, 1988.

Works by Friedrich Nietzsche

The Anti-Christ. In *Twilight of the Idols* and *The Anti-Christ,* trans. R. J. Hollingdale. New York: Penguin, 1968.

The Antichrist. Trans. R. J. Hollindgdale. New York: Penguin, 1990.

Beyond Good and Evil: Prelude to a Philosophy of the Future. Trans. Walter Kaufmann. New York: Vintage Books, 1966.

Beyond Good and Evil: Prelude to a Philosophy of the Future. Trans. R. J. Hollingdale. Harmondsworth, U.K.: Penguin Books, 1973.

The Birth of Tragedy. In *The Birth of Tragedy and The Case of Wagner,* trans. Walter Kaufmann. New York: Random House, 1967.

The Birth of Tragedy Out of the Spirit of Music. Trans. Shaun Whiteside. New York: Penguin, 1993.

Daybreak: Thoughts on the Prejudices of Morality. Trans. R. J. Hollingdale. Cambridge: Cambridge University Press, 1997.

Ecce Homo: How One Becomes What One Is. In *On the Genealogy of Morals and Ecce Homo,* trans. Walter Kaufmann. New York: Vintage, 1967.

Friedrich Nietzsches Werke in drei Bänden. Ed. Karl Schlechta. Munich: Carl Hanser Verlag, 1959, 1966.

The Gay Science: With a Prelude of Rhymes and an Appendix of Songs. Trans. Walter Kaufmann. New York: Vintage, 1974.

Human, All Too Human: A Book for Free Spirits. Trans. Marion Faber and Stephen Lehmann. Harmondsworth, U.K.: Penguin, 1984, 1996.

Human, All Too Human: A Book for Free Spirits. Trans. R. J. Hollingdale. Cambridge: Cambridge University Press, 1986.

Kritische Studienausgabe. 15 vols. Ed. Giorgio Colli and Mazzino Montinari. Berlin: DTV/Walter de Gruyter, 1967–77, 1988.

Le livre du philosophe. Paris: Garnier-Flammarion, 1993.

Nietzsche: A Self-Portrait from His Letters. Ed. and trans. Peter Fuss and Henry Shapiro. Cambridge, Mass.: Harvard University Press, 1971.

Œuvres philosophiques complètes: Textes et variantes établis par Giorgio Colli et Mazzino Montinari. Paris: Gallimard, 1984.

On the Future of Our Educational Institutions. Trans. Michael W. Grenke. South Bend, Ind.: Saint Augustine's Press, 2004.

On the Genealogy of Morals. In *On the Genealogy of Morals and Ecce Homo,* trans. Walter Kaufmann and R. J. Hollingdale. New York: Random House, 1967.

"On Truth and Lies in a Non-Moral Sense." Trans. Daniel Breazeale. In *Philosophy and Truth: Selections from Nietzsche's Notebooks of the Early 1870s.* Atlantic Highlands, N.J.: Humanities Press, 1979.

The Portable Nietzsche. Ed. and trans. Walter Kaufmann. New York: Penguin, 1976.

Selected Letters of Friedrich Nietzsche. Ed. and trans. Christopher Middleton. Chicago: University of Chicago Press, 1969.

Thus Spoke Zarathustra. Trans. Walter Kaufmann. New York: Penguin House, 1954.

Thus Spoke Zarathustra: A Book for Everyone and No One. Trans. R. J. Hollingdale. London: Penguin, 1969.

Twilight of the Idols. In *Twilight of the Idols and The Anti-Christ,* trans. R. J. Hollingdale. London: Penguin, 1974, 1990

Untimely Meditations. Trans. R. J. Hollingdale. Cambridge: Cambridge University Press, 1983.

La volonté de puissance, 1 and 2. Trans. Geneviève Bianquis. Ed. Friedrich Würzbach. Paris: Gallimard, 1995.

Werke: Kritische Gesamtausgabe. Berlin: Walter de Gruyter, 1967–.

The Will to Power. Trans. Walter Kaufmann and R. J. Hollingdale. New York: Vintage Books, 1968.

Other Works

Agamben, Giorgio. *Remnants of Auschwitz.* Trans. Daniel Heller-Roazen. Cambridge, Mass.: Zone Books / MIT Press, 2002.

Ansell Pearson, Keith. *How to Read Nietzsche.* London: Granta, 2005.

Aristotle. *Nicomachean Ethics.* Trans. J. A. K. Thomson. London: Penguin, 2004.

Austin, John L. *How to Do Things with Words.* 2nd ed. Cambridge, Mass.: Harvard University Press, 1975.

Benjamin, Walter. "Theses on the Philosophy of History." In *Illuminations,* trans. Harry Zohn, 250–64. New York: Schocken, 1991.

Bensussan, Gérard. *Le temps messianique: Temps historique et temps vécu.* Paris: Vrin, 2002.

Bernasconi, Robert. "Before Whom and For What? Accountability and the Invention of Ministerial, Hyperbolic, and Infinite Responsibility." In *Difficulties of Ethical Life,* ed. Shannon Sullivan and Denis Schmidt. New York: Fordham University Press, 2008.

——. "Rereading *Totality and Infinity.*" In *The Question of the Other,* ed. Arlene Dallery and Charles Scott, 23–34. Albany: State University of New York Press, 1989.

——. "The Third Party: Levinas on the Intersection of the Ethical and the Political." *Journal of the British Society for Phenomenology* 30, no. 1 (1999): 76–87.

Boothroyd, David. "Levinas and Nietzsche: In-between Love and Contempt." *Philosophy Today* 39, no. 4 (1995): 345–57.

——. "Skin-nihilism Now: Flaying the Face and Refiguring the Skin." In *Nihilism Now! Monsters of Energy,* ed. Keith Ansell Pearson and Diane Morgan, 198–215. New York: St. Martin's Press, 2000.

Butler, Judith. "Ethical Ambivalence." In *The Turn to Ethics,* ed. Marjorie Garber, Beatrice Hanssen, and Rebecca L. Walkowitz, 15–28. New York: Routledge, 2000.

——. "Giving an Account of Oneself." *Diacritics* 31, no.4 (Winter 2001): 22–40. Revised edition, in *Giving an Account of Oneself.* New York: Fordham University Press, 2005.

Casey, Edward. "Levinas on Memory and the Trace." In *The Collegium Phaenomenologicum: The First Ten Years,* ed. John Sallis, Guiseppina Monetam and Jacques Taminiaux, 241–55. Dordrecht and Boston: Kluwer Academic Publishers, 1988.

Caygill, Howard. *Levinas and the Political.* London: Routledge, 2002.

Chanter, Tina. "Neither Materialism nor Idealism: Levinas' Third Way." In *Postmodernism and the Holocaust,* ed. Alan Milchman, 137–54. Amsterdam: Rodopi, 1998.

Cohen, Richard A. *Ethics, Exegesis, and Philosophy.* Cambridge: Cambridge University Press, 2001.

——, ed. *Face to Face with Levinas.* Albany: State University of New York Press, 1986.

Conway, Daniel. "Autonomy and Authenticity: How One Becomes What One Is." *St. Johns's Review* 42, no. 2, *Essays in Honor of David Lachterman* (1994): 27–39.

——. "Nietzsche *contra* Nietzsche: The Deconstruction of Nietzsche." In *Nietzsche as Post-Modernist,* ed. Clayton Koelb, 91–110, 304–11. State University of New York Press, 1990.

Critchley, Simon. *The Ethics of Deconstruction: Derrida and Levinas.* Oxford: Blackwell Publishing, 1992.

De Greef, Jan. "Le concept du pouvoir éthique chez Levinas." *Revue philosophique de Louvain* 68 (1970): 508–20.

Deleuze, Gilles. *Nietzsche and Philosophy.* Trans. Hugh Tomlinson. New York: Columbia University Press, 1983.

——. *Nietzsche et la philosophie.* Paris: Presses Universitaires de France, 2005.

Derrida, Jacques. *Aporias.* Trans. Thomas Dutoit. Stanford, Calif.: Stanford University Press, 1993.

——. *De la grammatologie.* Paris: Minuit, 1967.

——. *L'écriture et la différence.* Paris: Le Seuil, 1967.

——. *Margins of Philosophy.* Trans. Alan Bass. Chicago: University of Chicago Press, 1982.

——. *Of Grammatology.* Trans. Gayatri Chakravorty Spivak. Baltimore, Md.: Johns Hopkins University Press, 1974.

——. *Writing and Difference.* Trans. Alan Bass. Chicago: University of Chicago Press, 1978.

Diprose, Rosalyn. "Arendt and Nietzsche on Responsibility and Futurity." *Philosophy and Social Criticism* 34, no. 6 (2008): 617–42.

——. *Corporeal Generosity: On Giving with Nietzsche, Merleau-Ponty, and Levinas.* Albany: State University of New York Press, 2002.

Franck, Didier. *Nietzsche et l'ombre de Dieu.* Paris: Presses Universitaires de France, 1998.

——. *Dramatique des phénomènes.* Paris: Presses Universitaires de France, 2001.

Godard, Jean-Luc, and Youssef Ishaghpour. *Cinema: The Archeology of Film and the Memory of a Century.* Trans. John Howe. Oxford: Berg Press, 2005.

Golomb, Jacob. "Nietzsche and the Marginal Jews." In *Nietzsche and Jewish Culture*, 158–191. London: Routledge, 1997.

——. *Nietzsche and Zion*. Ithaca, N.Y.: Cornell University Press, 2004.

Gooding-Williams, Robert. *Zarathustra's Dionysian Modernism*. Stanford, Calif.: Stanford University Press, 2001.

Granier, Jean. *Le problème de la vérité dans la philosophie de Nietzsche*. Paris: Le Seuil, 1966.

Heidegger, Martin. *Being and Time*. Trans. Joan Stambaugh. Albany: State University of New York Press, 1996.

——. *On the Way to Language*. Trans. Peter D. Hertz. New York: Harper and Row, 1971.

——. "Who Is Nietzsche's Zarathustra?" In *The New Nietzsche*, ed. David Allison, 64–79. Cambridge, Mass.: MIT Press, 1995.

——. "The Word of Nietzsche: 'God is Dead.'" *The Question Concerning Technology*. Trans. William Lovitt. New York: Harper and Row, 1977.

Henry, Michel. *Généalogie de la psychanalyse: Le commencement perdu*. Paris: Presses Universitaires de France, 1993.

——. *Genealogy of Psychoanalysis: The Lost Beginning*. Trans. Douglas Brick. Stanford, Calif.: Stanford University Press, 1998.

Husserl, Edmund. *Analyses Concerning Passive and Active Synthesis: Lectures on Transcendental Logic*. Trans. Anthony J. Steinbock. Dordrecht: Kluwer Academic Publishers, 2001.

Katz, Claire Elise. "Educating the Solitary Man: Dependence and Vulnerability in Levinas and Rousseau." *Levinas Studies: An Annual Review* 2 (2007): 133–52.

——. "Levinas Between Philosophy and Rhetoric: The 'Teaching' of Levinas's Scriptural References." *Philosophy and Rhetoric* 38, no. 2 (2005): 159–72.

——. "'The Presence of the Other Is a Presence That Teaches': Levinas, Pragmatism, and Pedagogy." *Journal of Jewish Thought and Philosophy* 14, nos. 1–2 (2006): 91–108.

——. "Teaching the Other: Levinas, Rousseau, and the Question of Education." *Philosophy Today* 49, no. 2 (Summer 2005): 200–207.

——. "Witnessing Education." *Studies in Practical Philosophy* 3, no. 2 (2003): 107–31.

Katz, Claire Elise, and Lara Trout, eds. *Emmanuel Levinas: Critical Assessments: Levinas and the History of Philosophy*. London: Routledge, 2005.

Kaufmann, Walter. *Nietzsche: Philosopher, Psychologist, Anti-Christ*. New York: Random House, 1968.

Klossowski, Pierre. *Nietzsche and the Vicious Circle*. Trans. Daniel W. Smith. Chicago, Ill.: University of Chicago Press, 1997.

——. *Nietzsche et le cercle vicieux: Essai*. Paris: Mercure de France, 1969.

Kress, Jeffrey, and Marjorie Lehman. "The Babylonian Talmud in Cognitive Perspective." *Journal of Jewish Education* 69, no. 2 (2003): 58–78.

Lampert, Laurence. *Nietzsche's Teaching: An Interpretation of* Thus Spoke Zarathustra. New Haven, Conn.: Yale University Press, 1987.

Leahy, David G. "Nietzsche, Levinas, and the Death of God." In *Faith and Philosophy: The Historical Impact*, 95–113. Aldershot, U.K.: Ashgate, 2003.

Lebovic, Nitzan. "The Beauty and Terror of *Lebensphilosophie:* Ludwig Klages, Walter Benjamin, and Alfred Baeumler." *South Central Review* 23, no. 1 (Spring 2006): 23–39.

Lingis, Alphonso. *The Community of Those Who Have Nothing in Common.* Bloomington: Indiana University Press, 1994.

——. "The Elemental Imperative." *Research in Phenomenology* 18 (1988): 3–21.

——. "Theoretical Paradox and Practical Dilemma." *International Journal of Philosophical Studies* 12, no. 1 (2004): 21–28.

——. "The Will to Power." In *The New Nietzsche,* ed. David B. Allison, 37–63. Cambridge, Mass.: MIT, 1981.

Patton, Paul. "Nietzsche and Hobbes." *International Studies in Philosophy* 33, no. 3 (2001): 99–116.

Rosenzweig, Franz. *On Jewish Learning.* Ed. and trans. N. N. Glatzer. Madison: University of Wisconsin Press, 1955.

Plato. *Republic.* Trans. G. M. A. Grube. Ed. C .D. C. Reeve. Indianapolis, Ind.: Hackett, 1992.

Roux, Wilhelm. *Der Kampf der Theile im Organismus.* Leipzig: Wilhelm Engelmann, 1881.

Sallis, John. *Crossings: Nietzsche and the Space of Tragedy.* Chicago: University of Chicago Press, 1991.

Schopenhauer, Arthur. *The World as Will and Representation.* Trans. E. F. J. Payne. New York: Dover Publications, 1969.

Schroeder, Brian. *Altared Ground: Levinas, History, and Violence.* New York: Routledge, 1996.

——. "Blood and Stone: A Response to Altizer and Lingis." *New Nietzsche Studies* 4, nos. 3/4 (2000–2001): 29–41.

——. "Breaking the Closed Circle: Levinas and Platonic Paideia." *Dialogue and Universalism* 8, no. 10 (1998): 97–106.

——. "Can Fig Trees Grow on Mountains? Reversing the Question of Great Politics." In *Difficult Justice: Commentaries on Levinas and Politics,* ed. Asher Horowitz and Gad Horowitz, 148–71. Toronto: University of Toronto Press, 2006.

——. "The Listening Eye: Nietzsche and Levinas." *Research in Phenomenology* 31 (2001): 188–202.

——. "Politics and Transcendence." In *Levinas, Law, Politics,* ed. Marinos Diamantides, 27–41. London: Routledge Cavendish, 2007.

Schroeder, Brian, and Silvia Benso, eds. *Levinas and the Ancients.* Bloomington: Indiana University Press, 2008.

Schroeder, Brian, and Lissa McCullough, eds. *Thinking Through the Death of God: A Critical Companion to Thomas J. J. Altizer.* Albany: State University of New York Press, 2004.

Sloterdijk, Peter. *Thinker on Stage: Nietzsche's Materialism.* Trans. Jamie Owen Daniel. Minneapolis: University of Minnesota Press, 1989.

Spinoza, Baruch. *The Ethics.* Trans. Samuel Shirley. Indianapolis, Ind.: Hackett, 1992.

Starobinski, Jean. "Le passé de la passion: Textes médicaux et commentaires." *Nouvelle Revue de psychanalyse: la passion,* no. 21 (Spring 1980): 51–76.

Stauffer, Jill. "Productive Ambivalence: Levinasian Subjectivity, Justice, and the Rule of Law." In *Mosaic: Essays on Levinas and Law,* ed. Desmond Manderson. New York: Palgrave Macmillan, forthcoming.

Visker, Rudi. "Is Ethics Fundamental? Questioning Levinas on Irresponsibility." *Continental Philosophy Review* 36 (2003): 263–302.

Waldenfels, Bernhard. "Response and Responsibility in Levinas." In *Ethics as First Philosophy: The Significance of Emmanuel Levinas for Philosophy, Literature, and Religion,* ed. Adriaan T. Peperzak, 39–52. New York: Routledge, 1995.

Warren, Mark, *Nietzsche and Political Thought.* Cambridge, Mass.: MIT Press, 1988.

Wright, Tamra, Peter Hughes, and Alison Ainley. "The Paradox of Morality: An Interview with Emmanuel Levinas." In *The Provocation of Levinas,* ed. Robert Bernasconi and David Wood, 168–80. New York: Routledge, 1988.

Wyschogrod, Edith. *An Ethics of Remembering.* Chicago: University of Chicago Press, 1998.

——. "Representation, Narrative, and the Historian's Promise." In *The Ethics of History,* ed. David Carr, Thomas R. Flynn, and Rudolf A. Makkreel, 30–31. Evanston, Ill.: Northwestern University Press, 2004.

Yovel, Yirmiyahu. *Dark Riddle: Hegel, Nietzsche, and the Jews.* University Park: Pennsylvania State University Press, 1998.

Contributors

SILVIA BENSO is professor of philosophy at Rochester Institute of Technology, New York. She is the author of *The Face of Things: A Different Side of Ethics* (SUNY, 2000) and is also the coeditor, with Brian Schroeder, of *Contemporary Italian Philosophy: Crossing the Borders of Ethics, Politics, and Religion* (SUNY, 2007).

BETTINA BERGO is the author of *Levinas Between Ethics and Politics* (Kluwer, 1999) and coeditor of the collection *Levinas' Contribution to Contemporary Thought* (*Graduate Faculty Philosophy Journal* 20–21, 1998). She has translated three works of Levinas and is the author of numerous articles on Levinas, Merleau-Ponty, feminism, and psychoanalysis.

DAVID BOOTHROYD teaches in the School of Social Research, Sociology, and Social Policy at the University of Kent, U.K. He is a cofounding editor of *Culture Machine* (http://culturemachine.net) and the author of *Culture on Drugs: Narco-Cultural Studies of High Modernity* (Manchester University Press, 2007). He is currently working on a book entitled *Ethical Subjects: The Ethical Encounters of Material Life*.

JUDITH BUTLER is Maxine Elliot Professor in the Departments of Rhetoric and Comparative Literature at the University of California, Berkeley. Her most recent book, *Giving an Account of Oneself*, appeared with Fordham University Press (2005) and considers the partial opacity of the subject and the relation between critique and ethical reflection. She is currently working on essays pertaining to Jewish philosophy, focusing on pre-Zionist criticisms of state violence.

RICHARD A. COHEN is the Isaac Swift Distinguished Professor of Judaic Studies at the University of North Carolina at Charlotte. His publications include *Elevations: The Height of the Good in Rosenzweig and Levinas* (University of Chicago Press, 1994) and *Ethics, Exegesis, and Philosophy: Interpretation After Levinas* (Cambridge University Press, 2001). He is the translator of many works by Levinas, including *Ethics and Infinity* (Duquesne, 1985) and *New Talmudic Readings* (Duquesne, 1999).

ROSALYN DIPROSE is associate professor of philosophy at the University of New South Wales, Sydney. Her most recent book is *Corporeal Generosity: On*

Giving with Nietzsche, Merleau-Ponty, and Levinas (SUNY, 2002). She is currently coediting a collection on *Merleau-Ponty: Key Concepts* (with Jack Reynolds for Acumen Press).

JOHN DRABINSKI teaches philosophy in the School of Humanities, Arts, and Cultural Studies at Hampshire College, Amherst, Massachusetts. In addition to numerous journal articles on Levinas, phenomenology, and political philosophy, he has published *Sensibility and Singularity* (SUNY, 2001) and is the author of *Godard Between Identity and Difference* (Continuum, 2007).

CLAIRE ELISE KATZ is an associate professor of philosophy and women's studies at Texas A&M University. She is the author of *Levinas, Judaism, and the Feminine: The Silent Footsteps of Rebecca* (Indiana, 2003) and the editor of *Emmanuel Levinas: Critical Assessments* (Routledge, 2005). She has published in the areas of feminist theory, philosophy of education, phenomenology, Jewish philosophy, and the history of philosophy.

ALPHONSO LINGIS is a professor of philosophy at Pennsylvania State University. His publications include: *Excesses: Eros and Culture* (1984), *Libido: The French Existential Theories* (1985), *Phenomenological Explanations* (1986), *The Community of Those Who Have Nothing in Common* (1994), *Abuses* (1994), *Sensation: Intelligibility in Sensibility* (1995), *The Imperative* (1998), *Body Modifications: Evolutions and Atavisms in Culture* (2005), and *The First Person Singular* (2006).

JOHN LLEWELYN, formerly reader in philosophy at the University of Edinburgh, is visiting professor of philosophy at the University of Memphis and the Arthur J. Schmitt Distinguished Visiting Professor of Philosophy at Loyola University of Chicago. His publications include *Margins of Religion: Between Kierkegaard and Derrida* (forthcoming, 2009) and *Appositions of Jacques Derrida and Emmanuel Levinas* (Indiana, 2002).

JEAN-MICHEL LONGNEAUX is professor of ethics and phenomenology in the Law School of the Facultés Universitaires Notre-Dame de la Paix, Namur, Belgium. He has published essays on the philosophy of Spinoza, Levinas, Nietzsche, palliative care, and two books: *L'expérience du mal* (Éditions Namuroises, 2004) and *Michel Henry: L'épreuve de la vie* (Le Cerf, 2001).

AÏCHA LIVIANA MESSINA is visiting assistant professor of philosophy at the Universidad de Chile, Santiago. She is the author of several articles and recently published, in dialogue with Jean-Luc Nancy, a study of the aesthetic desubjectivation at work in the creation of the literary and artistic double, *Poser me va si bien* (Éditions P. O. L., 2005).

BRIAN SCHROEDER is professor of philosophy and coordinator of religious studies at the Rochester Institute of Technology. His publications include *Altared Ground: Levinas, History, and Violence* (Routledge, 1996); *Thinking*

Through the Death of God: A Critical Companion to Thomas J. J. Altizer, ed. with Lissa McCullough (SUNY, 2004); and *Contemporary Italian Philosophy: Crossing the Borders of Ethics, Politics, and Religion,* ed. and trans. with Silvia Benso (SUNY, 2007).

JILL STAUFFER is assistant professor of philosophy at John Jay College, CUNY. Her publications include contributions to *Essays on Levinas and Law: A Mosaic,* ed. Desmond Manderson (Palgrave 2008); *Critical Beings: Law, Nation, and the Global Subject,* ed. Peter Fitzpatrick and Patricia Tuitt (Ashgate 2004); and the *Journal of Law, Culture, and the Humanities.*

Index